PEACE OF MIND
IN EARTHQUAKE
COUNTRY

PEACE OF MIND
IN EARTHQUAKE
COUNTRY ▪ How to save
your home and life

PETER YANEV

Foreword by Charles F. Richter

Drawings by Robert Higginbotham, Architect, A.I.A.

Chronicle Books/San Francisco

for Kay

Anyone who would deliberately attempt to ride out an ocean storm in an improperly designed or constructed ship would be considered foolhardy. Yet, here we sit, most of California's communities, in and below many of tens of thousands of old structures designed and built with little or no knowledge of earthquake engineering or foundation geology, waiting to ride out a severe earthquake next year or in five years or, with great luck, in twenty years.

Wesley G. Bruer
State Geologist of California

Library of Congress Cataloging in Publication Data

Yanev, Peter, 1946-
    Peace of mind in earthquake country.

    1. Earthquakes and building. 2. Dwellings—The West. I. Title.
TH 1095.Y36   693.8'52'0978   74-7406
ISBN O-87701-216-4

10 9 8 7

Printed in the United States of America.

Chronicle Books
275 Fifth Street
San Francisco, California 94103

Contents

Preface

In the 200 years since the first written record of an earthquake in the American Far West, Californians and Nevadans alone have experienced an average of 5,000 noticeable quakes every year. Another 500 jar the surrounding states of Washington, Oregon, Montana and Utah; while Alaska's record of tremors is comparable to that of California and Nevada. Most of these shocks are slight and cause no damage. Trees or bushes are shaken, window panes rattle, animals are startled momentarily, and a very few people take an unexpected pause in their busy day to be reminded of the ever-present danger of earthquakes in the Western states.

Approximately every four years, a major, potentially destructive earthquake strikes the region. The San Francisco Bay Area and the adjoining counties have experienced on the average 12 damaging earthquakes per century. The Los Angeles area and Southern California have similar records.

The other earthquake-prone Western states of Alaska, Washington, Oregon, Nevada, Montana and Utah have been more fortunate, rarely suffering severe earthquake damage. However, most of the large metropolitan areas in these states are severed by active or potentially active faults and live under the same shadow of imminent disaster that affects San Francisco or Los Angeles.

As ill-informed and ill-prepared as most Californians are regarding their earthquake problem, they are at least aware that there *is* a problem. The citizens and officials of the other seismically threatened states in the West seldom even know of the high risks they face. The San Francisco Bay Area, Los Angeles, Santa Barbara, Seattle, Salt Lake City and smaller cities and towns throughout the West remain in a dangerous and frightening position. Despite the long history of earthquake damage in these areas, and despite principles of earthquake-resistant construction and property location which have been known to builders and available to governments for at least three generations, the individual property owner and indeed most governing bodies remain blithely ignorant of the factors that determine earthquake risks and of the simple, relatively inexpensive corrective steps that could be taken.

Numerous books and films have pointed out the grave dangers of earthquakes again and again over the past 40 years. Countless articles and television features have excoriated officials (and citizens) in the Western states for their inaction in the face of the terrible earthquake threat. This book attempts another approach. I am addressing my information primarily to *you*, the *individual property owner*. I am telling you what the engineering profession has long known and too-often ignored—that the most dangerous earthquake hazards can be largely avoided and that earthquake deaths or damage can be prevented or minimized with just a little knowledge of geology and some relatively simple and inexpensive procedures in constructing or strengthening a home or small building.

This knowledge and these preventive procedures are available to you in this volume in simple and fully illustrated lessons. My hope is that you will apply this information to your own property and then urge it on your relatives, friends and neighbors, so that when the disaster strikes, you and they can be the Noahs who ride out the heaving waves of rock and soil and survive to supervise a city of stronger buildings and wiser citizens. I also hope, fervently, that as you are seeing to your own needs, you will join with others in demanding instant attention to the location and reinforcement of our schools and hospitals and other public buildings.

This book can result in considerable financial savings to you when the next big earthquake jolts the ground beneath your home or other property. Hopefully, through your new knowledge and civic actions, it may also save many lives.

Peter I. Yanev
Berkeley, California

Foreword

Mr. Yanev has produced a well-written book, of much potential value to the property owner or administrator in a region of active earthquakes. While applying especially to California and the West, it will be useful wherever the prevailing types of construction are similar.

In commending the book I do not wish to trespass on the territory of the professional engineer. My own opinions on earthquake risk and safety arose from discussion with those who are better qualified. The general tenor of Mr. Yanev's exposition accords well with my own best judgment; nevertheless, his position is his own, and he is exclusively responsible for engineering and other technical details.

The presentation is as accurate as brevity permits. Unavoidably, points are covered on which there are still differences in expert opinions. Nor is it to be expected that small errors and misprints can be wholly eliminated. Such minor imperfections need not diminish the value of the book to the general reader; the main outlines of the subject are correctly drawn.

Such a detail is the characterization of the earthquake magnitude scale. Magnitude is not defined in terms of energy; it is a measure of the extent of ground vibration, as measured by seismographs. In general magnitude increases with the energy of the shock, but estimating energy from the magnitude involves some rather arbitrary assumptions. The multiplying figure 31.5 cited in the text is neither exact nor universal. Especially for large shocks, the magnitude number more nearly represents power in the mechanical sense (horsepower or kilowatts).

In the last few years, conspicuous failures and near failures have shown the need for a new approach toward the earthquake-resistant design of large modern-style buildings, as well as of dams, bridges, and other engineering structures.

Engineers and administrators have responded vigorously. New and improved code specifications are being set up. A state-wide survey of dams is proceeding under authority of the California Department of Water Resources; new dam construction is being subjected to stringent requirements.

Discussion of earthquake risk at a given locality often overemphasizes its situation with respect to faults. This should not be allowed to obscure the fact that direct risk from faulting is very local and special. The risk of strong shaking, on the other hand, is general; even in a large shock the shaking may be nearly as heavy ten or twenty miles from the fault as within a few yards of it. In 1906, ordinary houses near the San Andreas fault, but not directly on it, were often relatively little damaged. Much depends on the degree of consolidation and stability of the ground, both with regard to shaking and to landslides. The reader should attend closely to Mr. Yanev's Chapter 3.

Californians must live with the risk of heavy shaking. Even if their homes are favorably located, they need to work, do business, shop and send their children to school, at other locations over which they have little choice. Persons who are utterly terrified by the idea of an earthquake should not try to live here; they only make themselves miserable and disturb other people. After all, the long-term risk to life and limb in our earthquakes is far less than the daily hazards that we all take on our streets and highways.

Losses of life and property in earthquakes are nevertheless largely unnecessary and preventable. In the past they have been due chiefly to the failure of houses and other structures which would never have been erected under any modern system of building regulation and inspection. Our greatest present earthquake risk consists in the continuance in use of antiquated and now unsafe structures.

Charles F. Richter
Altadena, California

How to use this book:

Eight steps for determining

and minimizing earthquake

hazards to your property

It is news to no one who lives in the Western United States that earthquakes remain the most unpredictable and frightening of the natural disasters that befall this earth. They strike without apparent warning, last only seconds, and, in those brief moments, can cause a range and severity of destruction, damage, death and injury comparable only to the devastation wrought by modern weapons of war. That said, I must quickly add that while earthquakes remain frightfully destructive and unpredictable, the physical *effects* of their sudden tremors are highly predictable; so that knowledgeable pre-earthquake planning and preparation can in most situations considerably mitigate their danger and destructiveness.

The protection of life and property during earthquakes is largely entrusted to the engineering profession, and geotechnical and structural engineers in the United States have begun to respond to the challenge in the past two decades. Present computerized analytical techniques have made it possible to design new structures to withstand tremendously high earthquake forces without structural collapse and with little or no structural damage. And such reliable earthquake resistance in newly designed buildings can be provided

11

for as little as one percent of their cost. Similarly, many older small buildings can be strengthened and secured simply and inexpensively—in many cases by the property owner himself.

This book directs attention to the information and safeguards which every present or prospective property owner in earthquake country should study and implement in order to minimize the dangers and the damage of a future earthquake disaster. The following chapters outline in simple terms and with numerous illustrations and examples:

- The causes and the effects of earthquakes;
- the varying risks of different areas within cities, counties and states in the earthquake-active regions of the West;
- the geologic, architectural and structural earthquake hazards that every renter and prospective buyer or builder should investigate before moving into or investing in a new home;
- the basic low-cost repairs and alterations that every property owner should make to upgrade the earthquake resistance and safety of his building and its occupants and furnishings;
- the considerations that will help the property owner or renter make a decision about the need for and amount of earthquake insurance;
- the steps to take before, during and after an earthquake to protect your family and property.

In short, this book is intended to qualify the reader to survive the inevitable "next" earthquake without serious personal loss.

The major hazards of earthquakes are in two broad categories: (1) geologic, and (2) structural. Both are avoidable in new buildings and correctable in many existing buildings, although in the case of some geologic hazards, the recommended remedy may be the bitter one of declaring a building site unsafe for human occupancy and abandoning it or using it for purposes other than a home.

Step 1: Locate your property with regard to known active faults

The geologic category of earthquake hazards arise, of course, from the formation of the land, and the most dangerous of such formations are the faults that criss-cross the most populous areas of the Western states. You can learn what you need to know about the sources, formation and hazards of faults in the background Chapters One and Two, which explain how earthquakes are caused, the terminology of earthquake measurement, and the appearance, effects and hazards of faults. Then you can proceed to the specific piece of the earth of most interest to you and discover its proximity to an active fault. This essential, even life-or-death information is contained in Appendix A, which lists and illustrates the locations of the known significant active faults in the Western states and provides a historical summary of the major earthquakes along these faults.

Those who have the good fortune or wisdom not to live on or too near a major fault can seek information about the proximity of their property to lesser or suspected faults in Appendix B, which lists the numerous detailed government-agency fault and earthquake maps and reports easily available to the public.

Step 2: Examine your building site and the appropriate geologic maps to determine soil conditions.

After you have established that your property is safely removed from dangerous fault traces, it is necessary for you to consider the geologic foundations of the property and the varying earthquake risks associated with bedrock, alluvial, landfill, and sandy and water-saturated soil foundations. The public is generally not aware that different soil foundations respond to a tremor with varying levels of vibrational intensities and other abnormal behaviors and, therefore, that different areas of a city, such as San Francisco or Los Angeles, face widely varying degrees of earthquake risk. Chapter Three deals with these risks and describes the geologic foundations of numerous urban areas in earthquake country. Appendix B lists other sources—government maps, geologic and engineering reports—for the areas not illustrated in the main body of the book.

Step 3: Examine your building site and appropriate geologic maps to determine landslide potential.

Along with living atop an active fault or a poor or unstable soil foundation near a fault, the most hazardous geologic situations in earthquake country are landslide-prone areas. Strong earthquakes always trigger numerous landslides, and therefore any property located in known slide areas carries the additional and significant risk of landslide damage. The final section of Chapter Three illustrates the tell-tale signs of landslide-prone soils and sites, discusses the risks, and notes some of the worst of the landslide areas in populous regions. Map and report references for other regions are provided in Appendix B.

Step 4: Locate your property with regard to the man-made hazards of inadequately constructed dams, reservoirs, neighboring buildings, etc.

In his rush to solve existing problems, man often creates new problems that are far more urgent. Dams present the greatest man-made danger to life and property in earthquake country. Several dams in California are located in or near active fault zones, and many minor dams have collapsed during the recurrent earthquakes of the region. In addition, several major dams have collapsed, while others have come to within inches of spilling a deadly torrent over a heavily populated valley or canyon. Reservoirs, water tanks, heavy power lines, large retaining walls, poorly designed neighboring buildings can be equally unstable and can wreak severe damage. Such structures present very real dangers to a property and must be considered when buying, building or renting property in seismic regions. Chapter Four offers some help and advice in this regard.

Step 5: Evaluate the architectural/structural characteristics and detailing of your building.

The architectural and structural characteristics and detailing of buildings are, after geologic considerations, the other major category of earthquake hazard. Structural materials, types of bracing and reinforcement and certain architectural features are directly related to the amount and the type of damage suffered by a building, its occupants and any persons or objects in the immediate vicinity of the building during an earthquake.

Chapter Five stresses the fact, well-known to engineers of modern high-rise buildings, that a few basic and rather simple principles govern the earthquake resistance of buildings and the extent of vibrational damage. The scope of this book is necessarily limited to houses and smaller residential and industrial or business buildings not exceeding three or four stories. However, the outlined principles, with some modifications, encompass all types and sizes of buildings.

Chapter Six outlines the specific types of buildings and structural materials that are either hazardous or recommended for seismic areas. You will learn, for example, that unreinforced masonry buildings are the least resistant to earthquake damage and are also the most likely to collapse. You will also learn that a properly braced wood-frame building is by far the safest small structure in earthquake country. A special section discusses the hazards and correctives for improperly supported mobile homes.

Chapter Seven deals with the architectural and structural features that are particularly susceptible to damage or collapse during an earthquake—for example, houses on stilts, inadequately supported split-level homes, roof-heavy buildings, poor foundation connections, and certain older homes. In combination with any adverse geologic conditions, these and other structural/architectural features and detailing can be ill-advised and dangerous to both you and your pocketbook.

In all of these chapters, the point is clearly made and repeated that a few relatively simple and low-cost repairs and alterations in most homes or apartment buildings can significantly increase their earthquake resistance and decrease the probability of any major damage from a quake and its aftershocks. The principles and the techniques of such improvements are discussed in detail and fully illustrated so that, in most situations, they can be implemented by a handy do-it-yourselfer. The recommendations include remedies for existing buildings of many types as well as for structures still in the planning stage.

Step 6: Examine your home for hazardous and damage-prone utilities, appliances, furnishings and exits.

Chapter Eight suggests the practical and simple measures that can be taken in advance to minimize the risks of falling objects, fire and broken gas and water lines in and around your home.

Step 7: Determine the need for earthquake insurance.

Chapter Nine introduces the subject of earthquake insurance, discussing the different types of policies available to the homeowner and renter, the varying costs of these policies, the companies that sell them, and the considerations that will help you determine the necessity of insurance and the amount of coverage advisable for your situation. In some cases, the right insurance rate could make some higher-risk properties desirable investments. On the other hand, since most policies have a costly deductible clause, the purchase of insurance might be unwise for a building that is unlikely to suffer more than minor damage.

Step 8: Follow the proper precautions before, during and after an earthquake.

The subject matter of the final chapter—How to Behave Before, During and After a Quake to Protect Your Family, Yourself and Your Property—is obvious but of vital importance. Not only you, but every member of your family, should be well-versed in the information and recommendations of this chapter.

In short, a few basic principles govern the extent of damage to buildings during earthquakes. The most fundamental of these is the land upon which the building stands or will stand, and anyone living and/or investing in the Western states should make the effort to determine the geologic conditions below his building site, the proximity of active faults and slide areas and the historic behavior of the land in any previous tremors. The other important factor is the structural and architectural characteristics and detailing of the building. Many structural deficiencies can be resolved readily, and architectural problems can either be avoided on the basis of the information in this book or corrected through the reconstruction or reinforcement procedures illustrated here. And, finally, there are the ultimate safeguards—earthquake insurance and intelligent behavior before, during and after an earthquake. Surely, a thorough understanding of these basic principles, facts and remedies is a prerequisite for safety, sound real-estate investments and peace of mind in earthquake country.

PART I

A BRIEF PRIMER
ON EARTHQUAKES

CHAPTER 1

How earthquakes are caused and measured

Until this century, the causes of earthquakes remained a profound mystery to man. The first milestone in the progress of our knowledge of earthquakes dates to November 1, 1755, when a great earthquake struck near Lisbon. The city fell in ruins, 30,000 people perished, buildings trembled all over Europe, and mild shocks from the quake reportedly rattled chandeliers as far away as the American Colonies. After the quake, Portuguese priests were asked to document their observations, and their records represent the first systematic attempt to investigate an earthquake and its effects.

Before that time and for nearly two centuries afterwards, tremors in the earth were generally relegated to that category of natural misfortunes that insurance companies still call "acts of God." Aristotle proposed that the frequent quakes which shook the ancient Greek temples and cities were caused by gales that became trapped in giant subterranean caves. Anaxagoras reasoned that earthquake motion resulted when large sections of the earth cracked and tumbled into the hollow terrestial core. The Roman scholar Pliny advanced the idea that earthquakes were simply mother nature's method of protesting the wickedness of men who mined gold, silver and iron ores. Other ancient philosophers placed the blame on an ill-tempered Poseidon, god of the sea and the watery element.

The less-civilized northern neighbors of these philosophers—the tribes of what is now Bulgaria—believed that earthquakes struck when an enormous water buffalo, which carried the world on its back, readjusted its burden to ease its task. Other primitive peoples throughout the centuries have assigned the phenomenon to a multitude of monstrous mythic animals—giant hogs, catfish, tortoises, spiders, frogs, whales, serpents—whose occasional restlessness caused the world to tremble. As charmingly preposterous as these notions are, the increasingly sophisticated scientists of later centuries had little better to offer. An Italian scholar in the sixteenth century suggested that the best earthquake protection was to place statues of Mercury and Saturn on a building. Even in the scientific age of the nineteenth century, most observers were, like their ancient predecessors, satisfied that earthquakes were not explainable except as a capricious force of nature or the stern work of an offended God. Man's fate was merely to wait and pray.

The source of earthquakes—the theory of continental drift and plate tectonics

Even today, the causes of earthquakes cannot be said to be completely understood. But there is now sufficient geologic evidence for scientists to conclude that the tremors are the effect of a re-balancing of forces arising from the collision of continuously moving plates of layered rock that float upon the earth's molten interior. This is the theory of continental drift and plate tectonics, which holds that the land surface of the crust of the earth was once concentrated in a single continental mass—a supercontinent. Perhaps 200 million years ago, the mass began to break apart, gradually forming into the fragments that largely define today's continents and ocean basins—a mosaic of about 20 extremely thick tectonic plates that drift across the molten mantle of the earth and form the planet's shifting crust.

The tectonic plates and their "piggy-back" continents and oceans are still sliding apart in a continuation of the free-floating motion of the original break-up. As some of these plates meet and collide around the globe—roughly at the intersections of continents and oceans—they cause islands and mountain ranges to rise, land masses to emerge from or sink beneath the seas, volcanoes to erupt and the adjustments of plate frictions which we know as earthquakes.

The newest and thinnest of these tectonic plates are beneath the ocean floors, where they are still being formed from molten materials flowing from the earth's interior. This flow emerges in narrow and deep rift valleys which form the inner boundaries of the sub-oceanic tectonic plates and which divide a vast and continuous mountain range that traverses the length of all the ocean basins like a global seam. The molten materials from the interior of the earth well up through the hot rock of the rift valleys and solidify to build the edges of the oceanic plates. Then in a process known as "sea-floor spreading," these oceanic plates are pushed slowly but steadily from the rift valleys at a yearly rate of two to five inches, pressing the outer edges of the young tectonic plates against the established and heavier plates that make up the continental land masses. It has been demonstrated, for example, that the Atlantic Ocean is spreading from the Mid-Atlantic rift at about two inches a year, so that within the lifetime of a man, the continents of Europe and North America will have moved further apart by about six feet.

As the oceanic plates meet the continental plates, a tremendous friction is created which gives way in the gradual buckling of the earth's surface (the creation of mountain ranges), the plunging of the thinner, weaker oceanic plates into deep-sea trenches beyond the continental shelves, and the violent upheavals of volcanoes and earthquakes. Along the western coast of South America, for example, the thinner oceanic plate is forced downward by the heavier continent; and as it is propelled below the continental plate and melts into the earth's core, the still-growing Andes mountains are pushed upward. At the same time, the force of this collision causes a temporary lock between the rocky layers of the two plates. The inevitable and frequent failures of this bond cause the deep and powerful earthquakes typical of Chile and Peru. A similar type of collision occurs between two continental

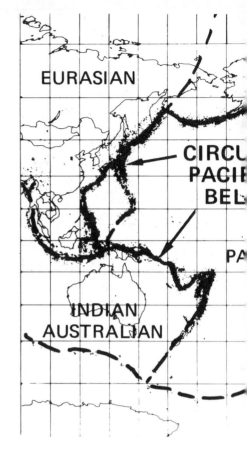

The dark areas on this map indicate the distribution and density of the 42,000 earthquakes recorded throughout the world from 1961 to 1970. These belts of seismic activity mark with dramatic clarity the turbulent boundaries of the drifting, colliding tectonic plates that form the earth's crust. The mid-oceanic lines of activity represent the towering mountain ranges and deep rift valleys where the younger tectonic plates are renewed and pushed outward, altering the sea floors a few inches every year. About 80 percent of the planet's earthquakes (and most of the largest quakes in history) occur along the Circum-Pacific seismic belt, which loops completely around the Pacific Basin. The Alpide belt, which extends from Java through the Himalayas and the Mediterranean, is responsible for about 17 percent of the world's seismic activity. The remaining 3 percent of all earthquakes

plates as well. For example, the sub-continent of India is a separate plate which is moving northward against the Asian mass. The soaring Himalayas and the deep and destructive tremors in India and Pakistan are the result.

Major faults—severe breaks in the rock layers of the earth's upper crust—are formed at the line of collision between tectonic plates. A related system of lesser ruptures in the bedrock spreads in all directions from the main line of collision like the cracks in old, settling concrete. Thus, the San Andreas fault system of California is the result of the ancient and continuing collision of the North Pacific plate and the North American continent. Many millions of years ago, the more massive westward moving continental plate overrode the opposing Pacific plate, driving the latter downward into the earth's crust and responding to this tremendous

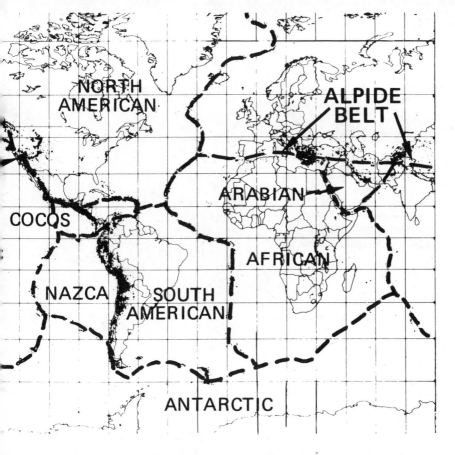

strike along the Mid-Atlantic Ridge and in scattered pockets of seismic activity throughout the world.

stress by pushing up the Sierra, the Cascades and the continental divide and by causing the violent blow-outs of such volcanoes as Shasta, Lassen, Rainier and Hood. At the same time, some of the plunging Pacific plate was scraped off against the continent at the San Andreas fault zone, so that the coastal surface of western North America grew outward by about 100 miles in a very gradual accretion of new materials that formed much of California and its Coastal ranges. Thus, the southwestern third of the state is made up of relatively new geologic materials riding the Pacific tectonic plate, while the remainder of the state forms the western edge of the North American plate.

Today, these two plates have changed directions slightly, so that they are essentially sliding past one another along the San Andreas fault. The great Pacific plate carries the

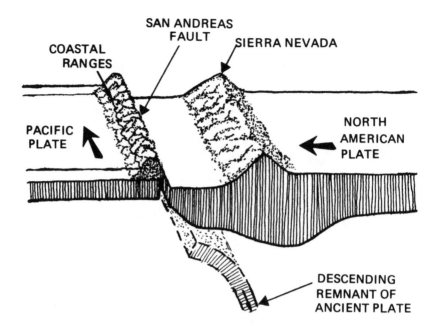

SAN ANDREAS FAULT

COASTAL RANGES

SIERRA NEVADA

PACIFIC PLATE

NORTH AMERICAN PLATE

DESCENDING REMNANT OF ANCIENT PLATE

California's San Andreas fault is one segment of the line of intersection between the North Pacific and the North American tectonic plates. Both plates are moving slowly north and westward at different rates, producing the frictions and temporary locks along the fault that are released in the sudden shifts of shattered bedrock that result in earthquakes, the surface distortions of the fault zone and the gradual growth of the coastal ranges. The Sierra Nevada ranges were formed in the geologic past, when the two plates were colliding directly and the thinner Pacific plate was forced downward, buckling the continental plate, lifting the mountain range and forming the westernmost portion of California with the accretion of materials from the oceanic plates.

ocean floor, a part of California and all of the Baja Peninsula northwestward in relation to North America, while the North American plate, pushed by the sea-floor spreading at the mid-Atlantic ridge, also moves west at a slower rate. The two plates finally collide directly in the Far North, along the Aleutian archipelago, where the Pacific plate is driven downward. It is estimated that at the present rate of movement, the Los Angeles area, riding the Pacific plate, will draw abreast of San Francisco Bay in about 10 million years.

The mechanism of earthquakes—
the theory of elastic rebound

If this movement along the San Andreas were unhindered by the constant and tremendous friction of the two tectonic plates, Californians and Westerners generally would have little to worry about. However, the rocky edges of the plates have a certain amount of elasticity and therefore tend to hold their basic positions along the fault. Portions of the fault frequently remain locked in this way, and under tremendous strain, for several years, decades or even centuries. Finally, when the accumulated strain exceeds the frictional force that binds portions of the plates and prevents their natural movement, the distorted and shattered rocky layers along the two sides of the fault suddenly slip past one another in an explosion of movement that allows a new position of equilibrium for the opposing plates.

This slippage, termed "elastic rebound" by scientists, can produce a series of powerful vibrations and shock waves that toss and sometimes rupture the earth's surface and may shift the positions of the two sides of the fault by several feet both horizontally and vertically. Earthquakes, such as the 1906 San Francisco quake along the San Andreas fault, are the result of these violent adjustments of a temporarily locked fault. More commonly, these adjustments, which may occur along a fault several times in a day without breaking the ground surface, are very slight and recognized only by sensitive instruments.

Two types of earthquakes are associated with the different types of plate collisions. Shallow-focus earthquakes, with an average depth of five to ten miles below the surface of the earth, result from the friction and slippage of primarily *laterally* moving plates and are typical of California and most of the seismic regions of the American West. Deep-focus earthquakes usually occur where the plates are directly colliding and one plate is forced below the other. For example, the great Chile quake of 1960 and the major Peru quake in 1970 were both at a depth of about 25 miles. Many other earth-

Types of faults and faulting

● *The quiescent fault.* A few faults may move relatively freely and very slowly along the plane of the drifting tectonic plates. This movement is termed fault creep and it will be damaging to structures above the fault only over a long period of time.

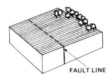

FAULT LINE

The Calaveras fault and a portion of the San Andreas near Hollister have moved in this way in the past several years. Other faults become locked with the friction of the colliding plates and move only when the rocky layers of the plates become strained beyond endurance and slip apart with the violence of an earthquake.

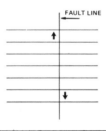

FAULT LINE

● *The strained fault before an earthquake.* The gradual movement of the tectonic plates has created a strain in the rocky layers of the fault where the two plates are col-

liding. The frictional force of the collision locks the two sides of the fault and prevents any movement. The limited elasticity of the rocky layers allows the strains of this locked fault to accumulate for years and even decades. Finally, the

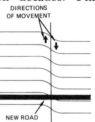

DIRECTIONS OF MOVEMENT

NEW ROAD

rocks give way, allowing the two sides of the fault to realign and causing the upheaval of an earthquake and surface displacements.

● *The adjusted fault after an earthquake.* The fault has moved into a new, unstrained position, causing

---

quakes in South America have occurred at depths greater than 75 miles.

The depth of an earthquake is closely related to its destructiveness; for the shock waves of the deeper earthquakes are generally dissipated as they rise to the surface and are therefore less damaging to buildings. On the other hand, the deep-focus tremors usually affect a much wider area.

surface displacements that have destroyed the continuity of the highway and fence and producing intense shock waves during the quake that have demolished buildings in the fault zone.

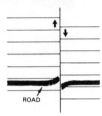

ROAD

• *The direction of faulting.* Faults typically move either *laterally, vertically* (thrust faulting), or in a

FAULT LINE
THE QUIESCENT FAULT

combination of vertical and lateral shifts. The San Fernando and White Wolf faults in California fit

this latter category of movement, which is quite common among faults. The faults of the San Andreas fault system move right-

VERTICAL FAULTING

laterally. Others, such as the Garlock fault in Southern California, move left-laterally. The Wasatch

HORIZONTAL FAULTING
(RIGHT LATERAL)

fault in Utah and the Kern River and Pleito faults in Southern California are vertical, or thrust faults.

COMBINED VERTICAL AND
HORIZONTAL FAULTING

Shallow-focus earthquakes are felt over a smaller area and are therefore sharper and frequently more destructive. For example, earthquakes in the Puget Sound area of Washington have depths typically three to five times greater than equally large earthquakes along the San Andreas fault in California, and historically, these shocks have been considerably less destructive than those in California.

Faults, fault zones, faulting and creep

Fault is the term used to describe not only the demar-
cation of opposing tectonic plates, such as the major trace of
the San Andreas, but also the related web of numerous crustal
breaks that result from the stresses of the plate collisions and
the wide-spread subterranean damage of frequent earthquakes along the collision course. The sub-soil of much of
California, for example, is made up of a whole network of
blocks that were formed and now move in different directions
as a result of the forces of the North American and Pacific
plates and the activity of the San Andreas fault. Each of these
blocks is separated by a large fault, most of which are *active*
(moving or potentially moving) and therefore capable of the
strain and then the abrupt slippage which produces an earthquake. In addition, throughout each of these crustal blocks,
there are the lines of strain which form lesser faults, also
under pressure and capable of slippage and eruption.

Thus, the plane along which the slippage and tremors
occur may be a major fault most recently active, or it may be a
newly created line of fracture among the weakened rock of
older and presumably *inactive* ("healed" or unstrained) fault
traces. For example, few geologists even suspected any
earthquake potential along the minor fault in the San Gabriel
Mountains behind Los Angeles until it ruptured on February
9, 1971, thrusting some of the mountains six feet higher,
killing 64 persons, and demolishing hundreds of buildings in
the San Fernando Valley.

Faults are generally narrow, from only a few inches to
several feet. However, a fundamental fault system, such as
the San Andreas, includes not only the most recent and active
break of a few inches or feet but also a broad *fault zone* of
shattered rock and partially "healed" traces of previous breaks
and surface ruptures. The San Andreas fault zone is usually at
least 100 yards wide and is more than 1½ miles wide at
numerous locations along its 650-mile length. In Southern
California, south of San Gorgonio Pass, the San Andreas fault
zone and its many branches encompass most of the width of
the state. Other major faults in the West are not so dramati-

This drawing of the San Andreas fault system in Central and Southern California illustrates a few of the numerous small crustal blocks and fault divisions created by the stresses of the tectonic plate collision and the frequent upheavals along the San Andreas. These lesser faults generally parallel the lateral northwesterly movement of the San Andreas and the continental and Pacific plates. However, this parallel movement is interrupted along the intersection with the Garlock fault, where the southern group of blocks encounter the deep crustal roots of the Sierra Nevada and are deflected to the west.

cally large, but each of them also generally encompasses a wider zone of past activity and potential future ruptures.

When the stresses of a fault are released in an earthquake, the highest intensity of shock waves and vibrations are felt along the fault line nearest the point of slippage. However, much of the length of a fault may also be affected by a major quake, so that destructive vibrations can occur along a fault for many miles on either side of the earthquake center. In addition, the shock waves disperse from the fault like the rings produced by a pebble dropped into still water, so that significant shocks and damage can affect areas 20 or more

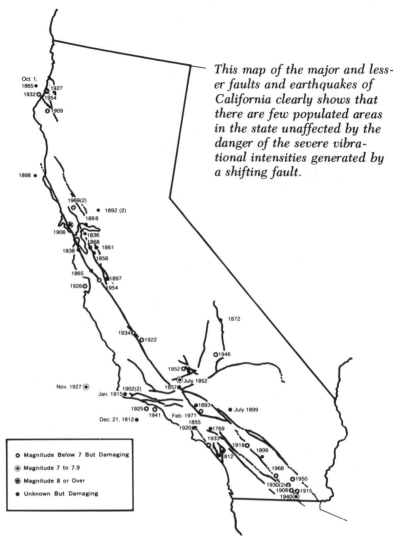

This map of the major and lesser faults and earthquakes of California clearly shows that there are few populated areas in the state unaffected by the danger of the severe vibrational intensities generated by a shifting fault.

miles on either side of the fault. The intensity always diminishes with distance, of course, but an unstable, vibration-prone soil many miles from the fault can produce more damage than a strong, rocky geologic formation only a few hundred feet away from the source of the quake.

All of the sound and energy waves generated by an earthquake are modified by reflection and refraction through the different layers of rock and soil and the various geologic formations (mountains, hills, water, plains) that make up the surface of the earth surrounding the fault. The combination of "pushes and pulls," "ups and downs" and reflections and refractions of these waves by the ground itself create the chaotic and violent surface motions that can literally and very quickly shake a house down.

During a strong tremor, the ground surface directly along a fault—and *only* along the fault traces—may rupture and shift laterally or upward by several feet. The 1906 quake resulted in lateral shifts of as much as 20 feet in several places along the fault, as well as lesser horizontal *and* vertical shifts and ruptures along 270 miles of the fault. Other earthquakes, such as the tremendously large shock in Owens Valley, California, in 1872, or the more moderate Hebgen Lake, Montana, earthquake in 1959, have caused vertical displacements of 20 feet or more at the surface. This displacement of ground along a fault during a quake is termed *faulting* and results in the abnormal topographical formations of scarred, crumpled and upthrusted rock and soil that visibly delineate a major and recently active fault. It also results in the certain

The large surface displacements of the laterally moving San Andreas fault are vividly illustrated in this photograph of a hillside field near Daly City after the 1906 San Francisco earthquake. The fence crossed the San Andreas in a straight line before the earthquake, and the camera taking this photograph was directed at the original line of the fence at the top of the hill. The massive shift of the earth along the fault during the quake left the abrupt 10-foot crimp in the fence line. Naturally, any building straddling the fault during such a large displacement would have been torn apart. This field is now covered by tract homes.

A vertically moving, or thrust fault left this tall scarp in the rock and soil along the fault near Dixie Valley, Nevada, in 1954. Note that the wood-frame shack within the fault zone but removed by several feet from the fault trace survived the heavy shock waves of the quake with no apparent damage. If the structure had been directly astride the fault, it would be a pile of broken lumber.

destruction of any substantial structure subjected to the faulting. A small earthquake represents a localized readjustment of fault strain, and usually such shocks are not accompanied by the surface displacements of faulting nor by serious damage to buildings in the fault zone.

Another type of fault movement, termed *slow faulting* or *fault creep*, occurs when the two sides of a section of a fault avoid locking completely and move past one another at an infinitesimally slow and gradual rate of fractions of an inch per year. Occasionally, the creep may halt entirely for a time, or it may drastically increase its speed with spurts of discernible movement within a few days. Whatever the speed of movement, the gradual surface displacements of fault creep are destructive to buildings in the immediate vicinity of the fault. The fault creep may also be accompanied by barely perceptible or small micro-tremors.

Some scientists believe that the more or less continuous adjustment of fault stresses through creep will prevent

The first evidence that some faults are subject to a creeping movement was discovered by earthquake scientists fairly recently. During a routine investigation in 1956 of some foundation damage in the old Cienega Winery near Hollister, engineers found that the portion of the San Andreas fault beneath the winery was moving very slowly without any perceptible earthquake tremors. The photograph shows the offsets and damage caused by the creeping fault beneath a concrete ditch just south of the winery. The Calaveras fault, which crosses Hollister, is similarly subject to creep and has caused many surface deformations and some structural damage in that city.

Creep along the Hayward fault through Berkeley caused this three-foot deformation in a stone retaining wall. A new school has been built along the fault only a few hundred feet north of this location. The University of California stadium, as well as several other structures on the campus, also straddle this creeping fault; and slowly widening cracks discov-ered in the stadium indicate that the structure is gradually being split apart by the creep.

the violence of sudden large earthquakes. Others suspect that creep may presage a quake, or that the creeping fault may be subject to large earthquakes triggered by the eruption of a nearby "locked" fault. Most agree that creeping faults, such as the Hayward fault or the Calaveras and San Andreas faults near Hollister, are highly susceptible to large surface displacements in the event of a major quake.

How Earthquakes are Caused and Measured **35**

Foreshocks and aftershocks

A large earthquake is rarely a single shock. A few smaller tremors sometimes occur before the main large shock —these are known as *foreshocks*—and a number of sizable quakes occur after the main shock and are known as *aftershocks*. The entire sequence of seismic events, often within the span of several months, is considered to be one earthquake and is given a single name by seismologists.

Our present technology cannot distinguish foreshocks from the numerous other small earthquakes that occur daily in seismically active regions. Thus, foreshocks cannot yet serve as warnings of impending danger. However, the probability exists that seismologists may someday detect certain characteristics that distinguish among foreshocks and allow them to be used as early-warning signals for the size and location of a larger quake.

Aftershocks are caused by the continuing readjustment of stresses at different locations along a ruptured fault after the main shock. Because of the varied geology of the regions along a major fault zone, all of the accumulated energy is rarely released at once by a quake, and the process of localized readjustment and reaction continues indefinitely. A very large shock is often followed by several hundred and sometimes several thousand discernible aftershocks for months after the main event.

The San Fernando area, for instance, was disturbed by a minor aftershock on February 9, 1972, exactly one year after the severe earthquake. The main shock in 1971 was typically followed by 33 large aftershocks during the first hour alone. The strongest aftershock of the San Fernando quake struck on March 31, 1971, in the Granada Hills area. It was felt over much of Los Angeles and in eastern Ventura County, but fortunately the shock was slight and caused only minor damage. From the standpoint of building damage, some of the earlier aftershocks are likely to be more damaging than the main tremor. For example, a month after the major Kern County earthquake in 1952, an aftershock centered near Bakersfield was strong enough to cause more damage to the shaken and weakened city than the initial quake.

The measurement of earthquakes

Epicenters and hypocenters

All news media reports on an earthquake inevitably give detailed accounts of the location of the *epicenter* of the shock, and the public inevitably assumes that the epicenter is located in the area most seriously shaken by the earthquake. The epicenter *is* very definitely related to earthquake intensity. However, other factors, such as geologic foundations, length of the fault rupture and the extent of faulting, may be much more important to intensity and damage.

The location deep in the crust of the earth where a fault slippage first begins is known as the *hypocenter*, or *focus*, of the earthquake (generally 5 miles and no more than about 10 or 15 miles deep for typical destructive California shocks). The epicenter is the projection of the hypocenter on the ground surface and is always the point on the surface closest to the initial slippage. However, the epicenter should not be confused with the point in the affected area which experiences the strongest or the longest shaking; for depending on the angle of the fault through the bedrock, the surface point nearest the focus of the quake may be several miles away from the fault. And the fault is almost always the center of the greatest quake intensity and, therefore, the greatest potential for damage.

One side of the Bryant Elementary School in Helena, Montana, was seriously damaged in a moderate earthquake on October 12, 1935. The weakened brick structure was then progressively rattled to pieces by a series of aftershocks, so that by October 31, when the second photo was taken, the school was a total loss.

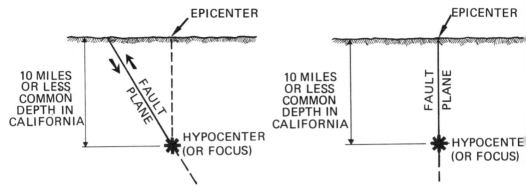

The drawing on the left shows the relationship between the hypocenter and the epicenter of an earthquake occurring on a vertical fault, such as the San Fernando. The other figure il-

lustrates a lateral fault, such as the San Andreas, in which the epicenter is projected directly above the hypocenter in the immediate vicinity of the fault zone.

Another way in which epicentral distance may be totally misleading from the standpoint of building damage is a failure to consider the response of an entire fault line to a quake at any point along its length. For example, in the 1906 earthquake, the epicenter was located near Olema, 27 miles north of San Francisco, but the intensity of the shock was equally strong along the fault in San Francisco and San Jose (more than 60 miles from the epicenter). There were also faulting and intense shock waves as far south as Hollister (100 miles from the epicenter). In other words, the damage caused by shock waves traveling from the epicenter of a quake may be small compared to the effect of the shock waves and surface displacements of the fault as it passes through a city some 100 miles away from the first epicentral break in the fault. If you wish to estimate the future earthquake hazard of a place, the *distance* from the active fault becomes the more important criterion, not the location of previous or future epicenters along that fault.

The Richter magnitude scale

The first question which comes up after an earthquake is "How big was it?" The answer can never be as straightforward as the question. Of necessity, earthquakes are measured

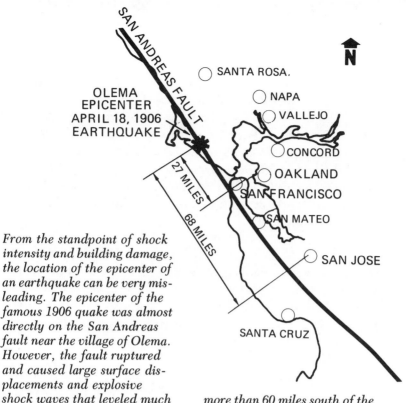

OLEMA
EPICENTER
APRIL 18, 1906
EARTHQUAKE

27 MILES

68 MILES

SANTA ROSA.

NAPA

VALLEJO

CONCORD

OAKLAND

SAN FRANCISCO

SAN MATEO

SAN JOSE

SANTA CRUZ

N

From the standpoint of shock intensity and building damage, the location of the epicenter of an earthquake can be very misleading. The epicenter of the famous 1906 quake was almost directly on the San Andreas fault near the village of Olema. However, the fault ruptured and caused large surface displacements and explosive shock waves that leveled much of Hollister, nearly 100 miles south along the fault from the epicenter. The most severe vibrational intensities were experienced not only in Olema but in San Francisco, 27 miles to the south, and in San Jose, *more than 60 miles south of the epicenter. Because of its deep and soft soil foundation, Santa Rosa was also subjected to ruinous vibrational intensities, even though it was 19 miles east of the epicenter and the fault line.*

by two rather complex scales—the Richter magnitude and any one of several intensity scales—and the two are often confused by and confusing to the public.

Earthquake *magnitude*, the amount of energy released by a quake, was originally defined in 1935 by Professor Charles F. Richter of the California Institute of Technology in Pasadena. Because there is no way to make a direct measurement of the released energy of an earthquake, Professor Richter based his scale on the alternations of a sensitive movement-measuring instrument—a seismograph—hypothetically located at a distance of 62 miles (100 kilometers) from the center of surface energy release (epicenter) by the shock. Since the distance from an earthquake epicenter to any one of many seismic recording stations would never be exactly 62 miles, complex mathematical tables are used to convert the seismograph records into the standard figures of whole numbers and decimals between 1 and 9. Advances in the seismological sciences since the introduction of the Richter scale have allowed for the comparative strength of an earthquake anywhere in the world to be reported within minutes of its occurrence, with only minor differences between the various reporting stations.

The Richter magnitude scale is also used by the media and the public, of course, for comparing the size of earthquakes, but the figures can be misleading without an understanding of the mathematical basis of the scale. The Richter scale is logarithmic, with each whole number representing a magnitude of energy release that is approximately *31.5 times* the lower number. This means that there is 31.5 times more destructive energy in an earthquake of magnitude 6 than in one of magnitude 5. The graph shown here, which measures earthquake energy in terms of tons of T.N.T., demonstrates the vast difference between a small quake, such as that in San Francisco in 1957, and a great quake like the 1906 disaster. It is also very important to note that the effects produced by the detonation of T.N.T. are much less damaging to structures than the equivalent energy release and shock waves of earthquakes.

The largest magnitude ever recorded is about 8.9 in two earthquakes in the Pacific—one off the Chilean coast, the other off the coast of Japan. Neither quake was particularly damaging since the intensity of each shock was largely dispelled before it reached land. It is very doubtful that a greater earthquake can occur, as there are certain physical principles that constrain any greater size. For one thing, even the strongest, most enduring rock has a limited breaking strength. Most faults would give way long before a quake of magnitude 9 could occur.

What may be the greatest quake to strike California in recorded history occurred in 1872 along the Owens Valley fault, east of the Sierra Nevada. The magnitude of that quake is estimated at 8.25+. The great 1906 San Francisco earth-

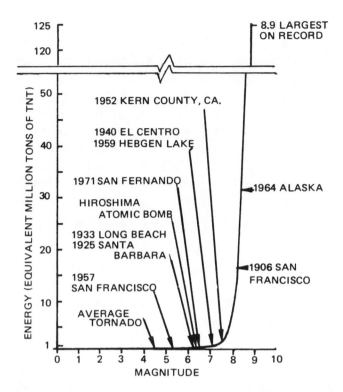

This graph dramatically demonstrates the vast differences in force or energy release between moderate quakes, such as the San Fernando, and great earthquakes, such as San Francisco in 1906 and Alaska in 1964. Note the incredible span between these latter great earthquakes and the magnitude 8.9 shocks, which are the largest on record.

quake is also estimated at 8.25, and the Tejon Pass shock of 1857 reached an estimated magnitude of 8+. The two most recent large and destructive American quakes, in Alaska in 1964 and San Fernando Valley in 1971, measured 8.5 and 6.5 respectively. A commonly accepted measure for earthquakes that relates magnitude and damage terms a "great earthquake" as one that has a Richter magnitude of 7.75 and above, a "major earthquake" at 7 to 7.75, and a "moderate earthquake" at 6 to 7. Thus, the San Fernando quake was in the category of the moderate-sized shock that can be expected approximately every four years somewhere in California.

Many people mistakenly believe that the occurrence of many small quakes in one area depletes the fault stresses and therefore annuls the possibility for a large shock. This is a myth and a physical impossibility, for with the Richter logarithmic scale, it would take about 500 shocks of the magnitude of the San Fernando earthquake (magnitude 6.5) to equal the energy released by the single great San Francisco earthquake of 1906 (magnitude 8.25). On the same basis, it would require about 1,000 San Fernando earthquakes to equal the energy of the 1964 Alaska earthquake (magnitude 8.5).

The Modified Mercalli intensity scale

Intensity scales measure the *effects* rather than the energy release of an earthquake. There are several intensity scales, all based on reports of ground and building damage and on interviews with people in different locations in the earthquake-affected areas. These scales were developed as the only means of evaluating the relative size of an earthquake before earthquake-recording instruments were available. Various categories of earthquake damage, ground effects, and personal sensations, emotions and observations were defined and were assigned numerical designations. Because the categories are mainly related to effects on people and buildings, intensity scales have become known as the "man-scaring, structure-busting" earthquake scales.

The Modified Mercalli (MM) intensity scale is the one most commonly used in the United States. The MM scale is denoted with Roman numerals from I to XII, with each number corresponding to descriptions of earthquake damage and other effects. Because the damage and ground effects are influenced by numerous factors, such as distance from the causative fault, local geology and ground conditions, the type of soil beneath the observer, the accuracy of the personal observations, etc., reported intensities vary considerably from site to site, with large differences sometimes occurring at locations only several hundred feet apart.

Since earthquake effects vary with these many factors, an earthquake cannot be assigned a single intensity number,

After a tremor, earthquake sci-
entists gather the public re-
ports of structural damage,
ground effects, interior dam-
age and personal observations
and sensations and then plot
this data on intensity, or
isoseismal maps, such as this
one from the Bakersfield after-
shock in August 1952. By
generalizing all of this informa-
tion into the Roman numeral
code of the Modified Mercalli
intensity scale, the scientists
can compile a useful visual de-
scription of the severity and
range of a given earthquake.

of course. Instead, the earthquake intensities observed at various locations are plotted on an intensity, or isoseismal map. The intensity map illustrated here for the magnitude 5.8 Bakersfield aftershock on August 22, 1952, is typical. The divisions (*isoseismal lines*) between the intensity zones form a circular pattern about the focal area of the quake, because the Bakersfield shock was relatively mild and localized. An intensity map of the main magnitude 7.6 Kern County quake on July 21 would cover a much larger area and would show elongated isoseismal lines reflecting the greater magnitude of the earthquake, the effect of the shock waves that emerged along much of the length of the White Wolf fault, and the considerable amount of faulting that ruptured the fault. The isoseismal lines between intensity zones are always at best a very rough approximation of the boundaries of the different intensities; for it would be impossible to include all of the reported variations in damage, observations and sensations for a particular quake.

Intensity maps like the one shown here are published by various public and private agencies very soon after a major or damaging earthquake strikes a populated area. In addition to these large-scale maps of the entire area affected by a quake, very detailed intensity maps of individual cities, and

How Earthquakes are Caused and Measured   **43**

Modified Mercalli scale of earthquake intensities

• The Modified Mercalli (MM) intensity scale, one of several similar measurements of earthquake effects and damage, was devised before seismographs were invented to give some kind of scientific dimension to tremors. The MM intensity scale remains useful in plotting maps which show the general range and severity of ground effects, structural and interior damage, and personal observations and sensations during an earthquake. Because the scale is largely dependent upon the observations and reports of the victims of an earthquake, these intensity maps are necessarily imprecise and approximate.

The MM scale is based on the following categories of earthquake effects and damage, coded by Roman numerals:

I. Not felt by people, except under especially favorable circumstances.

II. Felt only by persons at rest on the upper floors of buildings. Some suspended objects may swing.

III. Felt by some people who are indoors, but it may not be recognized as an earthquake. The vibration is similar to that caused by the passing of light trucks. Hanging objects swing.

IV. Felt by many people who are indoors, by a few outdoors. At night some people are awakened. Dishes, windows and doors are disturbed; walls make creaking sounds; stationary cars rock noticeably. The sensation is like a heavy object striking a building; the vibration is similar to that caused by the passing of heavy trucks.

V. Felt indoors by practically everyone, outdoors by most people. The direction and duration of the shock can be estimated by people outdoors. At night, sleepers are awakened and some run out of buildings. Liquids are disturbed and sometimes spilled. Small, unstable objects and some furnishings are shifted or upset. Doors close or open.

VI. Felt by everyone, and many people are frightened and run outdoors. Walking is difficult. Small church and school bells ring. Windows, dishes and glassware are broken; liquids spill; books and other standing objects fall; pictures are knocked from walls; furniture is moved or overturned. Poorly built buildings may be damaged, and weak plaster will crack.

VII. Causes general alarm. Standing upright is very difficult. Persons driving cars also notice the shaking. Damage is negligible in buildings of very good design and

even subdivisions, are usually plotted for the quake. The latter, in combination with block-by-block official accounts of earthquake effects and damage, can be very useful to an urban construction, slight to moderate in well-built ordinary structures, considerable in poorly built or designed structures. Some chimneys are broken; interiors and furnishings experience considerable damage; architectural ornaments fall. Small slides occur along sand or gravel banks of water channels; concrete irrigation ditches are damaged. Waves form in the water and it becomes muddied.

VIII. General fright and near panic. The steering of cars is difficult. Damage is slight in specially designed earthquake-resistant structures, considerable in well-built ordinary buildings. Poorly built or designed buildings experience partial collapses. Numerous chimneys fall; the walls of frame buildings are damaged; interiors experience heavy damage. Frame houses that are not properly bolted down may move on their foundations. Decayed pilings are broken off. Trees are damaged. Cracks appear in wet ground and on steep slopes. Changes in the flow or temperature of springs and wells are noted.

IX. Panic is general. Interior damage is considerable in specially designed earthquake-resistant structures. Well-built ordinary buildings suffer severe damage, with partial collapses; frame structures thrown out of plumb or shifted off of their foundations. Unreinforced masonry buildings collapse. The ground cracks conspicuously and some underground pipes are broken. Reservoirs are damaged seriously.

X. Most masonry and many frame structures are destroyed. Specially designed earthquake-resistant structures may suffer serious damage. Some well-built bridges are destroyed, and dams, dikes and embankments are seriously damaged. Large landslides are triggered by the shock. Water is thrown onto the banks of canals, rivers and lakes. Sand and mud are shifted horizontally on beaches and flat land. Rails are bent slightly. Many buried pipes and conduits are broken.

XI. Few, if any, masonry structures remain standing. Other structures are severely damaged. Broad fissures, slumps and slides develop in soft or wet soils. Underground pipe lines and conduits are put completely out of service. Rails are severely bent.

XII. Damage is total, with practically all works of construction severely damaged or destroyed. Waves are observed on ground surfaces, and all soft or wet soils are greatly disturbed. Heavy objects are thrown into the air, and large rock masses are displaced.

property owner in determining the range of shock wave intensities and damage that can be expected in his area during the next comparably sized earthquake. Appendix B lists these available earthquake reports and intensity maps by state and city.

Because the MM intensity scale and the Richter magnitude scale measure entirely different parameters, it is very difficult to compare the two. The magnitude scale records physical energy with instruments and therefore gives no consideration to the important factor of geologic conditions. The intensity scale, on the other hand, is necessarily less than precise since it is based solely on personal observations.

The table below provides a crude reference to the relationship between the two measures:

Magnitude	Intensity (MM)	Effects
1	I	Observed only instrumentally.
2	I-II	Can be barely felt near epicenter.
3	III	Barely felt, no damage reported.
4	V	Felt a few miles from epicenter.
5	VI-VII	Causes damage.
6	VII-VIII	Moderately destructive; some severe damage.
7	IX-X	Major, destructive earthquake.
8	XI	Great earthquake.

PART II

The geologic hazards of earthquakes—how to recognize and avoid them

CHAPTER 2

The hazards of faults and faulting

Buildings located in fault zones are exposed to the highest possible earthquake risk. This is unequivocally a fact -of life in earthquake country, and no measures—whether the most earthquake-resistant bracing and building materials nor the latest and soundest principles of reinforcement—can guarantee or even tentatively propose that any property astride a fault would survive a moderate quake without severe or total damage. It is illustrative that in a study of damaged and undamaged houses on two similar streets in Sylmar after the San Fernando quake, 30 percent of the houses within the fault zone had been posted as unsafe, as compared to only 5 percent of the houses adjacent to the zone. Similarly, 80 percent of the houses in the fault zone suffered moderate or worse damage, whereas only 30 percent of the buildings immediately beyond the zone suffered such damage.

The greatest hazard to structures in fault zones is that they are subject to ground-surface ruptures and displacements during an earthquake, and no building can withstand this faulting beneath it. A ground shift of only a few inches (vertically, horizontally or, most commonly, both) is sufficient to cause severe structural damage to buildings. A large quake, with its typical displacements in the fault zone of from several inches to several feet, could demolish the most well-engineered building.

This heavy four-story reinforced-concrete building straddled the fault that caused the Managua, Nicaragua, earth- quake in 1972. The mere eight inches of displacement at the surface of the fault was sufficient to "pancake" the building.

In addition, there is the problem of severe earthquake vibrations in a fault zone. Most structural damage to property during an earthquake is directly related to the intensity of the shock waves in the ground, and the intensity is inevitably the greatest along the fault. Thus, even if there were no faulting, any building located on or within the zone of a fault will be exposed to terrible vibrational blows. These motions are further intensified by the generally broken and unstable geologic foundations in a fault zone—the result of a long history of quakes and faulting.

Finally, some faults are subject to the more subtle form of movement called creep. This gradual movement of the opposing sides of a fault can take place in mere inches over many years, in which case damage to property would occur very slowly and might be barely noticeable for many years. More commonly, however, creep will occur in sudden week-long intervals during which the displacement may equal a fraction of an inch or more. The damage to property after a few such intervals can be considerable, and though the property can be maintained and repaired up to a point in keeping ahead of the creep damage, the property owner must eventually face up to the probability of serious structural damage from the creeping fault, as well as to the constant danger of a sudden quake that would bring larger and more destructive displacements along the fault under his building.

All of these facts about the hazards of building in fault zones have been known to geologists and soils and structural engineers for years. They have also known and meticulously mapped the locations of many of the most dangerous fault zones in the seismic areas of the Western states. Yet because of pressures from developers and landowners, because of ignorant or cynical governmental officials and outmoded building codes and zoning laws, and because of the public's ignorance, apathy and short memory, buildings continue to be constructed and bought and sold in fault zones. Many hundreds of homes and apartment buildings can be found actually straddling obvious evidence of a recent fault rupture.

People are commonly under the misapprehension that contemporary building codes in notoriously earthquake-prone areas, such as California, take the danger of faults and faulting into consideration. It is true that in California and throughout most of the Western states, the modern building codes recognize the high risk of earthquakes and set certain *minimal* standards of design and construction. However, in accordance with these building codes, almost all structures must meet the *same* standards. Permits for the construction of residential, commercial and public buildings in areas subject to earthquakes are still issued only on the basis of these minimal earthquake-resistant standards. There is rarely any recognition of the existence of the special geologic conditions and hazards of fault zones (as well as the high risk of landsliding, of landfill, alluvial and other soft soil foundations, and of dams and other man-made earthquake hazards, all of which we discuss in the next two chapters). Only in a handful of cities, including Los Angeles, is there any current plan to drastically revise building codes to account for the varying earthquake hazards of specific ground conditions.

Thus, the purchaser or owner of a property in a fault zone or on a particularly unstable site is almost always un-

How faulting damages buildings

● No building straddling a fault can withstand the abrupt surface ruptures and displacements of earthquake faulting without very severe damage. It is rare that a building can even endure the intense shock waves in a fault zone.

Unless the faulting is minute (less than a couple of inches), even the most well-built structure of the most flexible materials (wood or steel frame) will sustain heavy, difficult-to-repair and very costly damage. Foundations are cracked and thrust apart, vertical supports collapse or are knocked askew, floors and roofs sag or fall, and the interiors become a shambles of broken plaster, overturned furnishings and appliances and shattered glass and personal belongings. Rigid structures of masonry or reinforced concrete often collapse completely; a masonry or stone or stucco veneer on wood or steel framing almost invariably tumbles from the structural frame. The type and extent of faulting damage depends on the type and amount of fault movement, of course, as well as on the type of building. Generally, though, even moderate earthquake faulting will all but destroy any overlying structure.

The more insidious gradual damage of a creeping fault will not wreak such expensive and dangerous havoc, but a sudden interval of several inches of creep can leave a building uninhabitable. The inescapable conclusion, then, is that anyone holding property or living in an active fault zone with a history of past faulting is gambling his whole investment and perhaps his life on the slim hope that a large earthquake will not strike again in his area. No earthquake expert (and few insurance companies) will cast the odds favorably.

---

aware of the special dangers he faces and is comfortably suffused with the same half-baked notions and "what will be, will be" attitudes that affect the millions who reside on relatively safer sites in earthquake country. Until formal evaluations and gradations of geologic-based earthquake hazards become standard practice throughout the seismic regions of the West, a large percentage of these millions will continue to face grave danger to themselves and their properties, reassured by the unfounded belief that officialdom has done all that can be done to lessen the risks of that inevitable growling blow from deep within the earth. Hopefully, this book, in combination with the few knowledgeable legislators, engineers and planners, will finally bring home the point that it makes no sense

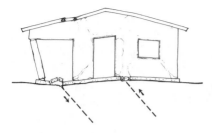

Vertical faulting thrusts the ground surface upward, destroying the foundation above it—which, in turn, breaks the vertical structural supports of the building. Very often, buildings straddling such fault movements are also pushed against adjacent structures, causing serious damage to both. In the top photograph of faulting damage in the San Fernando earthquake, the thrust of the fault was small. Even so, the structural damage to the house was extensive and very costly to repair. The other photograph is an example of larger faulting during the Hebgen Lake, Montana, earthquake in 1959. The damage to this barn was total.

to continue to build seemingly sound structures on unsound ground. The practice is a gross violation of all engineering principles; and with the example of San Fernando Valley and its collapsing freeways, dams and hospitals (or the example of Hayward, Daly City or Salt Lake City sometime sooner or later), the practice can also be termed a scandal.

The Hayward fault and the whole East Bay region of the San Francisco Bay Area provide a particularly instructive illustration of our total neglect of the special problem of fault zones in seismic areas. The Hayward fault has experienced significant faulting in historic times and continues to display the perceptible activity (including some creep) which indicates the ever-present risk of a large tremor. A *partial* list of

Lateral faulting shifts one or the other or both sides of the fault to a new position. The movement splits the foundation and in large displacements can tear an entire building apart. An illustration of what extremely large lateral faulting could do to a foundation slab can be seen in this 1906 photograph of a road which crossed the San Andreas near Point Reyes Station. The faulting displacement was more than 20 feet in this area near the epicenter of the earthquake. Lateral fault creep along the Calaveras fault in Hollister is gradually damaging not only retaining walls, such as the one in the photograph on the right, but also the homes and other buildings straddling the fault in that city.

the schools, important buildings and places of public assembly which are located directly above or very near to the fault would fill a full page in this book. Presumably, the newer of these structures were carefully designed and built for earthquake resistance. In most cases, however, particularly with the buildings straddling the fault, this care will have been largely futile when the fault experiences a large quake. As for

A network of tension cracks in
the ground surface and a
number of small pockets of
slight landslide movements
are both common earthquake
effects in a fault zone passing
through deep alluvial soil.
The fissures or settlements
will crack a foundation, and
this damage inevitably results
in some fractures in the structural supports of a building.
In the center photograph of a
house in San Fernando, downhill landslide displacements of
a few inches opened up the
narrow tension crack which
passed beneath the house and
continued on down the slope
behind it. The damage to the
foundation and the frame of
the house is not apparent

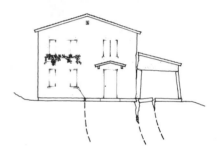

here, but it was so severe that
the house was declared unsafe
for occupancy. The right
photograph shows typical interior damage from these
types of faulting.

the thousands of homes, businesses and other buildings which
were built with less knowledge and care, the most optimistic
earthquake scholar would have to predict a broad swathe of
frightful devastation from San Pablo to Fremont in the event
of any surface shifts of the fault during even a moderate earthquake. Meanwhile, Fremont, proudly billing itself one of the
fastest growing cities in the nation, has until very recently

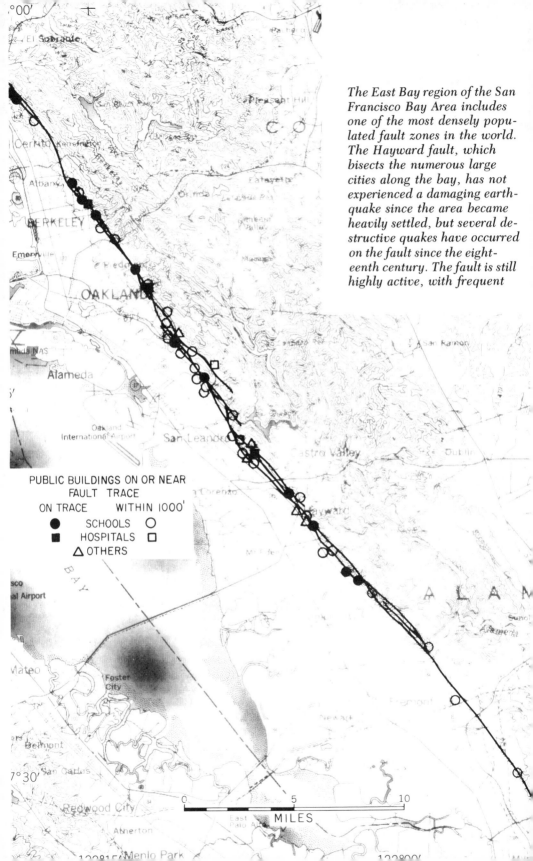

The East Bay region of the San
Francisco Bay Area includes
one of the most densely populated fault zones in the world.
The Hayward fault, which
bisects the numerous large
cities along the bay, has not
experienced a damaging earthquake since the area became
heavily settled, but several destructive quakes have occurred
on the fault since the eight-
eenth century. The fault is still
highly active, with frequent

PUBLIC BUILDINGS ON OR NEAR
FAULT TRACE

ON TRACE   WITHIN 1000'

● SCHOOLS ○
■ HOSPITALS □
△ OTHERS

0   5   10

MILES

displays of creep and small tremors, so that most earthquake experts rank the fault among the top five most dangerous earthquake zones in the United States. Note that the schools, hospitals and other public buildings marked on the map represent only a few of the hundreds of important buildings and thousands of homes that are in this fault zone.

recorded some of that phenomenal growth in bright new tracts carved into the earth directly above the surface traces of the Hayward fault.

Where the faults are—
determining the fault risk to your property

A look at a geologic map of California will show that few of the major population centers of the state are very far removed from an active fault. In the greater San Francisco Bay Area, Santa Rosa is only 19 miles from the broad and highly active San Andreas fault zone. Downtown San Francisco, the farthest point in the city from the fault, is only 9 miles away. Oakland is about 15 miles from the San Andreas and is traversed by the Hayward fault as well. San Jose is bounded on the west by the San Andreas and on the east by both the Hayward and Calaveras faults. The Calaveras fault also cuts through some of the heavily populated suburban cities of the East Bay, while the San Andreas crosses residential Daly City and then skirts the growing suburban cities of the San Francisco Peninsula.

Northeastern Los Angeles is also near the San Andreas fault, San Bernardino is located astride it, and all of metropolitan Los Angeles is criss-crossed by numerous other lesser faults related to the San Andreas. Santa Barbara is right on top of the Santa Ynez fault zone and its subsidiary fault traces. Sections of the Imperial Valley and lower Southern California

The San Andreas fault zone on the west side of San Francisco Bay is one of the most famous—and dangerous—in the world. The danger is graphically illustrated in these photographs taken in the western part of Daly City in 1956 and 1966. The sag pond, landslide, and other geologic features of the fault zone in the picture at the left are now obliterated by the landfill and concrete of a particularly overdeveloped surburban tract. Heavy property damage and some loss of life are a certainty when the next big earthquake strikes along this portion of the San Andreas. Fault zones such as this, and many similar areas in the East Bay and in Southern California, provided the ultimate rationale for pleasant and ecologically sound urban "green belts." But the irresponsibility of governmental leaders and the ignorance and apathy of the public allowed the opportunity to pass, and now it is too late in too many cases.

are bisected by the Imperial fault. In addition, there are numerous other faults in the state—near Eureka, in the Sacramento Valley, near Bakersfield—that are known to be active.

If that were not enough to sober the California resident, there is the problem of determining whether a given fault is active or inactive. The White Wolf fault, a short and relatively insignificant fault in the Arvin-Tehachipi area between Bakersfield and Los Angeles, was considered inactive for many years. Then on July 21, 1952, that theory was dramatically dispelled in the largest and most destructive earthquake in the nation in two decades. Similarly, the San Fernando earthquake occurred on the same type of fault —one which had been dutifully mapped on the more detailed geologic maps and then largely ignored as inactive. The quake in the Imperial Valley in 1940 took place on a fault which was unknown until it broke the surface of the rich agricultural landscape.

Numerous other large and assuredly active faults also exist throughout the other Western states—in Seattle-Tacoma, in Portland, near Anchorage, of course, and near Helena. A particularly treacherous fault zone—the East Bench—crosses Salt Lake City. The point is that it is impossible at the present time to predict the future behavior of the known faults, and new faults will continue to appear abruptly as they shake and rupture the ground in an unexpected tremor. Only one thing is certain—earthquakes and the associated faulting will continue to occur in the Western states, and there is nowhere, particularly in California and Western Alaska, where one can go to escape the risks of at least minor tremors. The other western states are generally less active than California and Alaska, but they are active, and potentially dangerous, nevertheless.

Still, the majority of damage from future shocks will occur along the *major* faults, such as the San Andreas, the Newport-Inglewood, the Santa Ynez, the Hayward, which are well-known and well-mapped. Professor Charles F. Richter, the noted seismologist, lists the most likely faults in California to experience *great* earthquakes in the future. In order of likelihood, they are:

1. A repetition of the 1857 Tejon Pass earthquake along the San Andreas fault in Southern California.
2. A repetition of the 1906 San Francisco earthquake on the San Andreas fault.
3. An earthquake in the Owens Valley, east of the Sierra Nevada, comparable to the great tremor of 1872.

4. An earthquake on some other large fault in California.

5. An earthquake in the central Coastal range, connecting the sections of the San Andreas which moved in the 1857 and 1906 shocks.

In category 4, most earthquake scientists would include, in no particular order, the Santa Ynez fault near and in Santa Barbara and the Hayward fault. They would also include a few faults outside California, including the East Bench fault in Utah and the highly active fault system along the Pacific coast of Alaska.

The first step in establishing the earthquake risk for a given site is to locate your property or the property you wish to purchase on a geologic map which shows the local active and inactive faults. The maps are essential because faults are not always obvious to the eye. The break always occurs initially deep below the surface of the earth, and it may never surface with ruptures or displacements, even during violent earthquakes. In addition, surface evidence of faulting can be absorbed and hidden by excavation and landfill, under the natural deposits of deep alluvial soils, or below the ocean or a lake surface. Or it may have been inadvertently or purposefully disguised by the bulldozers of land developers.

Certainly, neither individual property owners nor developers are going to be anxious to divulge the information that a fault runs under or near their property. Thus, until regulatory laws and building codes are reformed, the prospective buyer or builder or the present owner can rely only on professional consultants and/or on the information readily available in the maps of the U.S. Geological Survey and other state and local agencies. The maps are easy to obtain, are sometimes free, and are quite simple to read after a little study of the sample materials provided here. An extensive list of the sources and the numbers and titles of these maps is provided in Appendix B of this book, categorized by states and localities.

The second step in establishing earthquake risk for a given site is to determine the history of the nearest fault—the frequency, magnitude, intensity patterns and displacements

The trace of the East Bench fault in Salt Lake City can be clearly seen in the face of an excavation for an apartment building.

FAULT TRACE

The apartment building in Salt Lake City now straddles one of the most potentially dangerous faults in the United States. Regardless of the strengths of the building, a large earthquake and any faulting will almost certainly destroy the structure.

or surface ruptures of past quakes. All of these considerations are essential in weighing the risks of living or buying or building near (not *in*) a fault zone. You can do at least some of the initial research in Appendix A, which is devoted to a summary of the significant faults and quakes of the West and includes numerous maps of the major faults passing through urban areas of the Western states. Appendix A also contains necessarily brief reports and recommendations regarding past faulting, the varying intensities of past earthquakes, and the special geologic conditions and structural/architectural requirements affecting the larger urban areas near each fault zone.

How far from a fault zone is far enough?

This is one of those questions that everyone asks, assuming or hoping that it will bring a straightforward answer. It won't, of course; for unless your property is located within an active fault zone, the earthquake hazard varies, and simple distance is not always the most important factor.

In the background of this picture of an outlying street in Hollister, you can see a prominent scarp created by past faulting along the Calaveras fault.

How to identify signs of past faulting or fault creep

• The signs of past faulting abound in earthquake country, and those that have not been obliterated by the bulldozer are often easily recognizable. The Hayward fault through the hills of the East Bay region of San Francisco Bay is typical. In parklands, open fields, and undeveloped areas, the fault can be recognized as a series of low, steep scarps which resemble small quarry cuts in the gentler slopes of the hills. Numerous springs are often found at the bases of these scarp traces. In other sections, as in parts of Oakland, the fault and its zone forms a steep, narrow and straight canyon. Further south, through Fremont, the fault is marked by a series of natural sag ponds and other depressions, arranged in a very linear pattern. All of these geologic features are classical examples of recent movements along the fault.

Generally speaking, of course, the further you are from a fault, the better off you will be. However, the geologic foundation of your homesite also plays an important role. As you will learn in the next chapter, certain soil foundations intensify the shock waves of a quake. Certain soils, usually the same ones, are also prone to severe settlement during a quake—an action that few structures can withstand without serious damage. Thus, in a large earthquake in which the shock wave intensity remains strong many miles from the fault, a house on one of these unstable geologic foundations may suffer as much or more damage as a similar house on stable ground very near the fault zone.

In making a decision, then, about the relative risks of different locations all within *20 miles* or so of a fault, the main considerations should be the geologic foundations of the sites and the past history and future prospects of the fault. The way

In lieu of an earthquake, the signs of faulting damage to buildings can best be identified in a fault zone subject to creep. Numerous sidewalks, curbs, and retaining walls in Hollister, Hayward and Concord show a sudden offset or deformation where the creeping fault crosses the structures. Some sections of the Hayward Fault through the old city of Berkeley show creep deformations that exceed three feet, whereas the newer streets and curbs of Concord may show merely a couple of inches. Where houses straddle the slippage plane of the fault, patios are cracked, garage doors and retaining walls lean rakishly to one side, and underground pipes are bent and sometimes break. A few houses through Hollister have been tilted sharply by the fault. Most of the interior effects of creep—plaster

Creep on the Hayward fault near the center of Hayward has cracked the pavement and caused the garage to lean to the right.

cracks around doors and windows, doors and walls out of plumb—are identical to those produced by slight landsliding or local ground settlement beneath the structures, the topics of two display pages in the next chapter.

that you discover the former will be described in the next chapter. Information about the past history of a fault can be found in Appendix A. Generally, anyone living in coastal California or Alaska or in Utah should presume that they are "too near" a potentially explosive fault zone and should give primary consideration to the geologic foundation of his property, the strength of his building, and the need for insurance coverage.

There is one further consideration. It is quite fortunate for those who must live near a fault that the surface ruptures of faulting are almost always restricted to the relatively narrow area immediately adjacent—that is, within 500 feet or so—of the fault line. The San Andreas, for example, has typically ruptured and displaced the earth only within the narrow confines of the fault zone. Some faults, however, do not follow this linear pattern. Instead, they tend to fracture the ground surface over a broad area sometimes extending for hundreds or thousands of feet. Many people in the Sylmar-San Fernando area lost their homes to such ground displacements in 1971. And because the nearby fault had not previously been considered active, there could have been no advance warning of this hazard from geologic maps or earthquake experts.

This type of faulting is especially associated with flat plains or valleys backed or surrounded by mountains. The deep alluvial soil deposits in these flat areas are unable to contain the faulting to the narrow fault zone. The San Fernando Valley is such a region, as are the basins bisected by the White Wolf fault in Southern California and the Wasatch fault in Utah. Other such areas can be readily identified with geologic and fault maps.

The best recourse for people already living adjacent to a fault zone in such alluvial basins is to study carefully the detailed maps available for these areas from the government sources listed in Appendix B. If the maps indicate that faulting has occurred in a particular random pattern during a previous quake, you can assume that the pattern is likely to be repeated with the next tremor. And if that pattern crosses over or near your property, you should either relocate or obtain ample earthquake insurance and then seek professional help in reinforcing your home.

As we have noted, the problem of soil foundations and the possibilities of reinforcement and insurance are examined in detail in the following chapters. At this point in the book, you are merely reminded that proximity to one of the major active faults is not the sole or even the most important criterion for evaluating earthquake risk to your property. So long as a building is not located *within* the fault zone, it can survive an earthquake *if* (1) it is located on a stable geologic foundation, and (2) it is constructed or reinforced to be sturdily resistant to the forces of the shock.

What to do about a property in a fault zone

For the unfortunate thousands of people who find their property on or immediately adjacent to an active fault zone, a structural engineer or geologist will generally have little to

The line of faulting accompanying the 1971 San Fernando earthquake just caught the right-hand corner of the building, breaking the stairway. The land across the street is now developed and the traces of the fault are covered until the next earthquake on the fault leaves a path of damaged buildings. As a home owner or home buyer in an area crossed by a fault, you cannot rely on the inadequate zoning ordinances of a city or county or the honesty or knowledge of a developer. You must procure the available detailed fault maps of the area and establish for yourself the proximity of faults and faulting to your property.

say of reassurance. You should consult one, nevertheless to determine, first of all, whether the fault has demonstrated surface ruptures, displacements and/or creep in your area in the recent past. If not, there is a slim chance that the fault beneath or beside you will remain true to its history and that an earthquake on that fault would subject your home only to intense vibrations, and not to the foundation-splitting displacements of faulting. In this case, two further contingencies are important to the survival of your property during the quake and its aftershocks: (1) the *specific* geologic foundations of your property—a job for an experienced geologist; and (2) the strength of the design, structure and materials of your building—a task that an engineer must handle.

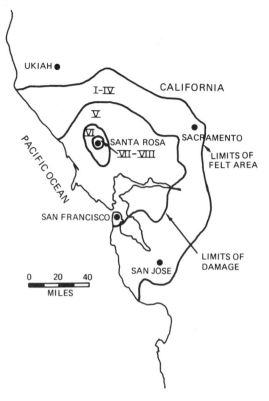

Because there were no surface ruptures or displacements in the Santa Rosa shock, the intensity map of that earthquake shows the circular pattern of ground effects and building damage arising from the epicenter of the quake.

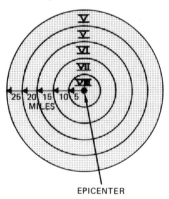

How far from a fault zone is far enough?

● Buildings located within a fault zone, and most especially those straddling the fault traces, risk severe damage and likely destruction from the ground ruptures and displacements of faulting. For those buildings beyond the fault zone, property damage is directly related to the intensity of the shock waves and ground vibrations, and this intensity level is usually closely related to (1) distance from the surface ruptures of the fault, or if there is no surface faulting, to (2) distance from the epicenter of the earthquake.

In order to understand the importance of the two factors of distance from a fault zone and the history of faulting in that zone, you can look at the typical damage-distance ratios of two very different tremors—the moderate, non-faulting Santa Rosa quake in 1969 and the great, dramatically faulting San Francisco quake in 1906:

The approximate distances represented by the intensity map for the Santa Rosa earthquake are shown in this graph. The maximum intensity of VIII affected an area of about five miles around the epicenter. The lowest damaging intensity (V) was experienced about 25 miles away from the epicenter. A stronger shock, with an epicentral intensity of XI, would have generated a damage rating of VII more than about 25 miles away.

66   The Hazards of Faults and Faulting

This intensity map of the San Francisco quake shows an elongated rather than circular pattern of ground effects and building damage. This elongated pattern results from the large-scale faulting along some 270 miles of the San Andreas. The violence of the surface ruptures and displacements along the fault generated a 270-mile-long continuous sequence of shock waves that nearly equaled the vibrational intensity in the area immediately surrounding the epicenter of the quake, a few miles north of San Francisco. The lengthy faulting also significantly increased the duration (and therefore the damage) of the vibrations. The Santa Rosa quake lasted about 10 to 15 seconds, whereas the 1906 vibrations exceeded 60 seconds.

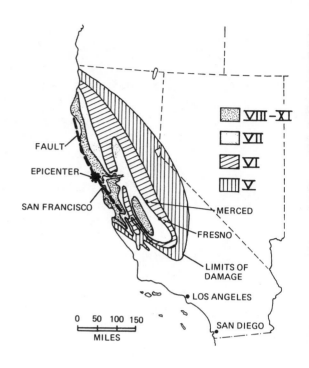

The distances affected by the monstrous San Francisco earthquake are shown in this graph. The highest intensity of XI was experienced for 270 miles along the rupturing fault and affected areas roughly five miles away from the fault. The very damaging intensity of VIII was generated over 35 miles from the fault, and the limits of building damage and reported experiences of feeling the quake extended as far south as Bakersfield (250 miles from San Francisco) and as far east as Reno, Nevada, more than 200 miles from the fault.

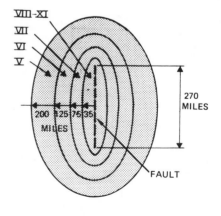

The Hazards of Faults and Faulting   **67**

As this book has repeatedly stressed, problems with the latter contingency are usually correctable at reasonable expense and may even be done by a knowledgeable do-it-yourselfer (with some professional guidance in this case of a fault-zone site). In regard to the former contingency—the geologic foundation—there is little point in spending much money on the structure if the geologic composition of your property is subject to faulting. There are rare geologic conditions within a fault zone—small blocks of unfractured rock, for example—that will lessen the vibrational impact of a tremor and make the risk moderate rather than intolerable. Extensive geologic investigations have revealed such conditions along the Hayward fault on the campus of the University of California at Berkeley, and new buildings have been sited and built with these conditions in mind. These careful geologic investigations are expensive, however, and are seldom worth the cost to an individual homeowner. Only the geologist can advise you on this.

In summary then, the rules regarding faults and your property are as follows:

1. If you are thinking of purchasing property or a building within an active fault zone, *don't*. If the fault is apparently inactive, hire a geologist for a careful investigation before you take the expensive gamble.

2. If you already own property within an active fault zone, determine from the materials in this book and from a geologic map whether the fault has experienced past displacements or creep. It would be advisable to hire a geologist to assist you in this research.

3. If the answer to 2 is "yes," there are really only three sad and costly alternatives:
   A. relocate the building to a safer site.
   B. abandon the building or, if possible, lease it for other than a living site. Of course, you could sell or also rent the building as a home, but this would be unconscionable, and if you were to try to salve your conscience by warn-

ing the new occupants of the risk, you would probably open yourself to liability in the event of a quake.

C. hire an engineer to advise you in strengthening the home to the best of his ability. Then, try to secure an insurance policy for earthquake damage and hope for the best. Properly reinforced and perhaps restructured, your home can probably be made safer for its occupants. It is very unlikely, however, that such measures could protect the building itself from expensive damage.

If it proves necessary, the decision to abandon your home or to take on the great expense of moving it to another location will inevitably be a difficult and bitter one. And until local governments become wiser and treat fault zone lands in the same way they sometimes handle recurrent flood zones—buying the land at minimal prices for parkland or leased pasture land and green belts—there seems to be no way to make such a decision less hurtful to your pocketbook. However, consider this: If a large earthquake should devastate your area, the resale value of your property will certainly plummet, especially now with the greater knowledge among the media about the relation of faults and earthquake damage. So, by moving yourselves or your home now, you are taking the loss on your own terms, which is far better than losing everything—building, furnishings, treasured objects, even lives—and then coping with the lost value of the property at the same time. Small comfort, perhaps, but a comfort nonetheless.

CHAPTER **3**

The relative hazards of various geologic foundations

During the early morning 1906 San Francisco quake, some people living on top of the famous hills of that city were not even awakened by the enormous tremor, and numerous unreinforced masonry buildings located on these bedrock hills survived the earthquake without significant damage. On the other hand, in homes atop the landfill along the bay and the alluvial soils between the hills of San Francisco, people were thrown out of bed by the shock and found themselves unable to get on their feet during the 60 seconds that the motion lasted. Many of the buildings in these flat, thick-soiled areas totally collapsed.

The reason for the sharper effects of the quake in alluvial and landfill foundations is that the intensity of earthquake vibrations increases as the rising earthquake waves enter a thick layer of soft soil or the unstable mixtures of soil and broken rock found in some landfills. These soft, unstable soils act much like jelly in a bowl, responding to and then amplifying the earthquake motions further, so that the shock waves are transformed from rapid, small-amplitude vibrations in the deep bedrock into slower and more damaging large-amplitude waves. The chaotically undulating motions of these waves can be devastating at the surface, particularly near the bases of rock outcroppings (the San Francisco hills) and in landfill and water-saturated soils (the bayside buildings). Dur-

The violent surface waves of the 1906 quake left their pattern on the badly fractured pavement of Dore Street in San Francisco. The waves and the intense vibrations also threw the buildings off their foundations or caused the ground settlement that left the structures severely raked.

ing the 1906 quake, surface waves of two or three feet passed over the earth, tipping and toppling buildings and creating a washboard effect in the cobblestone streets.

An earthquake-hazard map of California, Alaska, and much of the West would be largely a soil map. Such a map would show that aside from the actual fault zones, with their unstable broken bedrock, the highest earthquake-hazard areas are always the natural alluvial soils and man-made landfills in the valleys and near the coast and bays. The hills and mountains, which are composed mainly of solid bedrock with a thin soil surface, would appear on the map as the lowest risk areas.

Even a site on the bedrock of a *steep* hillside is safer than most others, unless the building is located on the broken rock and soil of a landslide area or the contractor has cut into the slope and then used the loose cuttings for landfill lacking the proper grading, compacting and drainage. Post-earthquake studies have invariably shown that structures built on solid rock near the fault or epicenter of an earthquake fare better than more distant buildings on soft soils. Only great earthquakes will reach damaging intensities on solid bedrock. However, a soil map drawn on a very detailed scale would also show numerous localized earthquake-danger spots on the hills and mountains; for river valleys and old lake bottoms, sea cliffs, and patches of landslide-prone fragmented rock produce pockets of high vibrational intensities.

The same highly detailed map would also show wide variances in risk from one homesite to another in a city or neighborhood, since urban areas are inevitably composed of a wide variety of natural and man-made soil foundations, including old and forgotten landfilled water courses, sand dunes, and water-saturated muds disguised by housing. During the San Fernando earthquake, different buildings within the small area of the Caltech campus in Pasadena, many miles from the fault, recorded vibrational levels that varied by a factor of two. This large difference in shock wave intensities is explained by the fact that various geologic foundations beneath the campus responded to the earthquake in considerably different ways.

The importance of the geologic foundation in minimizing earthquake damage can be demonstrated with a profile of the destruction caused by the 1906 quake. The intensity map shown here illustrates the distribution of ground and building damage in the city of San Francisco. The stability of rock foundations is clearly shown in the minimal structural damage on the hills of the city—Telegraph Hill, Russian and Nob Hills, Pacific Heights, Twin Peaks, Hunters Point and Potrero Hill. Note also that the summits of the hills were subject to the least shaking and destruction of any other part of the city. On the other hand, the flat alluvial areas between the hills were hard hit by the quake, with moderate to severe vibrational intensities and structural damage. The parts of the city that suffered the greatest amount of damage were the business district in the vicinity of the Ferry Building and most of the lower Mission district, which were built on landfill atop

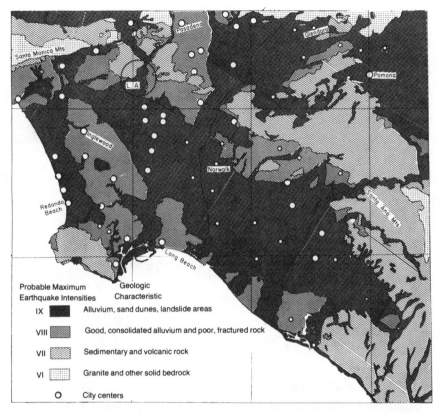

Probable Maximum
Earthquake Intensities

Geologic
Characteristic

IX ▉ Alluvium, sand dunes, landslide areas

VIII ▨ Good, consolidated alluvium and poor, fractured rock

VII ▧ Sedimentary and volcanic rock

VI ▨ Granite and other solid bedrock

O City centers

A soil map of the Los Angeles basin is a useful indicator of the varying intensities of shock waves that might be expected with an earthquake. The highest intensities (IX and up) would be experienced in and near the fault zones that crisscross the region, but comparable vibrational damage could be expected in the flat, alluvial soil areas if the quake were a large one. The lowest intensities and the least damage (VII or less) would occur in the hills and mountains, which are composed of bedrock with a thin layer of topsoil. A very detailed soil map would also show pockets of high earthquake hazard in the hills and mountains where developers have used deep landfill or careless grading in creating homesites.

the already unstable bay mud. Although these areas of the city were furthest (some 9 or 10 miles) from the fault, the land heaved and then settled drastically under the force of the shock waves, creating havoc among the light wood-frame

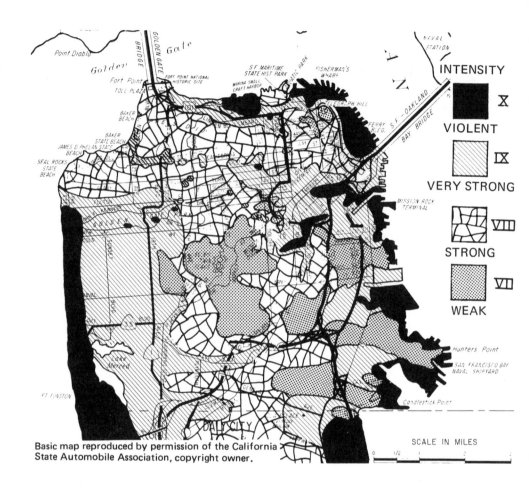

INTENSITY

X
VIOLENT

IX
VERY STRONG

VIII
STRONG

VII
WEAK

SCALE IN MILES

Basic map reproduced by permission of the California State Automobile Association, copyright owner.

This intensity map of the city of San Francisco during the 1906 earthquake indicates the widely varying effects of the shock in different soil foundations. The most violent areas were the ocean beaches of the city, which are soft soil and are also nearest the San Andreas fault. Other equally violent areas further from the fault are associated with the poorest ground conditions: landfilled swamps, water channels, bayside lands and deep natural soil foundations (alluvium) between the hills. Buildings on the bedrock of the numerous hills of the city were least affected by the powerful earthquake.

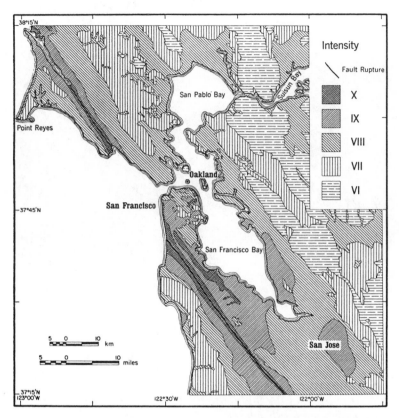

This intensity map of the Bay Area in the 1906 quake shows the high intensities all along the fault zone, in the alluvial area of San Jose, and on the bayside landfill and mud flats.

Note that the lowest intensities were recorded in the range of hills along the east side of the bay–the bedrock foundations furthest from the fault.

structures that abounded in the area. In addition, numerous fissures of several inches opened in this unstable ground, either toppling the buildings above with the shock of the displacement or allowing the high water table to surge above the surface. The latter results not only in flooding but also in the creation of a quicksand-like condition known as "liquefaction" which causes the foundations of heavy buildings to sink, tilt and break.

The sandy beach and dune areas along Lake Merced and near Ocean Beach were also severely shaken, partly be-

The building failures here are typical of the vibrational and settlement damage in 1906 in the alluvial and "reclaimed" bay lands of San Francisco. Note that some of the buildings, which were either better constructed or located on sounder soil foundations, survived the quake with little apparent damage. The photograph was taken before the fire destroyed the entire block.

cause of the nearness of the fault and partly because of the unstable water-saturated soils. At the time, this region of San Francisco was sparsely settled and damage was light. Today, an earthquake of the same magnitude would strike a densely settled area with many older homes and buildings lacking the most basic requirements of earthquake-resistant construction and design.

Santa Rosa suffered proportionally even greater damage than San Francisco in 1906 because of its geologic foundations, even though the city is more than 19 miles from the San Andreas fault—twice as far as the farthest point of San Francisco. The central business district of the town, which sits atop an alluvial plain, was almost completely destroyed by the heavy vibrations of the shock. The same comprehensive damage affected San Jose, which is located on a similar soil foun-

The central business district of Santa Rosa was leveled by the 1906 earthquake and the fire which followed it. The town is built over an alluvial plain which intensified the shock waves from the San Andreas fault, about 19 miles away.

dation nearer the fault but more than 60 miles from the epicenter of the quake. It is estimated that these and other localities relatively distant from the massively shifting fault experienced vibrational intensities equal to or sometimes greater than those in the most affected parts of San Francisco. Residents of the San Fernando Valley, the Los Angeles Basin, the valleys and flatlands of the Bay Area, and large sections of Seattle, Anchorage and Salt Lake City should take note of these experiences in 1906; for thick and soft alluvium deposits and a high level of seismic activity are common to these areas.

Problems with landfills

Like any soft soils, landfills—and particularly hydraulic sand fills and other poorly compacted fills typical of construction before the middle 1950s—introduce a much higher risk for earthquake damage than most other soil foundations. Indeed, improperly engineered landfill is often significantly

This is one of many large fissures that split the pavement in the Mission District of San Francisco during the 1906 earthquake. The crack resembles faulting but is only a local land failure due to poorly engineered landfill in a former swamp area. The structures straddling these fissures were without exception very badly damaged.

more damaging to structures than even some of the poorest alluvial soils; for the fill is often loose and insufficiently cohesive and will shake and settle drastically when the shock waves of an earthquake pass through it. Poor landfills are also frequently full of organic matter which decays and creates voids and weak spots that are prone to settlement. Filled refuse dumps, for example, are among the most dangerous sites in earthquake country because of the excessive amount of organic matter beneath the surface. Such sites, particularly when they are close to active faults, should never be developed and should be avoided if you are house-hunting. If you already own such property, relocation or extensive reinforcement and full insurance coverage should be the rule.

Even moderate ground settlement can severely damage a structure, cracking the foundation and plaster or plaster boards, breaking windows, and bringing down any weakly supported bearing walls or columns. The typically unreinforced supporting columns of a carport, for example, will quickly collapse under the burden of intensive tremors, a sudden ground settlement, and the weight of the roof. The effect of differential ground settlements, in which one part of a site (and building) settles more than another because of different geologic foundations (sand fill and clay, for example, or bedrock and a fill of soil and loose rock cuttings), can result in even greater structural damage and frequently the collapse of a building.

Modern methods of landfill engineering, which include careful compaction and selection of fill materials, have partially reduced the earthquake hazards associated with landfill foundations. During the 1957 San Francisco earthquake, for example, the well-compacted fill under the newest subdivisions of Daly City was apparently not a significant factor in the moderate structural damage to homes in the area, even though some of the fill was 35 feet deep. However, the earthquake was a minor one, so that these landfill sites were not subjected to great vibrational forces. Whether the filled areas are sufficiently well-engineered to protect structures during a large magnitude quake remains to be seen.

Certain hillside and hilltop developments, such as the tracts carved out of the hills in Southern California, are not always as secure and stable as their high elevation would suggest, and such sites should be approached with great caution if you are shopping for a home. This is most especially true when these areas are also near active faults. Steep hillside sites are obviously going to be largely graded and filled; and if the fill is poorly compacted or the grading is careless, these sites can be very risky, even in areas subject to only moderate-intensity quakes. A moderate quake (even a heavy rain) may cause such a fill to slip, taking the house down the hill with it or severely damaging the foundation and structural supports of the building. There is also the danger of a poorly graded or supported cut above the house surging down upon the walls and roof and destroying or badly damaging the structure.

Some high-elevation landfill sites will not be so obvious, though they can be equally hazardous. Developers of a large tract often level some of the hilly terrain and carelessly dump the refuse in small ravines or depressions to provide additional flat homesites. Thus, although you are located on the apparently stable ground of a hill, your home may actually be built directly over such a loosely filled ravine; and while your neighbor might come through a large earthquake with little damage, your home might be demolished by the ground settlement or intensification of earthquake waves resulting from the fill beneath you.

How to identify ground settlement

• It is essential to identify any signs of local ground settlements under buildings, for the foundations of such buildings will be weakened by the settlement and present a serious hazard during earthquakes. Walls or doors out of plumb; substantial cracks in basement slabs, floors, patios or walls; poorly fitting or obviously separating structural connections —all are signs of damage from ground settlement. Many other indications of damage are illustrated in the discussion of landslides later in this chapter. The shock waves of an earthquake always seek out the weakest structural elements and greatly magnify the existing structural damage. Thus, a cracked foundation will be rendered entirely by the quake or the sagging structural supports of a doorway will collapse. The damage can sometimes be corrected, but the assistance of a structural engineer is strongly recommended. The purchase of earthquake insurance is also a wise alternative. When purchasing a property, you should certainly compute the costs of needed repairs of settlement damage in the final price you pay.

Any *substantial* cracks in the foundation or in the driveway, sidewalks or patio of a building situated on a graded hillside or an apparently flat hilltop may be indicative of an inherent or man-made weakness in the site. If you notice such cracks around your home or suspect the existence of localized

The separation between these buildings is caused by differential ground settlements in the poorly filled former swamp area of the Mission District of San Francisco.

Ground settlements have distorted the sidewalk and the building foundation of this San Francisco building, causing the cracking in the masonry walls. Cracks such as these significantly reduce the earthquake resistance of the building.

fills in your development, call upon a geologist or soils engineer to aid you in investigating the subdivision records and the nature of your soil foundation. If you are shopping for a hillside or hilltop home, look for evidence of geologic instability. And if you find such evidence, it is probably best simply to look elsewhere. It is very costly and therefore seldom worthwhile to try to shore up a weak and unstable soil foundation.

Problems of hill-base sites

Very intense tremors and a large amount of structural damage are especially likely where the earthquake waves emerge from an alluvial soil and strike the bedrock of a hill. The earthquake force is increased because the shock waves are reflected and refracted at the point of contact between rock and soil, much like a wave of water rises to double its height when it meets the resistance of the shore. Thus, the alluvial base of a hill is a much higher risk area than an alluvial plain merely a few tenths of a mile distant from the hill.

One of the heaviest concentrations of damage in the San Fernando quake, for example, was along the base of the San Gabriel mountains. In these northernmost residential blocks of the Sylmar region, between the heavily damaged Olive View and Veterans hospital complexes, numerous houses were shifted from their foundations and damaged beyond repair. Many chimneys fell and nearly all the masonry walls in the area toppled. The evidence indicates that essentially all of this damage was due to the vibrations, since no faulting was observed in the area.

Similar or even greater damage could be expected along the base of hills which feature a fault, such as the East Bay region of San Francisco Bay. There, the Hayward fault parallels the base of a range of hills, and the flat, hill-nestled alluvial areas of such large cities as Hayward, Oakland, Berkeley, Albany, El Cerrito, Richmond and San Pablo should expect to bear some of the highest intensities of an earthquake along that fault.

A look around you may be sufficient to determine whether your property is located on the interface of alluvium soils with emerging rock. If you are not sure, consult the detailed geologic maps available for your area. A location in such an area, especially near a fault, requires the most stringent precautionary measures in constructing or reinforcing a building. Part III of this book details such measures, which

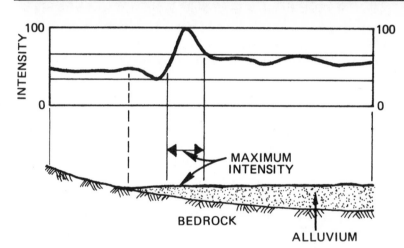

The earthquake waves rumbling through deep soil may be greatly magnified at the interface of the soil with the bedrock of a hill or mountain. Such hill-base sites are particularly susceptible to damage when a fault is nearby, as in much of the East Bay region of San Francisco Bay and in sections of the Los Angeles Basin. An example of such an area in Los Angeles is this photograph of the northeastern boundaries of Sylmar along the base of the San Gabriel Mountains. The homes here suffered the greatest damage of all the areas affected by the San Fernando quake.

would include bracing a structure for the maximum intensities of earthquake waves as well as strengthening chimneys and retaining walls and correcting any structural or architectural features that are particularly prone to vibrational damage. You should also brace any furnishings, appliances or valuable objects that may topple and purchase ample earthquake insurance.

Problems of bayside, riverside and old water-course sites

The flat alluvial lands along the shores of San Francisco Bay, the Santa Ana and Sacramento river deltas, Puget Sound and numerous other such bayside and riverside sites present a special earthquake problem. These areas are largely composed of thick deposits of a soft, silty clay which is highly compressible and unstable and has a high water content—all poor characteristics for high-intensity earthquake regions. The shock waves of an earthquake are amplified by this soft, water-saturated soil, and strong shocks can cause compaction of the clay and settlement of the ground surface. In addition, the high water content of such soils can produce the effects of liquefaction.

As we have noted, ground settlement can be every bit as damaging to a building as fault displacement. All comprehensive engineering reports on residential areas along the San Francisco Bay are agreed that both in large and some small earthquakes, the intensities and the damage will be as high in the bayside developments as they are in the fault zone itself. Such developments as Redwood Shores, Bay Farm Island, Foster City and the marina homes and apartments in Berkeley and Alameda face very great risks because they are largely on new landfill over the unstable bay mud. Records taken in the Redwood Shores development during the 1969 Santa Rosa earthquake indicated five to eight times stronger shaking than bedrock areas equally distant from the epicenter of the quake. Some of these developments also face the risk of flooding after an earthquake, because the perimeter dikes that protect them from high tidal waters are highly susceptible to earthquake damage and collapse.

In theory, at least, these waterside developments were constructed with this high risk in mind. A soils-engineering report on Redwood Shores, for example, recommends the "provision of adequate clearances between elements of the structure [to allow for maximum horizontal movement during a quake] and the proper connections of structural elements" in order to minimize the extent of earthquake damage. Although the advice in the report was sound, the building codes do not require such special provisions and it is therefore solely up to the developer to see that the recommendations are followed. Too often, the economics of construction dictate that such additional precautions be disregarded.

Before you buy a home or apartment in these or similar developments, you would be negligent of your own interests if you did not ask for a full report from the developer on the precautions his firm has taken to protect the buildings from severe earthquake damage and flooding. If necessary, have an experienced engineer accompany you in interviewing the developer and reviewing any written reports on earthquake risk. If you are building in these areas, see that the principles of structural earthquake resistance outlined in Part III of this book are fully incorporated into the plans for your home. The relatively small additional construction costs are very likely to prevent serious damage to your home in an earthquake, and the supplemental reinforcement will always result in a better, stronger, more durable structure. Earthquake insurance is recommended as well in these areas, the amount of coverage dependent on the professional assurances you have received and the precautions you have taken to lessen the risk of earthquake damage.

Riverside and old water-course sites face essentially the same problems as bay lands. Buildings located near or along present and former rivers, creeks, marshes, etc. usually entail a much higher than average earthquake risk. The strongest shaking in the destructive Long Beach earthquake in 1933 occurred in the vicinity of the coast adjacent to the mouth of the Santa Ana River. An earthquake near Puget Sound in 1965 caused considerable damage to buildings in the low-lying and filled areas along the Duwamish River in the Seattle area. The residential and commercial developments of Harbor Island, at the mouth of the Duwamish River, were also hard hit. Much, if not all, of this island was man-made,

During the 1906 earthquake, the ground along numerous rivers in Northern California lurched dramatically toward the river channels, destroying or severely damaging any structures in the vicinity. This example of a riverside ground failure was photographed along the Salinas River near the village of Spreckels, more than 100 miles from the epicenter of the quake and about 20 miles from the San Andreas. The riverside settlements along the Russian River, 140 miles to the north, were particularly hard hit. It is imperative to consult a soils (foundations) engineer before building or purchasing a home in such areas.

perhaps 60 or more years ago, and the soil is not seismically stable by any standards.

The 1906 shock in San Francisco caused some spectacular land failures along several filled creekbeds within the city. During that same quake, much of the ground along the Salinas River in Monterey County lurched and settled severely, completely destroying the small structures located in the area of failure. Numerous buildings along the Russian River, north of San Francisco, suffered similar fates.

Buildings located on old river beds, estuaries and other former water courses are among the worst locations for construction in earthquake country. These soils are usually very unstable, with numerous weak seams and channels. In addition, the landfill that usually accompanies development of such areas can intensify the instability of these lands. Numerous buildings in San Francisco that were located over and along old creek channels and swamp areas were destroyed or severely damaged by large ground settlements during the 1906 quake. Another most instructive example of such a localized failure occurred in Eastern Turkey in a magnitude 7 earthquake in 1966. A regional school campus had been built across a former river channel there. The majority of buildings actually on the old channel completely collapsed because of the amplified earthquake motions in the soft, unstable soil, whereas similarly constructed buildings on a higher gravel bench above the old river channel survived with only slight or no damage.

The recommended precautions in such areas are familiar: If you own property in the area, take out ample earthquake insurance and enlist the aid of an engineer or a knowledgeable do-it-yourselfer in strengthening your building. If the costs of these correctives are exceptionally high (as they can be on very old or poorly designed and constructed buildings), a geologist or soils engineer will be able to advise you whether the specific soil foundations of your home warrant the extraordinary expense or whether certain typical geologic conditions make lesser alterations sufficient.

Problems of coastal sites

In addition to landslides, the most typical earthquake problems for property along the ocean coasts are land settlements, the increased earthquake intensities caused by oceanside cliffs, soil liquefaction (also a problem with property located near large inland bodies of water), and *tsunamis*, or seismic sea waves.

Ground settlement

Historically, severe ground settlements along the coast during an earthquake have been the cause of widespread property damage. In some cases, this settlement is the result of fault displacements; in others, it is simply the effect of compaction resulting from the shock waves and the high water content of the soil. The great Alaska earthquake in 1964

In the coastal residential areas of Peru during the large 1970 earthquake, settlement and compaction of the soil caused a rise of the water table and flooding of many of the homes.

is the most recent example of heavy property damage due to coastal ground settlement. Many miles of the Pacific coast were partially or fully submerged, and several small towns were destroyed. The foundations of the coastal town of Kodiak permanently slumped some five feet, and faulting and compaction in the Portage area lowered the town about eight feet and made it inaccessible during periods of high tide. The highway from Anchorage to Portage, which was constructed on an embankment fill along the coast, was completely submerged. Since both the town and the highway had to be moved to new locations on higher, more stable ground, the private and public property losses and expenses were substantial.

Fortunately, California, Oregon, and Washington have not experienced any large-scale land settlement or submergence during past earthquakes, probably because of the nature of the faults and the faulting along the coasts. However, smaller scale ground settlement and even some localized submergence remain a distinct threat along the San Andreas fault zone, on the filled lands of San Francisco Bay and Puget Sound, and in beach communities and developments near the San Andreas and along the other major faults in Southern California.

When purchasing property in these areas, and particularly along the coast of Alaska, great care should be taken to select sites which are not subject to excessive settlement. Published studies of past quakes and government geologic maps will help you determine such sites. When in doubt, avoid such areas or enlist the aid of a geologist or soils engineer in evaluating a property. If you already own such a property, the best recourse is to try to insure it for maximum damage from earthquake *and* flooding damage and then hope for the best. There is little point in any significant expenditures toward strengthening the structure, for these corrective measures will be of no avail in the event of a severe settlement of several feet and the corresponding rise of the water table or of tidal waters.

Ocean cliffs

Ocean cliffs in the vicinity of large faults, such as the San Andreas in Northern California, the Santa Ynez near Santa Barbara or the Newport-Inglewood fault zone in the Los Angeles area, present special risks during earthquakes. Because the cliffs are unsupported by ground and rock on one side, they experience more earthquake motion than the ground some distance from the cliff. In addition, as the shock waves emerge from the ground, they are reflected back from the cliff face and cause further amplification of the vibrations. The Westlake Palisades section of Daly City suffered the highest amount of damage of any area during the relatively minor San Francisco earthquake in March of 1957. Earthquake experts relate the greater damage in this residential area to the sea cliff that bounds the development on the west. The earthquake waves, rising almost vertically from the nearby San Andreas, were reflected and intensified by the steep cliff, resulting in the peculiar concentration of damage in that area. Structures along such cliffs should be designed

The heaviest building damage and the highest earthquake intensities were recorded along the ocean cliffs of Daly City during the 1957 San Francisco quake. The cliffs reflected and magnified the shock waves emerging from the San Andreas.

for the highest earthquake forces and should be fully insured, particularly if the cliffs are near a major fault zone.

Soil liquefaction

Soil liquefaction is another very common effect of

This dramatic example of the effects of liquefaction in sandy or other water-saturated soils occurred in Niigata, Japan, during the large earthquake centered near there in 1964. The apartment buildings suffered only light structural damage; but the soil liquefaction left some of them tilted at 80 degree angles. The occupants evacuated some of the buildings by walking down their faces. Liquefaction occurs when the intense ground vibrations of an earthquake cause the settlement and compaction of sandy soil and the rise of the water table, creating a quicksand-like effect.

earthquakes in low-lying coastal areas or, as we have noted, wherever soft soils and high water tables exist (near bays, lakes, rivers and delta and marshlands, for example). The compaction of the soil from earthquake vibrations causes the water to flow upward, and the usually sandy or muddy soils become liquefied into a kind of quicksand. By far the most dramatic example of liquefaction occurred in the coastal city of Niigata, Japan, during a magnitude 7.3 earthquake in June of 1964. Although the epicenter of this major earthquake was about 35 miles from the sea-level city, liquefaction developed over large sections of the city, and numerous buildings, automobiles and other heavy objects gradually settled into the "quicksand."

The Relative Hazards of Various Geologic Foundations   **91**

Many tall apartment buildings settled several feet and tilted at such a rakish angle that the occupants made their escape by walking down the walls.

Studies have shown that numerous areas of California, Alaska and Washington are susceptible to equally spectacular effects—in particular the landfill areas in former delta or marsh regions, such as sections of Santa Barbara, Livermore and Pleasanton; the filled or diked lands bordering San Francisco and other bays; ocean beach developments; and the landfill sites near the mouths of rivers in Puget Sound and throughout Los Angeles. In owning, purchasing or building a structure—and most especially a large and heavy building —in such areas, you must seek the advice of a geologist or soils engineer regarding the possibility of liquefaction. The problem is expensive to correct, if it can be corrected, and the best recourse is not to build on such unstable land.

Tsunamis

Tsunamis, seismic sea waves, are caused by faulting or other abrupt ground movements on the ocean floor or shore during large earthquakes. In the open ocean, the waves are not much above normal in height, but they move at very high velocities—sometimes reaching 400 miles per hour—and when they approach a shoreline, the slope can raise them to heights of as much as 50 feet. The most recent destructive *tsunami* to hit the Pacific Coast of the United States was generated by the great Alaska earthquake. It reared more than 30 feet at its highest point and devastated many of the coastal settlements of Alaska—including Kodiak, Seward, Valdez, Whittier and Cordova—causing a large proportion of the deaths associated with that quake. It also damaged settlements along the coasts of Washington and Oregon and inundated a major portion of Crescent City, California, killing several people and causing $11 million in property damage. The damage resulted not only from the impact of the wave but from the debris—logs, sections of collapsed buildings, cars, fishing boats—carried on the water.

Tsunamis present a distinct hazard to the coast of Alaska and Hawaii and to the sea-level and beach com-

The waterfront and business districts of Kodiak, Alaska, were devastated by the tsunami that followed the huge Good Friday earthquake in 1964. Several 20-foot high waves struck the town, hurling the destructive debris of fishing boats, buildings and cars several blocks inland.

munities of Washington, Oregon and California. Bayside developments are endangered as well, for although no Pacific Coast *tsunami* within historic times has raised the actual sea level more than a few inches, an extraordinary but possible rise of two or three feet in San Francisco Bay, if coupled with a high tide and an on-shore wind, could cause significant flood damage to the residential developments protected by perimeter dikes. Certainly, the hazard of *tsunamis* should be taken seriously by anyone considering the purchase of property along the Alaskan water fronts; for the state's record of frequent major shocks makes it especially vulnerable to these destructive sea waves.

Landslide hazards

Natural landslides and rockslides occur frequently throughout the Western states and particularly in the drier regions of the West Coast, Alaska, Nevada and Utah. The reasons for these concentrations of landslide-prone areas are the hilly terrains, young and weak soil materials, poor geologic foundations aggravated by faulting, and periodic heavy precipitation. The "landslide season" inevitably comes during the wet winter months when the rains saturate the ground, the water table rises dramatically, and the "lubricated" hillside slopes abruptly begin to slide freely along discontinuities in the rock or topsoil.

The landslide problem is particularly acute in the Los Angeles basin of Southern California, where more than 4,000 large landslides have been mapped by the U.S. Geological Survey during the past 10 years. This concentration is probably higher than in any other area comparable in size; but the San Francisco Bay Area and the Anchorage area follow closely, and the heavily populated areas of Utah are not far behind. During the winter of 1968-69, the nine counties of the Bay Area suffered a total of $25.4 million in landslide damage unrelated to earthquakes.

Earthquakes increase the landslide potentials and actualities in great measure, of course. Major shocks will trigger literally thousands of large and small landslides and rockslides throughout a stricken region. In fact, much of the property damage and the most dramatic scenes of earthquake destruction in Alaska and San Fernando Valley were the result of landslides induced by the tremors. In the Alaskan quake, extensive sections of the waterfront areas of Anchorage, Valdez and Seward were carried away and destroyed by the surging rock and mud. And in San Fernando, more than 1,000 landslides, ranging in size from 50 to 1,000 feet, were triggered by faulting and the quake's vibrations. Fortunately, the California shock occurred when the soil was reasonably dry. During a wetter winter, many of the residential hillsides that were visibly ruptured by the quake would have become landslides, and the moderately shaken and damaged homes might have been totally demolished.

The Turnagain Heights slide in Anchorage during the 1964 quake was the largest and most spectacularly destructive single landslide within a metropolitan area in recent memory. During the tremor, a long bluff overlooking the sea broke into

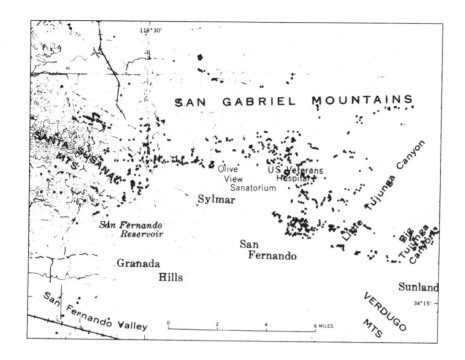

The darkened areas in this map of the San Fernando Valley represent the more than 1,000 landslides and rockslides generated by the 1971 earthquake in the still lightly developed San Gabriel Mountains. The slides, which varied in size from 50 feet to over 1,000 feet, were responsible for a large proportion of the building damage during the quake. The number of slides was minimal for the size of the earthquake, because the shock occurred during a dry year. A similar earthquake along the heavily settled Newport-Inglewood, Whittier, Wasatch and Hayward faults during a rainy winter could result in a high death toll and millions of dollars of damage to property.

thousands of earthen blocks and flowed outward toward the water, sweeping away a land mass nearly two miles long and 800 to 1,200 feet wide. The end of the slide extended far out beyond the previous shoreline, and the head of the slide formed new bluffs as high as 50 feet. More than 70 buildings, among them the finest homes in the city, were carried some 500 to 600 feet by the slide, and all were destroyed. Another

The tremendous size and destructiveness of the Turnagain Heights landslide in Anchorage can be seen in these aerial and "upslope" views of the aftermath of the earthquake. Published studies before the earthquake had indicated that the area was highly susceptible to slide damage, particularly during earthquakes.

slide, which occurred in the middle of the business district along Fourth Avenue, dropped 11 feet almost vertically. All of the buildings in the area had to be removed, and most were complete losses. The city experienced several other smaller slides as well, causing tilting, broken foundations and other heavy structural damage.

For our purposes, there are two interesting and important lessons in this dramatic and tragic ground failure in Alaska. First, the slide risk in Anchorage was eminently predictable. The geology of the area had been investigated and recorded in great detail by the U.S. Geological Survey in 1959, and a published map indicated that landslides and slumps had occurred in the area in the past. Referring specifically to the Turnagain Heights area, the geologic report stated:

> Shocks, such as those associated with earthquakes, will start moving material that under most conditions is stable. . . . Stronger shocks may be enough to exceed the shear strength of the dry material and cause it to move.

Had the city government been more conscientious and the home builders and buyers more alert, the destruction might not have occurred.

The second lesson is that the geologic and seismic conditions that resulted in the Anchorage slides are to be found along innumerable bluffs and hillside "view" locations in Washington, California, Utah and other areas of Alaska. As in Alaska, the forewarning maps and reports are readily available for most of these areas. And keep in mind that earthquakes only magnify the possibility of a landslide. In most cases, the danger is already there, and a heavy rain storm could bring the slide down.

The causes of landslides may be grouped into two general categories: natural geologic deficiencies, and man-made problems. Natural geologic flaws are usually responsible for the large slides, whereas the smaller, localized slides that affect a single or a small cluster of buildings tend to be the result of man-made problems. The danger from earthquakes is equal for both categories.

The most common natural condition for landsliding is a hillside, hilltop or bluff in which the geologic foundation of rock or stable soil is layered by thin clay seams—sometimes so thin as to be virtually indetectable—that give way when they become water-saturated or the lateral forces of an earthquake

Typical causes of
localized landsliding

● Landslides in hillside subdivisions are not always the result of naturally unstable slopes. Frequently, the slides will occur where a basically stable soil foundation has been disturbed by careless and poorly engineered grading or landfill. Home buyers and builders should consult the available geologic maps to be sure that a hillside property has no past history of sliding and no apparent potential for failures. In addition, they should be aware of the characteristics of poor grading or fill and should investigate the stability of the slope above and below the house before committing themselves to the sale.

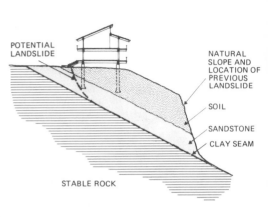

POTENTIAL LANDSLIDE

NATURAL SLOPE AND LOCATION OF PREVIOUS LANDSLIDE

SOIL

SANDSTONE

CLAY SEAM

STABLE ROCK

The building site here has the natural ingredients of a landslide area: (1) The gradual rise of the natural slope is abruptly broken by a steep incline –an indication that a slide probably occurred at that point in the past. (2) A thin seam of clay lies between the bedrock and the upper soil levels. Clay is very susceptible to sliding in such circumstances, especially when it becomes water-saturated and "lubricated" by heavy rainfall. Only a careful geologic investigation –usually with drill holes –will reveal these thin clay seams, but many potential slide areas have been recorded and marked on the landslide and geologic maps of various agencies.

---

break the very weak frictional bond holding the clay. The *flow slide* is another common form of natural landsliding, generally occuring in association with earthquakes. Flow slides are triggered by liquefaction under sloping ground. As we have learned, liquefaction is an upward flow of the ground water due to an earthquake's compaction of a water-saturated soil. The liquefied soil simply flows away from its base in a muddy morass. The massive landslides in Anchorage were primarily of this type. On a much smaller scale, the slumps that occur-

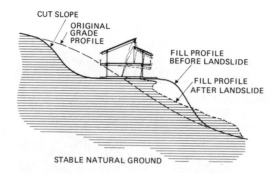

CUT SLOPE
ORIGINAL GRADE PROFILE
FILL PROFILE BEFORE LANDSLIDE
FILL PROFILE AFTER LANDSLIDE
STABLE NATURAL GROUND

Here, naturally stable ground has been disrupted by improperly graded or compacted landfill. New hillside developments are frequently stacked in a parallel series of cuts into the slope and landfills below the cuts to provide flat building sites. If the fill is not carefully engineered, it will be very subject to settlement of sliding during an earthquake.

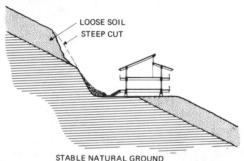

LOOSE SOIL
STEEP CUT
STABLE NATURAL GROUND

In this case, there is no problem of landfill. Instead, the cut slope above the house was graded too steeply, and the loose soil along the cut tumbled down during the motions of an earthquake. Such a slide occurs because the poorly graded cut exposes and removes the support from the inclined soil layers or from a weak clay seam.

red along the shore of Lake Merced in San Francisco during the minor 1957 shock were flow slides.

The generally more localized, man-made slides occur on naturally stable slopes that have been disturbed by poorly engineered grading and landfill for homesites. Typically, a stable slope is cut and filled for a flat lot without the provision of support for the inclined soil layers at the uphill face of the cut. A great deal of rain and/or a moderate earthquake can loosen the freshly exposed inclined soil layers and send them

How to read and interpret landslide maps

● Anyone owning or purchasing property in known landslide-prone areas, in canyons, on slopes that are not obviously rocky, and on coastal or riverside cliffs or slopes should consult a landslide map to determine the stability of the site. Numerous maps of past landslides and landslide-prone areas are available to the public either without cost or for a very minimal charge. Appendix B includes a list of many of these maps and the agencies which publish them. The maps can also be examined at many libraries and government offices, some of which are also listed in the Appendix. The two maps here are typical of those available.

A detail from Map MF-360, Landslide Susceptibility in San Mateo County, California *(U.S. Geological Survey, 1972). The entire county is zoned for landslide risk. Zone I represents minimal risk; zone IV, a serious landslide potential. The "L" notations on the map indicate areas either actively sliding or with a past history of sliding. Note that some of the "L" areas are heavily settled. Maps on a scale such as this are intended primarily for planning subdivision-sized blocks of land in undeveloped areas. The slide locations are indicated approximately and numerous small slides are not included. Therefore, this type of map is not particularly useful for the siting of single buildings. Still, the maps may be helpful to an individual property owner in obtaining a general understanding of the landslide risk for an area. And if your property or a property you wish to purchase is located within the higher zones–grade III or IV–on the map, it would be essential for you to seek the services of a geologist or soils engineer in investigating the site. The fees of these professionals are minor compared to the total cost of purchasing and developing the property–or salvaging it after a slide.*

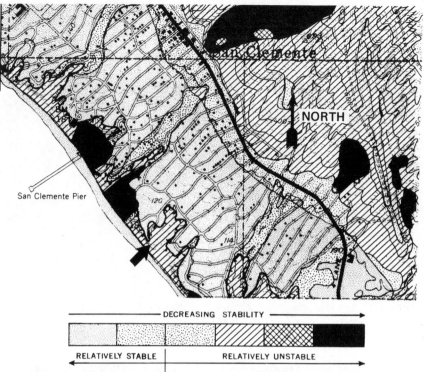

San Clemente Pier

DECREASING STABILITY

RELATIVELY STABLE

RELATIVELY UNSTABLE

A *detail from* Landslide Susceptibility in San Clemente, California (*California Division of Mines and Geology, 1968*). *This map of a portion of the San Clemente area is much more detailed and may be used by an individual property owner with greater confidence and precision. A distant but large earthquake along the Newport-Inglewood fault north of San Clemente could easily trigger some of the unstable areas.*

Many city and county offices have these detailed maps of all landslides which have been recorded and/or have damaged property in the past. Since slide damage is easily and frequently bulldozed and rebuilt by developers, you should always consult a de-

tailed landslide map when purchasing property which shows signs of instability or which is located in the kind of terrain susceptible to sliding.

Even a detailed map such as this is not likely to show the localized pockets of landslide hazard created by faulty landfill and grading. Only the very large landfill subdivisions are generally noted on landslide-susceptibility maps. Thus, a property owner in a hillside or bay or riverside development that is likely to include some landfill must very zealously pursue the information he needs from the developer, from city and county records or from a local geologist or soils engineer.

The photograph on the right shows a view of one of the residential areas plotted on the San Clemente map (see the arrow). The slope-stability rating for this area was "moderately unstable." Note the house under construction and the old slide debris at the base of the cliff. The other picture shows the same area after a landslide has damaged several of the expensive homes. In comparing the two photographs, you should note that the first was taken from ground level, well below the houses, whereas the other was taken from above the damaged houses. Obviously, the use of landslide maps and/or consultations with a local geologist or soils engineer could have prevented the costly mistake of constructing these houses in such a high-risk area.

The large depression in the middle of this gentle coastal slope is an example of the thousands of landslides caused by the 1906 earthquake in Northern California, from Point Arena to Salinas.

This slide was triggered near the town of Half Moon Bay, just south of San Francisco. Many similar areas in the hills of that growing suburban city are now densely developed.

sliding down upon the building below. Similar failures can occur with downhill fills that are graded improperly. With the latter, water saturation or a light shock may cause the uncompacted landfill to slide, or the fill may overload the natural soil foundation at the bottom of the cut-slope, causing a failure of the whole hillside.

Many other factors are involved in the incidence of both natural and earthquake-caused landslides: the slope angle of the ground surface, the nature of the bedrock, the slope of the geologic layers, the existence of any surface or underground waterflows, the level of the water table, the type and amount of vegetation that exists or is planted or removed, the proximity of active faults, the amount of rainfall, etc. Some landslide problems are correctable at a reasonable expense, particularly those that are man-made and can be

How to identify signs of landsliding

Extensional cracks in the street above the house indicate the head of the slide. Note that the asphalt is cracked in parallel *fissures and the gutter is fractured.*

The weight of the sliding soil and house has buckled the sidewalk below the house.

avoided in the first place by good engineering practices. If you are building a home on a bluff or steep slope in earthquake and landslide country, you should, of course, have professional help from a geologist or soils engineer in determining whether the site is basically stable. Then, a structural engineer experienced in the problems of landsliding can aid you and your contractor in designing and building a sound foundation for your structure without harming the basic stability of the natural geology.

If you wish to purchase or already own property on a

Although it is not at all obvious to the eye, the house is leaning in the direction of the landslide. The tilt is visible only in the framing of doors and windows which open parallel to the slide. Here the door no longer fits well—a gap of about ½-inch can be seen in the downhill corner. If several doors, windows or cabinet doors show the same gap in the same direction, a homeowner must assume that the house is leaning and may be slowly sliding.

Typical cracks in the stucco of the same house. Such cracks tend to concentrate around openings (doors, windows, etc.) and in retaining walls.

site that suggests a landslide potential, you should, again, seek the assistance of local professionals in evaluating the site. Local geologists and soils engineers are likely to be familiar with the reliability and building techniques of the contractor who built the home in question. In addition, a professional evaluation is necessary because geologic conditions can vary drastically over surprisingly small distances and it is therefore often impossible to determine slide hazards from available landslide maps.

Several types of landslide restraints are possible in certain circumstances, but generally the costs would be excessive for most individual property owners. Also, landslide control by modern engineering techniques becomes less and less feasible depending on the size of the potential slide area, the size and instability of any sliding that has already occurred, and the proximity of active faults. Finally, the success of a slide-stabilization program usually depends on constant surveillance and costly maintenance, and there can never be a full guarantee that sliding will not eventually occur anyway.

Thus, in all circumstances, the best advice to follow is that of a local professional. First, investigate an area thoroughly with the help of fault, landslide and other geologic maps and histories and check for any surface signs of landslide potential. Then if there is any suspicion of instability, especially in the hilly areas in the vicinity of active faults, call in a geologist or a soils engineer. At the same time, it would be wise to call upon your insurance representative to purchase adequate earthquake coverage. Keep in mind, also, that if a landslide potential does not exist or can be eliminated, your hillside property represents one of the best possible investments for earthquake country.

CHAPTER 4

The man-made hazards to your property—from dams to neighboring buildings

Certain public and private structures, such as dams, tall neighboring buildings, water tanks and power lines, can present a special earthquake hazard to homes and small apartment and commercial buildings. For the purposes of this book, these man-made hazards are categorized in the "geologic" section because they exist as a more or less permanent part of the landscape and there is generally little the individual property owner can do about them except to avoid them in buying or building a home.

If there is a "lesson" in this chapter, and in this book as a whole, it is that the property owner in earthquake country must approach the task of shopping for, buying, or building a home with a special expertise and caution that are not required in other regions of the country. He must know about the geologic and man-made foundations of his building; he must look for the signs of faulting or settlement or landsliding damage; he must understand the principles of earthquake-resistant construction and materials (the subject of Part III of this book); and he must look beyond the boundaries of his property to the special man-made "geologic" hazards that may threaten his home in an earthquake.

Lake Palmdale and smaller Una Lake are reservoirs created from the natural depressions, sag ponds and scarps of the San Andreas fault zone near Palmdale in the desert of Southern California. The fault can be seen to extend in a line from the dams through Leona Valley. Several smaller sag ponds lie in the distance along the trough of the fault. Sag ponds are formed when the fracturing and tilting of the ground from faulting brings underground water to the surface and then blocks the drainage channels. Since the sag ponds are generally enclosed on all sides, they provide ideal sites for reservoirs but unfortunate and dangerous locations for the dams that create these reservoirs. Lake Temescal in the Oakland hills is another example of a reservoir formed by enlarging and damming a sag pond along a fault zone, in this case the Hayward fault.

Dams and reservoirs

Of all structures, dams and the reservoirs which they impound present the greatest danger to large, populated areas during an earthquake. The failure of a dam during an earthquake can ravage more buildings and claim far more lives than the shock waves and faulting of the earthquake itself. Ironically, most major fault zones, such as the Hayward and San Andreas or the Newport-Inglewood and the San Jacinto, provide the narrow canyons and natural sag ponds that are ideal for large reservoirs, so that numerous dams serving the cities of the West have been built along or directly over the most recent scars of earthquake faulting. Heavily populated and highly seismic urban centers like the Los Angeles Basin and the San Francisco Bay Area also contain hundreds of smaller reservoirs within the city boundaries. The majority of these dams in the urban areas are old, and only a few, such as the 50-year-old San Pablo Dam east of Berkeley, have been specifically reinforced for high earthquake stresses. Thus, dam failures are virtually inevitable during future large earthquakes.

Certainly the most frightening dam failure in the recent past was the nearly total collapse of the Lower Van Norman Dam in the Mission Hills overlooking San Fernando Valley. The massive 142-foot-high earthen dam, constructed in 1915, had been perfunctorily reinforced for earthquake hazard several decades later. However, the intense 15-second San Fernando tremor exceeded the strength of the structure and broke away almost the entire upstream surface, knocking the thousands of tons of concrete facing and dirt and rock into the reservoir. Fortunately, at the time of the quake, the reservoir was only slightly more than half full, and the slump of the dam still left a slim five-foot margin of earth above the crest of the water. If the water level had been higher, or if the quake had lasted an additional five seconds, or if a large aftershock had struck before the reservoir could be lowered to a safe level, a flood of water would have swept down the hills and through a 12-square-mile area with some 80,000 sleeping residents.

Other areas of California have not been so lucky. A similar failure of the earthen Sheffield Dam during the Santa Barbara earthquake in 1925 resulted in the flooding of the lower area of that city. A breach in the wall of the small Baldwin Hills Reservoir in December of 1963, following several years of creep along the Newport-Inglewood fault zone in Los Angeles, resulted in a disaster that claimed five lives and

This aerial photo of the Lower Van Norman Dam in San Fernando was taken one day after the earthquake had sheared the sloping concrete facing of the dam into the reservoir. Fortunately, the reservoir was only half full at the time of the quake. Even so, the slump of the earthen crest of the dam brought the water to within five feet of spilling. Some 80,000 people were threatened in the spill area of the dam and had to be evacuated until the water level could be lowered. Dam failures such as this present one of the greatest earthquake hazards to property and life, and the purchase of a home in the flood zone of an earthen dam in earthquake country can be a very poor and very dangerous investment.

approximately $15 million in property damage. Only the diligence of the reservoir's caretaker and the quick evacuation of the residential area below the reservoir prevented a much greater death toll. The Baldwin Hills reservoir was a modern structure, constructed in 1951 when the dangers of faulting were well-understood. Yet it was built over the very fault zone responsible for the large, destructive and carefully investigated Long Beach earthquake.

Even a carefully reinforced dam that is well-removed from a fault can present an earthquake hazard to nearby residents. A sudden earthquake-induced landslide into a reservoir, for example, can damage the dam or turn the spill over

Creep along a branch of the Newport-Inglewood fault through Los Angeles caused the failure of the 10-year-old Baldwin Hills Reservoir in 1963. The slow faulting under the dam slightly ruptured the concrete lining, and the water then eroded a wider channel which caused the collapse of a large section of the dam. Several houses in the spill area outlined in the photograph were washed away by the flood, and many others were severely damaged.

The houses on the right side of Cloverdale Avenue in the Baldwin Hills area of Los Angeles were completely washed away by the flood from the creep-damaged Baldwin Hills Dam. The rem-nants of foundations and a swimming pool can be seen in the foreground. Some $15 million in property loss and damage resulted from the de-cision to build a dam directly over an active fault trace.

The Man-Made Hazards to Your Property   **111**

the dam into a destructive flood. Similarly, the mere rocking motion of earthquakes, particularly the large ones that are predicted for the San Francisco and Los Angeles areas, can generate large waves in a reservoir that overflow the dam and bring serious flood damage to any structures in the spill area or near the shores of the reservoir. Such waves, called *seiches*, topped the Hebgen Dam near West Yellowstone, Montana, during the earthquake there in 1959. This is how the foreman of the dam described the waves:

> . . . I walked over to the edge of the dam and all we could see was blackness. There was no water. No water above the dam at all . . . and I couldn't imagine what had become of it. By that time the dust had started to clear, and the moon had come out a little. And then here came the water. It had all been up at the other end of the lake. . . . We could hear it before we could see it. When it came over the dam, it was a wall of water about three to four feet high completely across that dam, and it flowed like that for what seemed to be 20 minutes . . .

Three distinct waves overflowed the full length of the 720-foot dam and surged down into the unpopulated valley below. A similar series of seiches (or a dam failure) in the Mount Sutro Reservoir above the Sunset District of San Francisco could pour millions of gallons of deadly flood waters over the small homes and apartments surrounding the reservoir.

What can you do about the dam hazard in earthquake country? Nothing short of moving if you already own property in the natural flood channel of a dam or reservoir. Or if you must or prefer to gamble with the unfortunately high odds for disaster in most such locations, you should certainly purchase insurance that will cover both earthquake *and* flood damage, since most earthquake policies do *not* cover related flooding. Finally, you would be doing yourself and your neighbors a very good turn if you organized a vehement and persistent campaign to force state or local officials to undertake all possible measures—new analyses, tests and reinforcement procedures for dams and a permanent policy of lower levels for vulnerable reservoirs—to make the probability of dam fail-

In the rural areas of the West, there are countless small privately owned dams which do not fall under the jurisdiction and code requirements of the state or county. Such dams are usually built with little or no attention to sound compaction of the earth and other engineering precautions essential for earthquake country. As a result, these dams are very likely to fail during a tremor—as did this small earthen dam near Anchorage in 1964.

ures or landslide or seiche flooding less likely.

If you are purchasing or building a new home, the proximity of a dam—and especially the flood channels of the dam and reservoir—should be a major consideration in your choice of a site. The dual dangers of earthquake and flooding present too high a risk of death and destruction, and you simply should avoid properties that face both possibilities.

Dikes and levees

Typically, dikes and levees are built over and surround some of the worst possible geologic terrain for construction in earthquake country. The previous chapter noted that the water-saturated alluvial or sandy soils along rivers and estuaries, the landfilled areas over the mud of bays and marshlands, and the water-saturated sand dunes along the seashore are subject to especially intense vibrations and to the ground effects of settlement, landsliding and liquefaction during an earthquake. Any of these effects is likely to destroy a dike or levee, so that any buildings which remain standing after the quake may be subjected to the additional damage of flooding.

Generally, very little regulation or engineering analysis goes into the planning and construction of privately financed dikes and levees. Therefore, anyone living in marina developments or other low-lying waterside sites protected by such structures should make it his business to know more about their engineering and earthquake resistance. A talk with the project engineer and with a local civil engineer or the city engineering department may reassure you that all possible measures have been taken to protect the dike or levee from earthquake damage. Even so, both earthquake and flood insurance is a must for a property owner in this type of development. And for those who are still shopping for a home or investment, you would be well-advised to pass up the attractions and glamour of these waterside homes and look for a property that does not carry with it the double risks of very severe earthquake damage plus flooding.

Water tanks

Three types of water tanks present earthquake hazards to residential property: the municipal or private ground-level tank, the elevated municipal or industrial tank, and the rooftop water tanks commonly found on old commercial buildings and old, usually rural homes. The large, ground-level storage tanks of wood or concrete are probably the most hazardous of the three because they hold a very large amount of water and because they are frequently located on hilltops surrounded by residential buildings. Although the quantity of water may not be sufficient to destroy housing, the rapid flow of the water and collected debris can certainly erode the foundations of a home, flood a basement, and cause other substantial property damage. The purchase of property below or near such a structure is not recommended; for these tanks, and particularly the older ones, are highly subject to earthquake damage. If you already own such a property, be certain to carry adequate

Dikes and levees are generally even more vulnerable than dams to earthquake damage. This failure of the Isleton levee in the Sacramento River delta in 1972 was not caused by an earthquake, but it is a striking example of the damage which could occur during a sizable earthquake in the Sacramento and Santa Ana River deltas or the diked marinas and bayside developments of San Francisco Bay, Puget Sound and western Los Angeles.

insurance for water damage.

Old elevated tanks also have a very poor history of survival during earthquakes, since those built before the 1950s are seldom braced properly for the stresses of an earthquake. In every major shock there have been numerous instances of the collapse of these structures. Residential buildings are usually not located near enough to these old towers to be threatened by their collapse, but if your present home or other building is the rare exception to this generalization, you should lobby with the city or county for the reinforcement of the structure.

Property in the spill area of large water tanks, such as this one near the Hayward fault, *is subject to the dual hazards of vibrational and flooding damage.*

The small rooftop water tanks are an earthquake hazard because their position at the highest point of a building subjects them to greater vibrational accelerations than any other part of the structure. And since these tanks are often old, corroded and improperly designed for resisting tremors, it is not at all surprising that they frequently collapse during even moderate earthquakes, causing structural and water damage to the building below. The rooftop tanks present an additional hazard (and the risk of expensive litigation) if they are also located too near the edge of a roof, so that they fall upon other buildings (or upon people) during a quake. Rooftop water tanks should be frequently inspected for corrosion or cracking, properly located away from the edge of the roof, and carefully braced to prevent collapse during a shock.

The older, elevated water tanks are seldom reinforced properly for the shock of an earthquake, and every major quake has resulted in the collapse of such towers. This 100,000-gallon, 100-foot steel tank fell during the Kern County quake in 1952.

Inadequately reinforced roof-top water tanks frequently topple during an earthquake and cause structural and interior damage either to the building supporting the tank or to adjacent structures. This photograph of roof-top and interior damage is from the Puget Sound quake in 1965.

Oil fields, oil tanks and refineries

Since oil fields, oil tanks and refineries are generally far removed from residential areas, it is not likely that your home is directly threatened by any of these structures during an earthquake. However, oil spills are usually accompanied by fires, and the fire hazard can be a serious one in the more arid regions of earthquake country. Keep in mind, as well, that these oil-based fires can be water-borne, so that a waterside location near a refinery is far from ideal.

Local building codes generally require no special precautions in the location or design of oil-industry structures, and there are several instances of extensive private property losses due to fires originating in oil installations after an

This photograph of the fire in a petroleum tank yard on the docks of Seward, Alaska, was taken 24 hours after the earthquake. Such oil-based fires can spread across water, making any waterside property near an oil field or refinery a risky investment for earthquake country.

earthquake. A large oilfield fire destroyed a major portion of the Paloma Cycling Plant near Bakersfield after the Kern County earthquake, and oil-facility fires burned the dockside buildings of Seward and Valdez in the aftermath of the most recent Alaska quake.

High-voltage power lines

High-voltage power lines are generally separated by at least a narrow strip of land from any residential or commercial development. But in the more arid regions of earthquake country, the lines still present the danger of grass fires caused by the sparking of severed wires. In addition, the tall towers are subject to collapse during a severe earthquake, and falling debris and hot wires are a real danger to nearby buildings. These hazards are perhaps less urgent than some of the others listed in this chapter, but they should nevertheless be a consideration in buying, building and insuring a home.

The pounding damage to these commercial buildings in Anchorage can be seen in the cracks and shattered corner of the building on the right as well as the extensive damage to the facing and windows all along the adjoining wall of the other building. Pounding damage occurs because adjoining buildings respond with different movement to the shock waves of an earthquake. Row houses with varying roof lines are also subject to this type of damage.

The damage to the concrete-block wall of this building in San Fernando Valley was caused by pounding from the adjacent lower roofline. Such pounding damage can be avoided or minimized if the wall adjacent to a lower roofline of the same or a separate building is stiffened with horizontal beams or with a floor slab located in the same building. This gap can then be partially filled with a protective crumple-section joint of thick stucco, neoprene or other material.

Semi-attached or taller neighboring buildings

Two semi-attached or adjacent buildings with only a small gap between their adjoining walls can seriously damage one another during an earthquake. Because the two buildings are structurally independent, they respond to the tremors in two different ways and therefore pound against each other. This pounding can be especially severe at the roof level of the lower of two adjacent buildings.

Row houses are usually not subject to this type of damage because they are connected and move as a unit during a quake. An exception are the *corner* row houses, which may experience heavy earthquake damage because they lack support on one side and are therefore free to deform and twist off their foundations. If the row houses follow the slope of a hill and are at different levels, the corner houses will also be subject to pounding at the roofline from the adjoining house.

Earthquake insurance is recommended for corner row-house properties, and for the second house from the corner if the roof levels are different. Other buildings suscep-

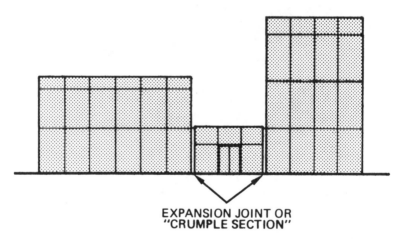

**EXPANSION JOINT OR
"CRUMPLE SECTION"**

A joint of neoprene, 3/4-inch stucco, or some other readily crushable substance provides a crumple-section joint which will protect closely adjacent buildings from serious pounding damage. The crumple section must allow some lateral movement of the buildings—about six to eight inches —and must extend to the foundations in order to be effective.

The collapse of an unreinforced and poorly connected brick wall caused this interior damage to a lower adjoining building in Bakersfield. A woman in this shop was killed by the falling debris.

tible to pounding damage (including independent parts of the same building) should be separated by "crumple sections" made up of neoprene, ¾-inch stucco or some other easily crushed material which will absorb the pounding. These crumple-section joints should allow some lateral movement (about six to eight inches) and should be inserted down to the foundations in order to be effective. After an earthquake, the damaged crumple sections can be easily and inexpensively replaced.

In addition to the problem of pounding, a low building next to a taller building is threatened with damage from debris falling from its neighbor. This is particularly a problem in the larger cities, where a one- or two-story home may be separated by only a few feet from a much taller apartment or commercial building. If the taller building has unreinforced brick or concrete-block walls or veneer, precarious architectural features (such as balconies, chimneys, parapets or Spanish tile roofing), or a water tank or an air-conditioning enclosure on the roof, the lower building may be very seriously endangered.

In the circumstance that you are building a home or small building next to a taller and old or poorly designed or masonry building, it is advisable that you leave as much space as possible between the two structures. Generally, if the taller building is not more than five to seven stories high, a 10 to 15-foot separation will be sufficient to protect your property. Another possible solution in putting up a new building is

One possible protective measure against the collapse of the masonry wall or parapet of a taller adjacent building is the construction of a new cantilevered wall—as in this Bank of America building in Bakersfield. The protective wall probably saved the bank from the type of destruction that killed a woman in the dress shop across the street.

illustrated in the photograph here, which was taken shortly after the Bakersfield aftershock. The engineer who designed the new bank building had the foresight to include in his plans a strong cantilevered wall which very likely prevented a collapse of the masonry parapets of the old neighboring building onto the roof of the bank.

If you wish to buy or already own a building adjacent to a taller and threatening structure, your best recourse is, first, to get earthquake insurance and then to check with the city engineer's office to see if the dangerous projections or rooftop structures of your tall neighbor meet local building-code requirements. Most California cities, for example, now have earthquake ordinances (rarely enforced) for the removal of potentially dangerous appendages or objects. If your city codes do not deal with this problem, you are faced with the task of convincing your neighbor that both buildings will benefit from the removal of such hazards and the strengthening of unreinforced masonry or masonry-veneer walls. Give him your copy of this book, and, if necessary, have your lawyer remind him of the possibility of lawsuits in the event of property damage or personal injury due to his negligence in not removing or correcting clearly hazardous conditions in his building.

PART III

The architectural and
structural hazards
of earthquakes—
how to avoid
or correct them

CHAPTER **5**

The principles of earthquake resistance in buildings

Two recent and similar earthquakes—the moderate San Fernando shock in 1971 and the somewhat smaller Managua, Nicaragua, quake in 1972—demonstrated anew that the most practical approach to problems of public safety and the prevention of serious damage during tremors is the earthquake-resistant design and reinforcement of buildings. The Southern California earthquake (magnitude 6.5) resulted in scattered, severe destruction and the death of about 60 people, mainly in the collapse of old, unreinforced masonry buildings. The magnitude 6.25 shock in Central America killed more than 5,000 people and demolished large sections of the city. The better performance of the buildings in the Los Angeles area can be attributed primarily to the more advanced state of earthquake engineering and superior materials of construction in this country.

Knowledge about the effects of earthquakes on buildings has steadily advanced during the years since the Long Beach quake in 1933, and the basic principles of earthquake-resistant design and construction have been well-established since the 1950s. Inevitably, the chief constraint on the incorporation of these principles in new buildings is cost. The architect and engineer are pressured by the owner or developer to reduce construction costs as much as possible by staying *just* within the limitations of the local building codes.

Unfortunately, these codes are, at best, minimally effective in meeting some earthquake hazards. And at worst, as in Utah and some of the cities of the West Coast, they are criminally negligent.

Until the public and builders and government agencies realize that a very slight increase in the construction costs of a small building will provide a very substantially sturdier and quake-resistant structure, earthquakes will continue to claim lives and to inflict unnecessarily severe and expensive damage to property. Similarly, a very modest outlay of money and effort for architectural improvements and structural reinforcement can render most older, existing buildings, and particularly wood-frame structures, far safer both for their occupants and for the investment of their owners.

This chapter presents a brief outline of the basic principles of earthquake-resistant design and construction. The remaining chapters in Part III then explore these principles in more detail and explain how you can apply them either in evaluating the strengths and deficiencies of a building you own or wish to purchase or in constructing a new building or reinforcing an older one.

The effects of earthquake forces on a building

The superstructure of any building is designed chiefly to distribute and then to carry the weight of the building and its furnishings and occupants to the supporting foundation and into the ground. This basic structural system involves some distribution of a building's weight along horizontal planes (beams, roof and flooring, for example), but, obviously, the heaviest load supported by the superstructure will be along the vertical supports (walls and columns) leading to the foundation. As we have learned, earthquake shock waves generate opposing and chaotically irregular horizontal and vertical vibrational forces in the ground. The sudden ground motions push and pull upon a building's foundation, which causes the walls of the building to expand and compress (responding to the vertical shock waves) and to bend and sway from side to side (from the lateral waves). The structure strongly resists these abrupt movements rising from its foun-

This new plywood-sided, and therefore shear-wall braced, home survived the San Fernando quake without harm, while the other house in the same area suffered very severe damage because of inadequate bracing in the garage walls and along the crawl space beneath the single-story portion of the building. Special lateral bracing is essential for all buildings in earthquake country.

dation, and the resistance creates a natural inertia which sharply snaps the building back and forth, up and down. The experience of lateral inertia in a building is precisely the same as the physical response of a person in an abruptly braking car, while vertical inertia is comparable to one's sensation in a rapidly rising or descending elevator.

Because buildings are, by their very nature, designed for large vertical loads (and because the intensities of the vertical shock waves are usually weaker in typical tremors of the western United States), the vertical forces of an earthquake are generally resisted effectively by routinely designed and constructed buildings. The horizontal earthquake movements, however, can easily exceed the lateral strength and flexibility of a conventionally built structure, and it is usually these lateral vibrations that result in cracked and broken studs and columns, separation of the superstructure and foundation, and the collapse of all or part of a building. These lateral earthquake waves can also literally burst the mortar seams of brick or concrete-block walls that are underreinforced and/or improperly connected to the framing of a building.

A building is also especially vulnerable to the lateral shock waves because the *vertical* inertia of the structure compounds its normal weight and thrusts this greater weight upon the supporting columns and walls. The strain of this weight, plus the lateral blows of the quake, can defeat any building that is improperly or inadequately designed and reinforced for these conditions. Thus, in earthquake country, and especially in areas that can anticipate very high earthquake intensities, special techniques of reinforcement—of *lateral bracing* and extraordinarily sound and durable *connections* between all of the structural components—are necessary to enable a building to absorb and distribute the lateral forces of a tremor without collapse or severe damage. In addition, four other factors—the *foundation*, the *building materials*, the *architectural and structural design and detailing*, and the *workmanship*—are important to the earthquake resistance of a building.

Lateral bracing

The most efficient and reliable means of ensuring that the shock waves and inertial load generated by an earthquake will be resisted and carried from one component of a building's superstructure to another and then back to the

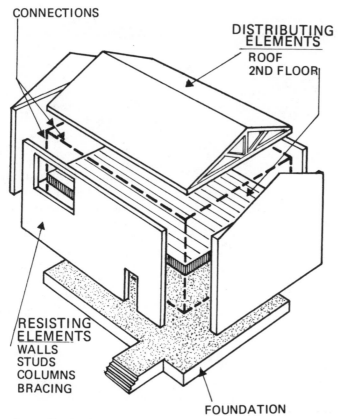

CONNECTIONS

DISTRIBUTING ELEMENTS
ROOF
2ND FLOOR

RESISTING ELEMENTS
WALLS
STUDS
COLUMNS
BRACING

FOUNDATION

The effect of earthquake forces on a building

The basic structural components of any building are four:

• The *distributing structural elements* are those that lie in a horizontal plane. These *diaphragms* (roof and floors) and *joists* (beams and trusses) tie the walls together and disperse the static weight of furnishings, occupants and the elements themselves to the walls and foundation.

• The *resisting structural elements* are the vertical components of a building (walls, columns, studs and bracing). These elements support and transfer the load of the distributing elements to the foundation.

• The *foundation*, which supports and ties together the walls and transfers the weight of the building to the ground.

• The *connections* (nailing, blocking, joints, etc.), which tie all of these components together.

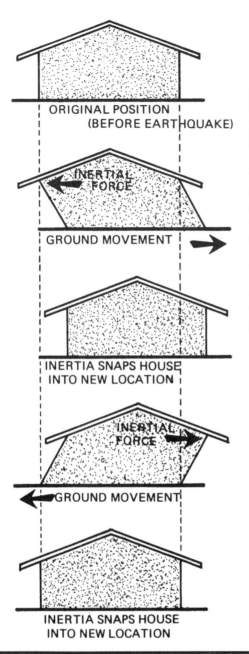

ORIGINAL POSITION
(BEFORE EARTHQUAKE)

INERTIAL FORCE

GROUND MOVEMENT

INERTIA SNAPS HOUSE
INTO NEW LOCATION

INERTIAL FORCE

GROUND MOVEMENT

INERTIA SNAPS HOUSE
INTO NEW LOCATION

During an earthquake, the shock waves cause lateral and vertical ground movements, or vibrations, which are transferred to a building through its foundation. The vertical earthquake movements cause the walls of the building to expand and compress (and to bulge and buckle if the shock is strong enough). This movement is usually not damaging, since buildings are, by their nature, able to withstand a large vertical load. The lateral earthquake waves, however, are very destructive, since they cause the walls to bend and sway to the point of shattering the wall materials or breaking the connections between the walls and the other components of the building. Both building movements—the swaying and the expansion/compression —are the result of the physical principle of *inertial force*, which causes a naturally stable structure to snap back into its original position when it is deflected by the earthquake movement.

foundation and the ground is a special system of lateral bracing for the walls. Such bracing strengthens the connections between the horizontal and vertical components of a structure and stiffens the vertical components (the walls, columns and

The effect of lateral earthquake movement on a building is clearly shown in this drawing of a three-story structure. The movement emerges from the ground and travels through the foundation to the walls—in effect, one floor at a time. When the waves have reached the roof, they return to the foundation and ground in the same way. Of course, the earthquake does not wait for a complete foundation-to-roof-to-foundation cycle to be completed before another ground movement strikes in the opposite direction. Thus, the actual behavior of a building during the several seconds of an earthquake is usually extremely erratic.

The earthquake waves inevitably focus on any weak connections or materials, and once the structural components and connections of a building begin to fail, the behavior of the building changes drastically. It is subjected to a chaotic mixture of new stresses and loads for which it is not designed, and the damage compounds until the building fails.

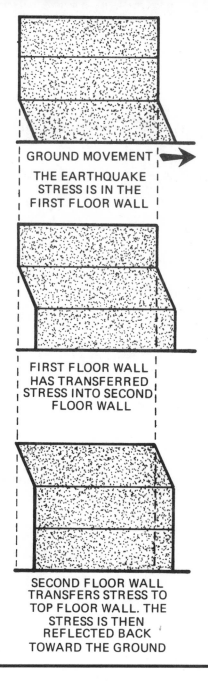

GROUND MOVEMENT ⟶
THE EARTHQUAKE STRESS IS IN THE FIRST FLOOR WALL

FIRST FLOOR WALL HAS TRANSFERRED STRESS INTO SECOND FLOOR WALL

SECOND FLOOR WALL TRANSFERS STRESS TO TOP FLOOR WALL. THE STRESS IS THEN REFLECTED BACK TOWARD THE GROUND

studs) against damaging deformations. That is, lateral bracing has very little to do with the actual load strength of a building's walls, columns and studs. Rather, it provides the control which allows these vertical supports to remain rela-

Special earthquake bracing

● Because of the severe lateral stresses to the walls, columns and studs of a building during an earthquake, a special lateral bracing system is essential. The primary function of the bracing is to strengthen the walls and other vertical supports, so that their deflection under the force of the lateral earthquake waves will stop short of breaking the supports. The bracing may also provide an easier, more direct route for the transfer of the earthquake forces to the foundation. The three most common techniques of earthquake bracing are the *frame-action, shear-wall* and *diagonal* systems.

The box-shaped, frame-action bracing of steel or reinforced poured concrete

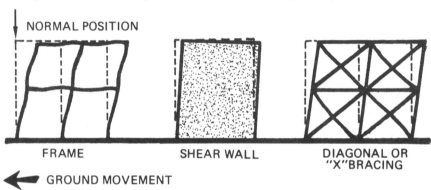

NORMAL POSITION

FRAME   SHEAR WALL   DIAGONAL OR "X"BRACING

GROUND MOVEMENT

tively stable and entirely intact during the onslaught of the lateral vibrational motions of the quake. The walls are then able to support and transfer the additional inertial weight of the building into the foundation and the ground. Besides preventing the collapse of a building, lateral bracing also limits the damage to exterior veneers, plaster and plasterboard, window and door frames, and fixtures and furnishings, because it reduces the building's internal motion.

Lateral bracing for earthquake resistance may follow three basic patterns: *frame-action, shear-wall* and *diagonal.* Frame-action bracing, used most often in large buildings, comprises a series of connected, box-shaped frames of steel or reinforced poured concrete which resist the lateral earthquake forces by flexing at each corner of the frame. The bending action in the columns and beams of the frame absorbs *is common in large buildings. Of the three types of bracing, it allows the most flexibility and movement, which can be a disadvantage—particularly to the occupants and furnishings of the swaying building.*

Shear-wall bracing is a solid, continuous wall of plywood or reinforced poured concrete serving either as the main bearing wall or as a second backing wall attached to the framing of the building. When this type of bracing is added as a supportive wall for the frame, it adds very great strength to the vertical superstructure. Most important, shear-wall bracing is very stiff and unbending—thereby reducing the lateral deformations of the walls. This technique of bracing also provides a solid surface for the easy

transfer of the earthquake forces back to the foundation.

Diagonal bracing is the most common technique for wood-frame houses and other small buildings. A sturdy strip of lumber or a special strap of steel is securely nailed at a 45-degree angle across the studs. Very often, two strips are attached in this way to form an x-brace. Both the diagonal and the x-bracing stiffens the framing of the building against excessive deformations and provides a more direct path for the transfer of the earthquake forces to the foundation. Diagonal bracing is less effective than shear walls, but if it is well-designed and connected, such bracing will protect a home from substantial damage.

some of the energy of the earthquake waves and thereby reduces the lateral strain to the frame and walls of the building. Frame-action bracing is generally very effective in tall buildings. It has only one disadvantage: If the frame is too flexible, the bending action during a quake will cause large lateral deformations in the walls, leading to shattered or distorted exterior veneers, broken windows and plaster or plasterboard, falling ceilings, toppling furnishings, bent air and elevator shafts, and the pounding of adjacent buildings.

Shear-wall bracing entails the use of solid, continuous walls of plywood or reinforced poured concrete to tie together, stiffen and stabilize the vertical frame of a building or to tie together the columns of a building by serving as the actual main bearing walls of the structure. This type of bracing adds great strength to the frame, allowing it to endure the lateral earthquake forces and to support the additional inertial weight of the roof and floors. Because the shear-wall bracing is relatively stiff and unbending, it also limits the lateral deformations of the building and thus further reduces the probability of architectural or interior damage.

Wood-frame buildings can be made especially earthquake resistant by the addition of solid plywood sheathing to brace and tie together the studs and supporting columns. The plywood panels allow the naturally flexible wood supports to deform just enough to absorb the earthquake forces without cracking or becoming disconnected or lessening their load-bearing strength. The shear-wall bracing of large buildings is generally made of poured, steel-reinforced concrete walls.

Diagonal bracing is the type most commonly used in wood-frame houses and other small buildings in seismic regions. It entails long, sturdy strips of lumber or straps of steel which are securely attached at a 45-degree angle across the studs of a building. Either a single diagonal or two crossed diagonals (called *x-bracing*) may be used.

Like the other lateral bracing systems, diagonal bracing stiffens the supporting frame of a structure against damaging deformations during a tremor. This type of bracing also increases the earthquake resistance of a building by enhancing the endurance of the studs and columns with a more direct, diagonal path for the transfer of the inertial weight of the structure to the foundation. Overall, diagonal bracing is considerably less effective than shear walls of plywood, but if the bracing is well-designed and connected, it can protect a home from substantial earthquake damage in many situations.

The foundation

Because earthquake movements and shock waves are transmitted from the ground through the foundation of a building and then into the superstructure, a weak or poorly connected or poorly located foundation may fail even before the shock waves reach the rest of the building. When this occurs, the damage is usually very severe and difficult and expensive to repair. Thus, a strong, well-designed and connected foundation is essential in earthquake country.

The building materials

As noted earlier in this book, certain building materials perform better than others under the duress of earthquake motion. Generally, wood and steel construction is preferred in earthquake country (1) because these materials are relatively light, which lessens the inertial weight that the walls must support; (2) because the materials are tremendously flexible and can deflect with the shock waves without cracking or breaking. (Of course, too much flexibility can also be a disadvantage, which is the reason that special lateral bracing is required.) New concrete-block and other masonry buildings can also be made reasonably safe, providing that special reinforcement procedures are carefully followed. Similarly, stucco over wood frame presents special reinforcement requirements to prevent earthquake damage.

The architectural and structural design and detailing

Engineers and architects who understand how buildings behave during earthquakes (and surprisingly many do not) go to a great deal of trouble to design a building and to specify unusual detailing which will increase the durability and stability of a building. For example, certain critical columns may have additional bracing which is not required by the local codes, or the pattern of reinforcing steel in masonry buildings is carefully planned to prevent any weak spots, or a tall exterior chimney is securely braced to the frame of a building, or shear plywood walls rather than open stilts are recommended for a hillside home. It is very important that these details or design recommendations be fulfilled exactly as planned in building or reinforcing a home. Careless or "penny-wise" or esthetic rejection or execution of these important features is likely to result in expensive damage during strong earthquakes.

The workmanship

Closely related to the detailing of a building's design and construction is the quality of the workmanship. Sloppy and careless workmanship leads to weaker buildings; and numerous collapses or other severe cases of earthquake damage can be blamed on the poor quality of the work. For example, if a contractor places reinforcing steel in the cavities of a concrete-block wall but neglects to fill the cores of the blocks with concrete to form shear-wall bracing, then his negligence will likely lead to the buckling or collapse of the wall during an earthquake. Anyone building or reinforcing a home must be aware of and attentive to the workmanship, either supervising it himself or hiring a reliable and knowledgeable engineer to watch over the construction.

The preceding, then, are the fundamental and closely related factors that govern the amount of damage which a given structure will or will not experience during an earthquake. A building is earthquake-resistant only when all of the structural components are properly tied together with good connections, when the selected materials of construction are flexible and durable, when the bracing system is adequate for the type of structure and the seismic conditions, and when all of the features of the design and engineering of a building are faithfully and properly executed. The following chapters explore all of these factors in detail.

CHAPTER **6**

The best and the worst: types of construction and earthquake resistance

The basic structural materials of a building—wood, brick, concrete block, poured concrete, steel, and the numerous combinations of these materials—are, with the lateral bracing system and other reinforcement measures, the most significant factor in the resistance of the structure to earthquake damage. The same types of buildings that failed in 1906 also failed in 1933 in Long Beach, in 1952 in Bakersfield, in 1964 in Alaska and in 1971 in San Fernando. The same types of buildings will continue to fail until building codes, builders and property owners pay some heed to history and the principles of physics and earthquake engineering.

Wood-frame buildings

A carefully designed and constructed modern wood-frame building is by far the most desirable small-property investment in earthquake country. As noted in the previous chapter, the high earthquake resistance of wood buildings is primarily the result of the lightness and flexibility of the material. The lightness means that the inertial load resulting from the building's resistance to the ground movements will be relatively small; the flexibility enables the supporting components of the building—the walls, columns and studs—to deflect with the lateral shock waves of the tremor without cracking, breaking or becoming disconnected. Another advantage of wood-frame structures is that the quality of the building material and the connections is more easily controlled than, for example, the mortar which holds a masonry building together. Similarly, since wood buildings are not so readily damaged by a tremor, they are better equipped to withstand the aftershocks, which can be more damaging to weakened brick or concrete structures than the main shock.

Wood-frame buildings are not by any means quakeproof, of course. The damage to single-family wood-frame dwellings in the moderate and relatively localized San Fernando quake, for example, came to a staggering $115 million, excluding the land and contents. It is notable, however, that much of this damage resulted not from any inherent weakness in the wood but from deficiencies in the building site or from poor design or construction. All engineers would agree that a wood-frame building is most likely to suffer serious earthquake damage when one or more of the following conditions are present:

- A poor site of soft, unstable ground.
- A weak or poorly located or inadequately connected foundation.
- Structurally weak architectural features.
- An old, poorly maintained building, or a new building poorly constructed.
- Insufficient lateral bracing or an inadequate number of load-bearing walls and columns.
- Improper placement or inadequate connections of lateral bracing and other structural detailing.
- Small thin vertical supports, such as the stilts used for some hillside homes.
- Heavy roofs, such as clay tile.
- Non-continuous corner columns and other critical supports in a two-story building.

Besides a sound geologic site and a strong, well-sited and connected foundation, the most important condition for a durable and safe wood-frame building is a lateral bracing system. Such special earthquake bracing is now generally required for all new wood-frame construction in most areas of California and coastal Alaska, Washington, and Oregon. Lateral bracing is also a common code requirement along the Gulf and Atlantic coasts, which are subject to the strong lateral forces of hurricanes.

Diagonal bracing is the usual minimal code requirement in these areas. As noted in the previous chapter, this type of lateral bracing entails the mounting of a series of lumber strips or metal straps at about a 45-degree angle across the studs of a building. The diagonal bracing is not nearly as strong as shear-walls of plywood, but it is adequate if:

- the area has not been historically subject to extremely high magnitude quakes (over 6) and/or is not within 10 miles of a large and active fault zone;
- the building is not located on an unstable or exceptionally soft geologic foundation or at the interface of alluvium and bedrock;
- the building is single-story and architecturally conventional (no lengthy glass walls, no split-levels, no stilt mountings);
- the building does not have an exterior veneer of stucco or masonry.

The lumber diagonals should be good-quality 1 x 4s and should be long enough to span from the *top plate* (horizontal cross beam or joist) at the roof-line of the columns and studs down to the *sole plate* (floor joist) or foundation sill. The studs and plates should be notched so that the diagonals will lie flush; then the 1 x 4s should be nailed securely to each of the studs and especially to the top plate and the sole plate or sill. The studs around large door and window openings should always be crossed by a diagonal brace to strengthen these weak points in the wall. A system of x-bracing (two crossed diagonals) is always preferable to a single diagonal.

Shear-wall bracing—a continuous covering of plywood paneling over the studs—is recommended in lieu of diagonal bracing in areas subject to strong tremors and/or in unusual or split-level and multi-story houses. If diagonal bracing must be chosen because of its lower cost, then special steel straps (1 to

In diagonal bracing, the strips of lumber must be a single length reaching from the top plate at the roof-line or the next floor to the sole plate or the foundation sill. The bracing should be securely nailed to all the studs, and it should be concentrated around large openings, such as this picture window. Note the extensive use of steel framing devices for securing the connections along the roof beams. The detailed drawings below show an acceptable nailing procedure for the diagonals.

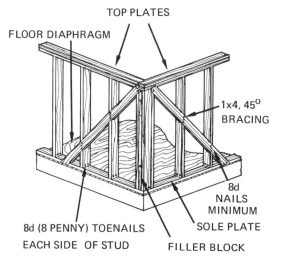

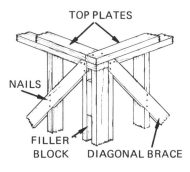

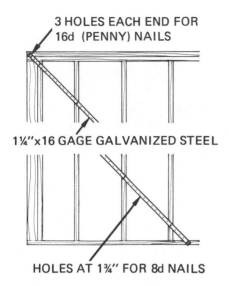

3 HOLES EACH END FOR 16d (PENNY) NAILS

1¼"x16 GAGE GALVANIZED STEEL

HOLES AT 1¾" FOR 8d NAILS

Specially designed steel straps, which can be purchased in varying lengths, serve very well as diagonal bracing for a small wood-frame building. The straps are also most convenient for reinforcing the bearing walls of an existing building.

1¼ inches wide) can be used in addition to lumber diagonals. The added strength of the steel diagonals can be a great asset in high intensity areas.

The metal straps are mounted in the same way as wood diagonals. Nails should be driven into all of the holes along the length of these straps where they intersect a stud and meet the top and sole plates or the sill. These metal straps are also most useful for reinforcing an *existing* building, since they are available in a variety of lengths and are easy to mount. Simply measure the roughly 45-degree-angle lengths of areas in your home where the studs are exposed and additional bracing is required—typically, the main bearing walls of the garage, attic or basement or in the crawl space under the building. Then, order the appropriate lengths of steel straps from a building-supply company and thoroughly nail these straps, preferably in an x-pattern, to the studs and top and sole plates.

As stated, shear-wall bracing is the stronger of the two most common lateral bracing systems for wood-frame buildings. It is, therefore, recommended for *all* wood-frame houses in earthquake country. Like any other bracing system, shear-wall bracing with plywood panels will be effective only if the wood is high quality and the nailing is adequate. If you are applying the plywood directly to the studs, it should be at

A *number of steel straps were added here to the wood bracing, which is a very good idea. However, in this case, the straps are not nailed down sufficiently. If the bracing is to be effective, there must be nails at each intersecting stud, not just at the ends of the straps.*

Three "don'ts" for diagonal bracing

• The best remedy for these types of mistakes is to prevent them in the first place through careful supervision of the construction of your building. However, if they occur anyway, or if you find such mistakes in an existing building, simply apply the principles of earthquake resistance and decide upon the course of action (further bracing, addition of anchors and framing devices, etc.) that will best reinforce the structure.

In this case, either the wood brace was too dry or of poor quality or too many nails were driven through it into the foundation sill. A severely split brace like this introduces a weak point which is very likely to pull out during a tremor. Such poor workmanship can be corrected by the addition of a metal angle or plate or wood blocking to strengthen the cracked board and the weak connection.

Here, the diagonal let-in brace has been cut off to allow room for the placement of a drain pipe. This kind of careless planning and workmanship can be responsible for severe damage to a home. The function of the brace is negated by this cut; the brace would be totally ineffective in strengthening the wall and carrying away the earthquake forces. A short metal strap should be added here to continue the diagonal brace into the foundation sill.

ALL JOINTS BETWEEN PLYWOOD
PANELS SHOULD HAVE STUDS OR
BLOCKING FOR NAILING

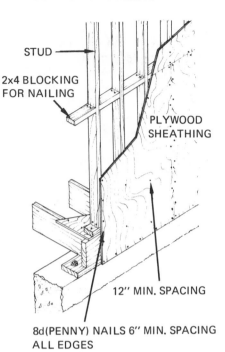

STUD

2x4 BLOCKING
FOR NAILING

PLYWOOD
SHEATHING

12" MIN. SPACING

8d(PENNY) NAILS 6" MIN. SPACING
ALL EDGES

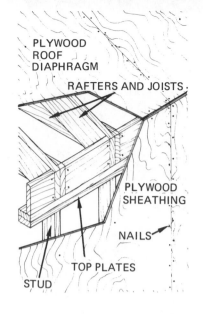

PLYWOOD
ROOF
DIAPHRAGM

RAFTERS AND JOISTS

PLYWOOD
SHEATHING

NAILS

TOP PLATES

STUD

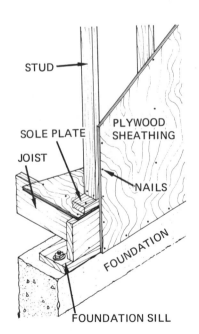

STUD

SOLE PLATE

PLYWOOD
SHEATHING

JOIST

NAILS

FOUNDATION

FOUNDATION SILL

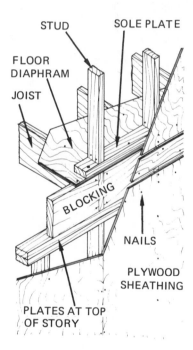

STUD

SOLE PLATE

FLOOR
DIAPHRAM

JOIST

BLOCKING

NAILS

PLYWOOD
SHEATHING

PLATES AT TOP
OF STORY

*These detailed drawings of
the connections of plywood
sheathing to the studs and
plates stress the importance of
careful and frequent nailing.*

Construction and Earthquake Resistance **143**

Plywood sheathing–shear-wall bracing–is superior to any other type of bracing for a small wood-frame structure. It provides a tremendous strength against damaging deformations of the walls during an earthquake, and it greatly enhances the dispersal of the earthquake forces back to the foundation. Plywood shear-wall bracing is commonly found in earthquake country both as an exterior architectural feature (with battens, for example, as in these "before" and "after" photographs of townhouses) and as a backing for stucco or some other exterior facing. Interior wood paneling will also function as bracing if it covers the length of a wall and is carefully attached to the studs and the top and sole plates.

least ⅜-inches thick and, whenever possible, the panels should extend from sole plate to top plate. If the ceilings are taller than the usual 4 x 8-foot plywood panels, use two panels of equal height. Never patch the few inches or feet above an eight-foot panel with a small piece of sheathing. This would introduce a break in the continuity, and a weak seam, very near the vital top-plate connection with the studs.

Plywood panels thinner than ⅜-inches will be effective if they are applied with gypsum board or some other relatively weak wall sheathing. The conventional "double wall" construction of sheetrock and stucco very common to the Western states is simply not strong enough for high earthquake-intensity areas, and such construction should be reinforced with an additional shear-wall of thin plywood. The main load-bearing walls of existing buildings of "double-wall" construction should either be faced with plywood siding or lined with a strong wood paneling.

Reinforcement for masonry veneer

• If you are building a wood-frame house or some other small structure of less than three or four stories, use plywood shear-wall bracing and all of the metal and anchoring devices available.

• If you own or will purchase a building sheathed with plywood, be certain that the sheathing is adequately nailed down and is either at least ⅜-inch thick or backed by sheetrock.

• If your building includes only diagonal bracing and it is located on a soft soil foundation and/or in a high intensity area, reinforce any exposed studs or the sheetrock of the most vulnerable exterior load-bearing walls with plywood sheathing or with interior wood paneling. Use metal framing and anchoring devices wherever possible.

• If, in the above situation, the addition of shear-wall bracing is inconvenient or too costly, substitute metal-strap diagonals wherever the studs are uncovered or can be easily exposed (removing the sheetrock in the garage, for example). Also, add metal framing and anchoring devices wherever you can.

The traditional wood clapboard siding of the majority of older houses and many modern structures can be almost as strong and earthquake resistant as shear-wall bracing with plywood, and in most circumstances, the wood siding requires only diagonal bracing behind it to form a very sturdy wall. Shear-wall bracing is always better, of course, but if the clapboard is a good quality lumber, and if the boards are fitted tightly together and are well-nailed and maintained, the walls should survive even the largest quake with little or no damage. Inadequate foundation connections or poorly designed columns are the factors most often responsible for damage to such walls. Wood shingle siding (and asbestos siding) does *not* provide the effect of shear-wall bracing, however, so that shingled buildings should include either steel-reinforced diagonal bracing or plywood sheathing.

Another valuable reinforcement technique in addition to lateral bracing is the use of the variety of steel framing and anchoring devices available. These devices greatly strengthen the connections between the different components of a wood-frame building's superstructure. They are also useful in providing continuity between these components, so that the building will move as a unit in responding to the earthquake

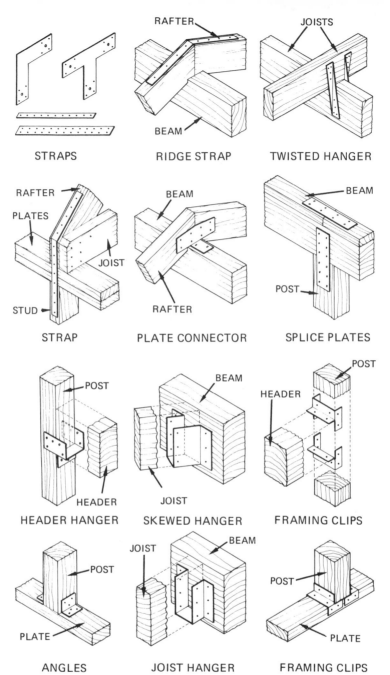

STRAPS

RIDGE STRAP

TWISTED HANGER

STRAP

PLATE CONNECTOR

SPLICE PLATES

HEADER HANGER

SKEWED HANGER

FRAMING CLIPS

ANGLES

JOIST HANGER

FRAMING CLIPS

Numerous special steel framing and anchoring devices add a little to the costs of construction but greatly strengthen the connections of a wood-frame house. They are highly recommended both in construction of a new building and in reinforcing an existing building.

The exceptionally strong and durable plywood sheathing kept this building intact despite the blows it suffered both from the huge Alaska earthquake and the landsliding that destroyed its foundation and knocked it down the hill. The building was severely damaged, but it presented little threat to the occupants at the time of the quake and slide.

shock waves. The framing devices add a little to the cost of the materials for construction, but they also save some money in labor charges, in that they take less time to apply than the conventional techniques of cutting and fitting blocks and of mitering structural connections. Most important, these steel devices will add significantly greater strength to the building.

Wood-frame buildings with stuccoed walls

Although stucco is an easily fractured material, it is not as fragile during earthquakes as one might think. If the stucco is applied to strong wire mesh that has been carefully lapped and securely nailed to plywood sheathing (or to the clapboard of older frame buildings), it will seldom fracture or fall in even a large earthquake, because it is quite flexible and strong. The problem is that many stuccoed buildings are constructed with sheetrock or plasterboard backing, neither of which is strong enough to withstand the lateral shock waves of an earthquake

The application of stucco directly to conventional wire lath and sheetrock without the additional structural backing of plywood sheathing can be an expensive mistake in areas that can expect high earthquake intensities. Multistory stucco buildings, in particular, are subject to extensive damage to the facing at the intersection of the different floors and in the areas around windows and doors. Note the stucco damage to a similar house and an apartment building in San Fernando Valley.

without significant deformations that crack and break the stucco. And if the stucco falls off the walls, not only is it expensive in itself to repair, but it usually indicates that even more serious and expensive structural damage has occurred.

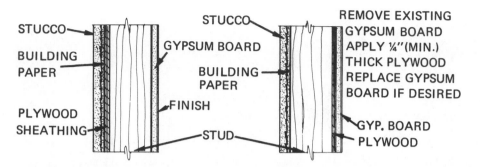

STUCCO

BUILDING PAPER

PLYWOOD SHEATHING

STUCCO

GYPSUM BOARD

BUILDING PAPER

FINISH

STUD

REMOVE EXISTING GYPSUM BOARD APPLY ¼"(MIN.) THICK PLYWOOD REPLACE GYPSUM BOARD IF DESIRED

GYP. BOARD

PLYWOOD

The wall cross-section on the left shows a recommended procedure of applying stucco to metal lath backed by plywood sheathing. The detail on the right illustrates a recommended procedure for strengthening existing stucco wllls. The wood sheathing stiffens the walls and lessens the deformations that break the stucco. Small buildings constructed after 1973 under the specifications of the Uniform Building Code (1973) may not require plywood sheathing, since the code calls for a heavier and much stronger welded wire lath.

Multi-story stucco buildings without shear-wall plywood bracing are especially susceptible to such damage because of the wider deflections of the building caused by the greater inertia of the upper floors.

The newest specifications for *single*-story stucco structures in the Uniform Building Code (1973) adopted by many communities call for a much heavier and welded wire lath. When this type of mesh is properly overlapped and welded and then mounted directly to the studs (with 16-gage staples every six inches), a carefully applied one-inch thick stucco covering will have a strength equivalent to ¼-inch plywood sheathing. Thus, single-story stuccoed houses built later than 1973 *and* under these new specifications (check with the city engineer) do not require a plywood backing. If you own a stuccoed wood-frame building without plywood sheathing —and if the building is more than one story or does not meet the 1973 code specifications—you should take one or more of the following steps:

- At the minimum, carry enough earthquake insurance to cover the likely damage to the stucco facing of the building.

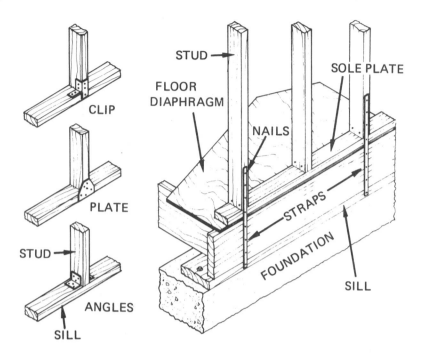

Steel anchorage devices, such as these, are useful in strengthening the connections between the wall and the foundation sill and in stiffening the wall against deformations that will crack the stucco facing along the foundation. These same devices can also be used around large door and window openings in order to minimize stucco damage.

- Wherever you can, strengthen the connections between the foundation sill and the studs with the special metal straps, angles and framing devices available for that purpose. Stucco damage always tends to concentrate at the sill, where the flexible wood framing deflects from the unyielding foundation. These metal reinforcements will help prevent or minimize such damage.
- Stucco damage also tends to occur around doors and windows, where the stress paths are interrupted and the earthquake forces tend to concentrate. The damage to these areas can be lessened by

The importance of lateral bracing is vividly demonstrated in this residential construction site in San Fernando. Note that the intact structures had the very slight lateral reinforcement of a wire *mesh and a building-paper backing in preparation for the application of stucco facing. The houses which had only the uncovered stud framing completely collapsed.*

the addition of interior wood paneling around these openings. This measure should not only eliminate the fractures around the windows and doors but also minimize the damage to the rest of the stucco covering of the building, since the window and door fractures frequently extend into a web of cracks and breaks all across the face of a building.

- If your building is more than one-story and is likely to be subjected to strong quakes, plywood sheathing is essential both at the base of the building and *overlapping* the connections between each floor. The sheathing at the base can be achieved with interior wood paneling, but the overlapping sheathing between floors will involve the considerable task of removing the stucco in at least a 4-foot strip around the building at each floor level and replacing the stucco with plywood. If this is too big and too expensive a venture, a less reliable alternative is to cover the main bearing walls on each story with interior plywood paneling. The addition of the metal straps and framing devices is also recommended in all multi-story buildings wherever you have access to the studs and top or sole plate.

Wood-frame buildings with masonry veneer

Masonry veneers are an appealing architectural feature, but, unfortunately they are also highly susceptible to earthquake damage. Unless specifically designed and reinforced for earthquake forces, such buildings always suffer far greater damage than clapboard, plywood or stucco-covered wood-frame structures. Most earthquake insurance policies reflect this fact by carrying addendums excluding masonry veneer from the coverage.

The basic structural strengths of veneered and other wood-frame buildings are the same. The problem with the former lies in the additional weight of the brick or stone facing. During an earthquake, this load generates greater inertial forces which can cause serious structural damage as well as certain damage to the veneer itself. In addition, the anchorages between the brick or stone and the wood frame are often weak or insufficient, so that the veneer will crack or be torn away from the frame during the tremor.

The four-inch brick veneer on this wood-frame dwelling in Seattle was peeled off by a moderate earthquake in 1965. The veneer had been properly attached to the frame with galvanized metal anchors, but the mortar in which the anchors were embedded was of poor quality.

This Anchorage post office was reinforced by plywood shear-walls, which prevented any serious structural damage, but the brick veneer was inadequately tied to the plywood. In addition, the strict vertical alignment of the bricks reduced their resistance to the earthquake forces.

Poor-quality mortar is another factor in the damage to masonry veneers. Lime mortar is particularly notorious for having no resistance when subjected to earthquake stress. There is little that a home builder or homeowner can do to assure himself that a consistently strong mortar mixture is being or has been used. If you are building a masonry-veneered home, be certain that the contractor understands that you do not want him to use mortar containing more than 10 percent lime and that you are concerned about the care with which the mortar is mixed. If you own or wish to purchase a veneered building, examine the hardness of the mortar. Weak mortar can be readily recognized by its tendency to scrape away easily and to crumble between the fingers. Scrape a coin across the mortar, and if it falls away easily, it is very likely to fail during an earthquake. For the home buyer,

Reinforcement for masonry veneer

• These views of masonry-veneer construction show the proper placement of anchors at least every one and a half square feet over the facing.

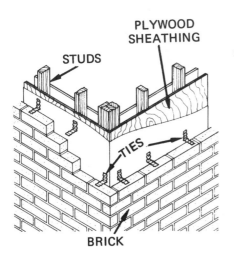

STUDS

PLYWOOD
SHEATHING

TIES

BRICK

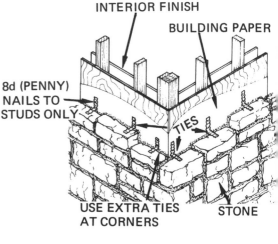

INTERIOR FINISH

BUILDING PAPER

8d (PENNY)
NAILS TO
STUDS ONLY

TIES

USE EXTRA TIES
AT CORNERS

STONE

the message here should be obvious. For the homeowner, the advice of a professional—a structural engineer—is essential.

The quality of the anchorage system for the veneer is a factor that is easily controlled by the home builder. Title 21 of the California building code for schools includes some very specific and sound requirements for all brick and stone veneer construction:

• All veneer, except for ceramic facing, should be anchored to its backing by means of non-corrodable metal ties designed to withstand a horizontal force equal to twice the weight of the veneer.
• There should be a tie anchor for each 200 square inches of wall area.
• Anchorage should be by 14-gage anchors in 22-gage anchor slots secured to the studs with 10d [10 penny] duplex nails at 12-inch maximum spacing.

These older wood-frame walls in San Fernando were stripped of their stone veneer by the tremor. It is probably fortunate that the heavy veneers were not anchored to the frames; for the collapse of the veneers might have taken large portions of the structure with them.

- Veneers on wood-frame walls should not be permitted more than 15 feet above ground level.

Because stone veneer is usually heavier than brick and is placed in irregular patterns, the anchors must be even more carefully placed. As a general rule, it is recommended that one anchor be placed, at least every one and a half square feet for veneer less than three inches thick. For veneer exceeding three to four inches in thickness, one anchor should be used every square foot. It is not advisable to cover large areas, such as entire walls, with stone veneer—particularly when the building is in an area which may experience high earthquake intensities. The very probable failure of the heavy veneer can seriously damage the frame of the building and may be a hazard to nearby property, to passersby and to the occupants. Small and low stone (or brick) veneered areas, such as partial walls and foundation coverings, do not present such hazards, of course. But such walls must be constructed carefully if substantial post-earthquake repairs are to be avoided.

Unreinforced brick buildings

Of all of the most common types of buildings, those constructed of brick which has not been reinforced by steel and poured-concrete framing have consistently suffered the most severe damage during earthquakes. The major weakness

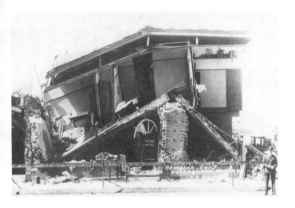

Long Beach had many unreinforced brick buildings before the 1933 earthquake, and virtually all of them were severely damaged or demolished by the moderate shock. Generally, the failure of the brick walls led to the disconnections of the diaphragms that brought the whole building down.

in these structures is that an unreinforced brick wall, unless abnormally thick, cannot withstand the strong lateral thrusts of an earthquake. The brick is heavy and extremely inflexible, so that the lateral motions create an overwhelming inertial load that cracks the usually weak mortar connections and bursts the bricks apart. If the building is more than one-story or has a heavy roof, the ponderous vertical inertial load will add to the stress until the walls collapse. Only the presence of numerous wood-frame interior bearing walls and partitions——typical of older brick residences, offices and apartment buildings—can prevent total collapse of the structure in such circumstances.

The quality of the mortar between the bricks is particularly important to the performance of unreinforced brick buildings during an earthquake. When the mortar is poor or old (usually both), the lateral earthquake stresses cause cracks to form in a zig-zag course through the mortar and around the bricks. During large shocks of long duration, such cracks may

Thirty-eight years after the lesson of the Long Beach disaster, the moderate San Fernando earthquake brought down the walls of another unreinforced brick building. The many wood-frame partition walls of this apartment building prevented the total collapse of the structure, but the falling bricks destroyed the interiors of the adjacent lower buildings and would have presented a terrible hazard if people had been on the street. Most of the fatalities in American earthquakes are attributed to the collapse of unreinforced brick structures.

propagate diagonally across the walls, gradually spreading from foundation to roof and rapidly reducing the strength of the walls. In California, mortar has been so bad that it has earned a nickname, "buttermilk mortar." After any of the large earthquakes in California, it has been possible to collect the fallen bricks from damaged buildings, wash off the remaining mortar with a hose, and re-sell the bricks as practically new. Even when the mortar is of good quality, a failure to thoroughly wet the bricks before encasing them in mortar will weaken the bond between brick and mortar. Bricks or stone should never be laid dry.

An old (pre-1933) unrein-forced brick service building of the Olive View Hospital complex in San Fernando collapsed during the earth-quake. The Los Angeles County Earthquake Commis-sion estimates that more than 20,000 similar buildings re-main as a threat to the citi-zens of that metropolitan area. San Francisco, Salt Lake City and Seattle also have thousands of such hazardous structures.

Old brick buildings have by far the worst earthquake record. A study after the Bakersfield quake found that only one of the 71 older brick buildings in the city survived the tremor undamaged, and more than 30 of the buildings had to be either torn down or substantially revamped by removing one or more of the damaged and dangerous upper stories. A major cause for the damage to older brick (and concrete-block) buildings is the lack of sufficient lateral ties between the unreinforced walls and the diaphragms (roof and floors). The failures of these connections result in the collapse of the masonry walls, particularly in the upper floors and along high architectural façades, such as gables and parapets. The prob-lem of diaphragm connections will be discussed in detail in the next chapter.

In general, old, unreinforced or faulty masonry build-ings are difficult and expensive to repair or reinforce. The cost of such work often exceeds 50 percent of the value of the buildings. When a new Long Beach, California, earthquake

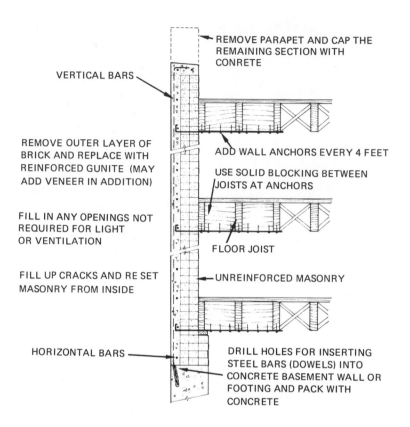

VERTICAL BARS

REMOVE PARAPET AND CAP THE REMAINING SECTION WITH CONRETE

REMOVE OUTER LAYER OF BRICK AND REPLACE WITH REINFORCED GUNITE (MAY ADD VENEER IN ADDITION)

ADD WALL ANCHORS EVERY 4 FEET

USE SOLID BLOCKING BETWEEN JOISTS AT ANCHORS

FILL IN ANY OPENINGS NOT REQUIRED FOR LIGHT OR VENTILATION

FLOOR JOIST

FILL UP CRACKS AND RE SET MASONRY FROM INSIDE

UNREINFORCED MASONRY

HORIZONTAL BARS

DRILL HOLES FOR INSERTING STEEL BARS (DOWELS) INTO CONCRETE BASEMENT WALL OR FOOTING AND PACK WITH CONCRETE

One method of strengthening unreinforced brick walls is the removal of the outer layer of brick and its replacement with four-inch thick gunite in which new diaphragm and joist anchors have been carefully embedded. Such repairs are expensive and, generally, it is better simply to phase out all such structures in earthquake country.

code in 1959 required reinforcement of all existing brick buildings, more than half of the owners chose demolition because of the high costs involved. On the other hand, when local codes have been less stringent, brick structures that have survived previous earthquakes with what appears to be only light damage to the brick walls have been "reinforced" by the "plaster and paint" method—the cracks are plastered

The quality of the mortar is very important to the earthquake resistance of brick buildings. The photograph on the left shows the typical cracking pattern when the mortar is old or of poor quality. This type of damage is the more dangerous, since a sharp aftershock can bring the weakened wall down. A strong mortar and proper reinforcements and anchorages will allow cracking mostly through the bricks themselves, as in the picture on the left. A brick building damaged in this way is less likely to collapse, but it is seriously weakened and the essential repair work will be costly.

over and the walls are then painted to cover the patching and the inherent weaknesses of the building. The idea that "older buildings are substantial because they have stood the test of time" can be a dangerous fallacy for earthquake country.

In general, very little can be offered in the way of encouraging advice to the owner of an unreinforced brick building in earthquake country. It is best for everyone concerned to phase out these buildings as soon as possible. However, if you own such a building and are willing to invest a substantial amount to protect the occupants and minimize earthquake damage, there are methods which will strengthen the building to a degree. One of the more common repair techniques entails the removal of the outer layer of bricks and their replacement with a four-inch thickness of gunite (spray-on concrete) reinforced with steel bars. The gunite is certainly not as attractive as brick, but it usually strengthens the walls adequately against collapse. At the same time, the connections between brick walls and the floor and roof joists are strengthened with metal anchors that are driven through the brick and embedded in the gunite. Often, it is also necessary to remove parapets and even the upper floors so that the repaired building can meet new earthquake codes.

If you are contemplating the purchase of an unreinforced brick building, don't buy until you have consulted a structural engineer who specializes in building renovation and earthquake hazard. He will be able to advise you on the feasibility and costs of making the structure safer. He will also likely advise you that the public and governmental agencies are becoming more and more aware of the high risks involved with such buildings and may well invoke a policy of large-scale condemnations of these buildings at any time in the near future. Certainly, it is more desirable to pay the moderate fee for an engineer's consultative services than to risk lawsuits, your entire investment and your life in a future earthquake.

Cavity-wall brick buildings

Cavity-wall brick buildings, as the name indicates, are constructed with a double wall of brick separated by a small gap. Such buildings are generally old and fairly unusual. There are a few examples in the older West Coast cities, but the largest number of cavity-wall structures are found in Salt Lake City. Even when the double walls of such buildings are tied together with anchors (which is not always the case), they have practically no resistance to the lateral forces of a quake and are readily damaged. The cavity and double wall of these buildings make the difficult and expensive reinforcement procedures described for conventional unreinforced brick structures even more complex and costly. Generally, then, the best way to handle these very hazardous buildings is simply to eliminate them. Consult an engineer specializing in earthquake reinforcement if you wish to tackle the formidable and expensive task of renovating such a structure.

Concrete-block buildings

When the hollows of concrete blocks are properly reinforced with vertical and horizontal steel rods and then care-

The earthquake damage to this unreinforced cavity-wall brick building in New Zealand was extensive and costly to repair, but it would have been far worse had the building not been supported by a reinforced concrete exterior frame. A few aging examples of this type of building are found in the American West, particularly in Salt Lake City. Unless such buildings are completely remodeled and reinforced, they present a very serious earthquake hazard to the occupants, to passersby and to adjacent structures.

fully grouted with poured concrete, the walls of concrete-block buildings form solid and continuous shear-wall units. Thus, reinforced concrete-block buildings can exhibit great strength and resistance under the stress of earthquake forces. Attention to detailing and workmanship is critical, however. Because the walls are an assemblage of separate block units joined by poured concrete and mortar, they can share many of the weak points of brick construction if the mortar is faulty or poorly executed, if the poured concrete grouting does not completely fill the cavities, if the steel reinforcing is inadequate, or if the connections with the diaphragms of the building are weak or insufficient.

In both of these Alaskan structures, the concrete-block walls were unreinforced and therefore highly subject to collapse with the lateral ground motions of an earthquake. The results of such inadequate design and construction are evident here. Neither the Anchorage apartment house nor the Valdez hotel were salvageable after the 1964 quake, and it was a miracle that none of the occupants were killed by the falling concrete blocks. Note the undamaged wood-frame structures on both sides of the hotel.

Any of these mistakes in structural design or workmanship can cancel the advantages of this type of construction. For example, a large percentage of the damage, injuries and fatalities in the Managua, Nicaragua, earthquake in 1972 were caused by the partial or complete collapse of poorly designed

The importance of good workmanship and careful supervision in all construction in earthquake country cannot be overemphasized. This detailed photograph of severe quake damage to a concrete-block structure illustrates what happens when the blocks contain no grouting, which makes the reinforcing steel completely ineffective in strengthening the wall.

and carelessly constructed concrete-block buildings. *Unreinforced* concrete-block structures are, of course, totally unacceptable—and dangerous—even in areas subject only to light earthquakes.

The following design and construction features enhance the strength of reinforced concrete-block buildings:

- The vertical reinforcing steel bars or rods should be continuous from the floor slab or foundation footing, through the wall, and into the collar beams of the roof or the next floor. The ends of the bars should be bent so that they cannot slip or be pulled from their anchorage.
- The vertical reinforcements should be inserted in the hollow of every other concrete block, or at least every two feet.
- The horizontal and vertical bars or rods should not be more than two feet apart, which means that approximately every third or fourth layer of concrete block should be topped with the horizontal reinforcements. The horizontal and vertical bars should then be connected with wire ties, so that there is a continuous mesh of reinforcing steel.
- Every hollow of the concrete blocks should be filled with carefully compacted concrete grouting. In order to obtain a strong bond between the blocks and the grouting, be sure that the blocks are

thoroughly pre-wetted according to the specifications of the supplier.

- Every layer of horizontal steel should be carefully embedded in a continuous beam (*bond beam*) of poured concrete.
- Additional horizontal and vertical reinforcements should be used at corners and at the intersections of all other walls, so that the walls are well-tied together and will act as one continuous unit during an earthquake.
- The walls should also be reinforced more heavily around any door or window openings. Historically, some of the most severe damage to this type of construction has been concentrated around improperly and insufficiently reinforced windows and doors.
- The two most common patterns for laying concrete block are the staggered *common-bond* arrangement and the parallel *stack-bond* pattern. Of the two, the common bond is more desirable, since the staggered joints enhance the resistance of the walls to lateral earthquake forces.
- The mortar used for the blocks should be very good quality.
- The reinforcement specifications of most local building codes are insufficient. Generally, the quantity of steel reinforcement should be increased significantly—by as much as 50 to 100 percent —over the requirements of the codes. The above specifications would usually be sufficient.
- Any exterior veneers over the concrete block must be anchored extremely well. A variety of new anchoring systems are available, and their use is strongly recommended.

The purchase of a reinforced concrete-block building in an area subject to high earthquake intensities is somewhat of a gamble; for unless you are present at the construction site, you cannot be certain of the adequacy of the reinforcement or the workmanship. Have a structural engineer check the plans

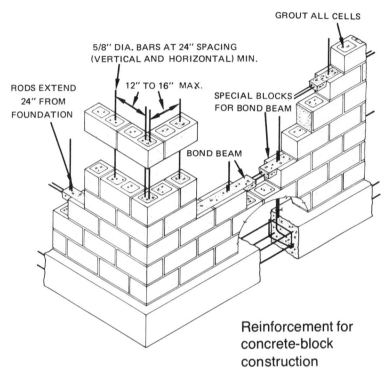

GROUT ALL CELLS

5/8" DIA. BARS AT 24" SPACING
(VERTICAL AND HORIZONTAL) MIN.

RODS EXTEND
24" FROM
FOUNDATION

12" TO 16" MAX.

SPECIAL BLOCKS
FOR BOND BEAM

BOND BEAM

Reinforcement for concrete-block construction

• The quantity of vertical and horizontal steel reinforcements should be increased by at least 50 percent, and perhaps doubled, over the requirements of most present-day local building codes. Special at-

for earthquake intensity equal to twice that required by the building code. If he finds that the reinforcing steel and concrete grouting are ample and well-placed, you can assume that the building represents a fairly safe investment. Even so, earthquake insurance should be considered.

The same rules apply for the present owner of a concrete-block structure. If the engineer informs you that

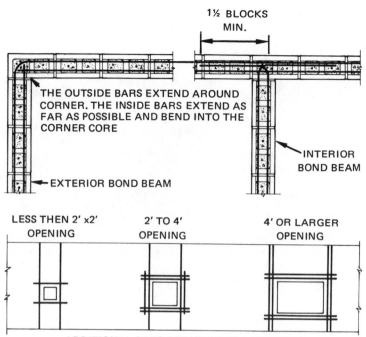

1½ BLOCKS MIN.

THE OUTSIDE BARS EXTEND AROUND CORNER. THE INSIDE BARS EXTEND AS FAR AS POSSIBLE AND BEND INTO THE CORNER CORE

INTERIOR BOND BEAM

EXTERIOR BOND BEAM

LESS THEN 2' x2' OPENING

2' TO 4' OPENING

4' OR LARGER OPENING

ADDITIONAL BARS AROUND WALL OPENINGS

tention should be given to the corners of the exterior bearing walls and the intersection of the bearing walls with other interior walls. In these areas, even greater quantities of steel bars should be added.

• The vertical steel reinforcements should be continuous from the floor slab or foundation footing to the beams of the roof or the next floor. The bars should also be bent at their anchorages at each end.

• The horizontal and vertical reinforcements should not be more than two feet apart and should be tied together with wire.

• Carefully compacted grouting should fill *every* cavity, and the horizontal reinforcements should be embedded in continuous beams of poured concrete.

• The blocks around window and door openings should be reinforced more heavily with steel bars.

your building is not adequately reinforced, you should investigate possible measures for strengthening the walls. Generally, however, these repairs can be very costly—even exceeding the market value of the building—and insurance is the only way to protect your investment. As for the protections of those living or working in or near the building, you should precisely follow the recommendations of the consulting engineer.

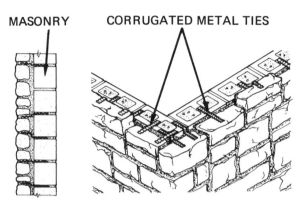

MASONRY　　**CORRUGATED METAL TIES**

The conventional anchoring devices for veneer facing on concrete block are embedded in the grouting. The spacing requirements are similar to those for masonry veneer on wood framing. These devices are not as effective under earthquake stresses as the anchors shown in the next illustration.

Reinforced brick buildings

Reinforced brick buildings are very similar in construction to concrete-block buildings. Two separate layers of brick are laid with connecting steel ties embedded in the mortar, and horizontal and vertical steel reinforcements are then inserted in the slight space between the two layers. The steel rods are tied together, and the space is then filled with poured concrete. Properly constructed buildings of this type have proven effective in resisting at least moderate earthquake forces and are acceptable for earthquake country provided that there is full-time inspection throughout the construction period by an engineer with considerable experience in earthquake reinforcement. If you own or wish to purchase a brick building, inspection by an engineer is essential.

Clay-tile buildings

Hollow clay-tile is similar to concrete blocks save for one important difference—the clay tiles are very brittle and easily shattered. Therefore, clay tile is simply not a sound building material for earthquake areas, even when it is well-reinforced with steel and properly grouted with concrete. Walls of tile have suffered severely during all past earthquakes, and the best course is to avoid such buildings or, if

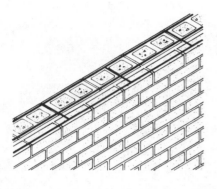

A variety of steel reinforcing and anchoring devices combine the tasks of horizontally reinforcing a concrete-block wall and tying a masonry veneer to that wall. Three such devices are shown here. If the mounting is proper, and the grouting and mortar are of good quality and carefully executed, these devices can be very effective in minimizing earthquake damage to both the walls and the veneer.

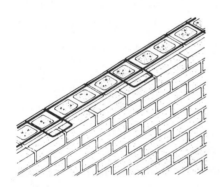

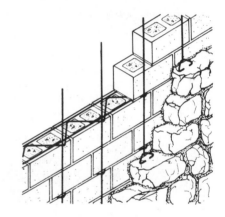

The strength of carefully reinforced and grouted concrete-block walls is well-illustrated in this detail of the damage to a concrete-block structure during the San Fernando earthquake. Note that the lateral ground motions and wall deflections merely chipped off the exterior face of the concrete blocks, leaving the steel-reinforced poured-concrete cores and preserving the structural integrity of the wall.

Construction and Earthquake Resistance   **169**

The stack-bond, concrete-block walls of the steam plant for the San Fernando juvenile facility were reinforced with vertical steel bars but lacked sufficient horizontal bars and concrete grouting. A staggered common-bond pattern might have prevented or lessened this damage. It is interesting to note as well that the main buildings of this facility were designed under the strict California state school code (Field Act), rather than the county code, and consequently suffered considerably less damage than this building.

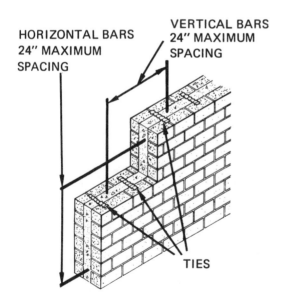

HORIZONTAL BARS 24" MAXIMUM SPACING

VERTICAL BARS 24" MAXIMUM SPACING

TIES

Brick buildings constructed with superior mortar and thoroughly reinforced with steel rods and ties carefully embedded in poured-concrete grouting have proved effective in enduring moderate quakes. Nevertheless, as a general rule, it is wiser not to buy or build a brick structure in earthquake country. The quality of the workmanship and the materials is always difficult to control in brick construction, and the heavy, extremely inflexible and brittle walls make even reinforced brick buildings somewhat risky to occupants and investors.

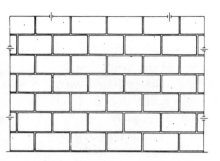

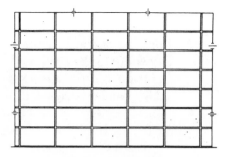

COMMON BOND

STACK BOND

The two most common patterns for concrete-block construction are the staggered common bond and the vertically aligned stack bond. The former is recom- *mended for earthquake country because of its greater strength and resistance to lateral earthquake forces.*

you own one, to carry insurance for the full value of the structure and its furnishings. In addition, you should seek the advice of a structural engineer in taking whatever measures you can to lessen the hazard to the building's occupants.

Unreinforced stone and adobe buildings

Stone and adobe buildings, and particularly those without any reinforcement or bracing, are designed to carry only vertical loads and have practically no flexibility or strength for resisting the lateral forces of earthquakes. The high casualty figures for earthquakes in South and Central America and Southern Europe and Asia are due primarily to

Because of their extreme brittleness and inflexibility, hollow tile structures, such as this guest house of the Veteran's Hospital complex in San Fernando, inevitably suffer proportionally greater earthquake damage than most other masonry buildings. Tile is not an adequate construction material for earthquake country.

this type of construction. Such structures are no longer built anywhere in the earthquake-prone areas of the United States, but many old examples remain standing, with previous earthquake damage disguised by "plaster and paint" work. A very minor earthquake may be sufficient to destroy such a weakened building. Major alterations are required to improve the resistance of these buildings; and except in the case of historical monuments, such alterations are neither economically feasible or warranted.

Reinforced-concrete buildings

Most modern large buildings in earthquake country are either reinforced poured concrete or steel-framed. Reinforced-concrete structures, when properly designed, can be highly earthquake resistant. However, because of their great weight and their dependence on careful detailing and workmanship, these structures have suffered considerably more earthquake damage than steel-frame buildings. The failure of the new Olive View Hospital in Los Angeles during the San Fernando quake is an instructive example. The hospital had been completed and dedicated only a few weeks before the earthquake, and it was designed and constructed in accordance with the latest building codes. It failed because the shear walls of concrete were eliminated on the ground floor to allow for more window space. In addition, the slim concrete supporting columns at the street level were inadequately reinforced with steel, and the combination of the heavy inertial load and the chaotic deflections of the ground floor shattered the columns and caused the entire structure to lurch to one side. Three of the four independent exterior stairwell structures totally collapsed because of the inadequate columns.

Several high-rise concrete buildings designed to standards similar to those of California have also failed or completely pancaked in recent earthquakes in Alaska, Venezuela and Japan. All of the failures are generally attributed to inadequate building code requirements, poor design, or a lack of careful supervision of the workmanship. The most prevalent problem is the so-called "Swiss cheese" effect in the

The reinforced-concrete Olive View Hospital in San Fernando was dedicated only weeks before the earthquake destroyed it, causing four deaths and several injuries. Three of the four separate stairwell structures also fell to the ground (one of them lies on the right), and two smaller concrete buildings in the complex suffered partial collapses. Such failures in new, presumably well-designed structures during a moderate quake demonstrate the weaknesses in the contemporary building codes and the urgent need for revision of these codes.

shear walls. The architect and engineer design a sound shear wall structure; but, then, as in the Olive View Hospital, there is a decision to add more window openings, or the designers neglect to consider the numerous additional openings that might be made by the plumbers, electricians, air-conditioning technicians, etc. Soon, the concrete walls are riddled with inadequately planned and reinforced holes, which weaken the strength of the building to resist earthquake forces.

Concrete buildings should be, and can be, exceptionally sound for seismic regions if local building codes and their enforcement are revised and if the construction is well-supervised. The fundamental strength of reinforced concrete structures is demonstrated in the photograph here of the Olive View Hospital; for despite the battering from the quake and the collapsing columns, the main structure remained virtually undamaged.

The virtually unreinforced poured-concrete Cummings Valley School in Kern County was described by investigators as "a classic in poor design, poor material and poor work-manship." The school, built about 1910, was a total loss. Actually, with proper design and construction, reinforced concrete can be a very durable material.

Concrete buildings without any steel reinforcement, or with minimal reinforcement, do not meet contemporary building codes, but a few such older structures can be found. Concrete buildings constructed before 1933 should be especially suspect. Of course, it is impossible to determine whether an old building is improperly reinforced without the engineering drawings and the aid of a structural engineer, and you would be very unwise to purchase an older concrete building without such professional help.

Steel-frame buildings

Steel buildings, when properly designed and constructed, are the most earthquake resistant structures known. Like wood-framing, steel has the ideal quake-resistant qualities of lightness and flexibility. However, steel is much stronger than wood, and steel buildings are generally designed and built with greater care. High rises and other modern steel buildings specifically designed for high earthquake loads have never collapsed in recent earthquakes, and it is highly improbable that they ever will. Collapse is a possibility only if severe geological failures, such as massive landsliding or faulting beneath the structure, should occur. Poorly braced steel buildings have suffered considerable damage to their interiors and architectural features, however, particularly in the upper stories. Because of excessive deflections in the higher floors during the ground motions, columns, floor beams and stair and elevator shafts buckle and twist, some connections fail, and veneers are often shattered.

Builders of steel or reinforced-concrete buildings exceeding three stories or about 50 feet should request special dynamic earthquake analyses of the structures to be performed by the structural engineers involved in the design. In these analyses, computers are used to simulate the actual behavior of the buildings during earthquakes of various magnitudes. The results often indicate certain peculiarities in the building which may be overlooked or neglected by the more common and extremely over-simplified "long-hand" analyses. The cost of such computer analyses is a worthwhile investment for major structures.

With the rising prices for lumber, steel is beginning to be used now for residential and other small construction. When such buildings are properly braced and connected, there can be no better property investment in earthquake country. Builders very near a large and active fault zone should certainly give serious consideration to the use of steel framing.

Mobile homes

In the mobile-home parks of the hard-hit Sylmar district of Los Angeles, virtually *all* of the coaches were shaken off their mountings by the San Fernando quake, and more than half of the homes sustained extensive and expensive damage. Many of the occupants also sustained moderate injuries in the falling coaches. The nature of the mobile home—essentially a small and relatively light structure sup-

With the rising prices of lumber, light steel framing for residential and other small buildings is becoming more economical. This type of construction substitutes steel columns and joists and steel x-bracing for the conventional lumber diagonals. The steel is as flexible as wood and considerably stronger so long as the various steel members are properly connected and braced. If costs permit, light steel framing for a new building is very desirable and is recommended without qualification for areas that may expect high earthquake intensities.

ported on stilt foundations—makes them susceptible to damage in even slight tremors, unless special precautions are taken to ensure that the supports are sturdy and that there are strong connections between the coach and the ground.

Most mobile homes are mounted on poured-concrete or concrete-block piers at intervals of about six feet along the frame of the coach. Screwjacks are then placed on each pier, raised until they are in contact with the undercarriage, and then adjusted to level the coach. Generally, piers at least 12-inches high are required by local codes, but often on sloping ground, the pier foundations are four or more feet high. These stilt foundations are precarious in the best of circumstances unless they are very well reinforced and tied. They can also be dangerous—in the San Fernando quake, the screwjack levelers were often unattached to either pier or undercarriage; and as the jacks were thrust aside by the tremor, the coaches dropped upon and were pierced by the concrete piers. Even more frequently, the piers had not been properly reinforced or anchored to the ground, and they simply rolled over or burst apart, toppling the coach to the ground.

Typically, mobile homes are thrown from their pier foundations during even small tremors, unless the foundations are strongly reinforced and well-tied to their footings and to the undercarriage of the coaches. The resulting damage *can be slight but bothersome or it can be quite severe, as in these coaches which were pierced and badly battered when the unanchored piers were thrust aside and the coaches fell upon their own foundations.*

As in the case of any building, mobile homes require numerous and strong connections to the foundation and a well-located, carefully constructed foundation if they are to endure an earthquake with minimal and mainly interior damage. The following procedures for reinforcing the foundation piers and footing and properly anchoring the structure will add a little to the costs of your homesite, but besides securing your coach against collapse, they should also considerably improve the resale value of the unit. Generally, if these procedures are carefully followed, earthquake insurance (at least for exterior damage) will not be necessary.

- Manufacturers generally recommend a maximum pier spacing of about 10 feet, but six-foot spacing is better in earthquake country, and the end piers should be no farther than four or five feet from the ends of the coach. Every other pair of piers should be perpendicular to length of the coach.
- Concrete footings at least 16 x 16 x 6 inches should be cast for each pier; and vertical steel bars, bent at each end and one-half inch in diameter, should be

Construction and Earthquake Resistance   **177**

embedded in each footing. The number and spacing of the bars should correspond to the hollows in the concrete blocks, and the bars must be long enough to extend two inches above the piers.

- The blocks should be laid with good-quality mortar and all of the hollows should be filled with carefully compacted concrete grouting. Each pier should then be topped with a four-inch-thick solid concrete cap cast over the top of the reinforcing bar.

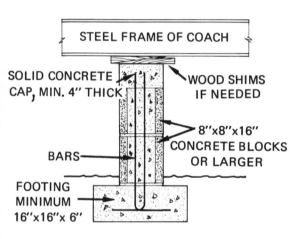

The piers for mobile homes should be constructed of concrete blocks bonded by good-quality mortar and reinforced in each cavity with a steel bar grouted in concrete. The steel bars should be bent at the lower end and embedded in a concrete footing at least 16 x 16 x 6 inches. A solid concrete cap should top the blocks, and creosote-treated wood shims, rather than screwjack levelers, should be driven tightly between the undercarriage and the cap if leveling is necessary.

- Creosote-treated wood wedges (*shims*) should be driven between the concrete caps and the undercarriage of the coach if leveling is necessary. These wood levelers are far less trouble and considerably more reliable than steel screwjack levelers.
- Strong ties of commercially available rust-resistant steel cable or strapping must be used to brace the coach against the ground motions of an earthquake. The ties are securely bolted to the undercarriage frame and then attached with a fastener and tensioning device to ground anchors (or with a slab

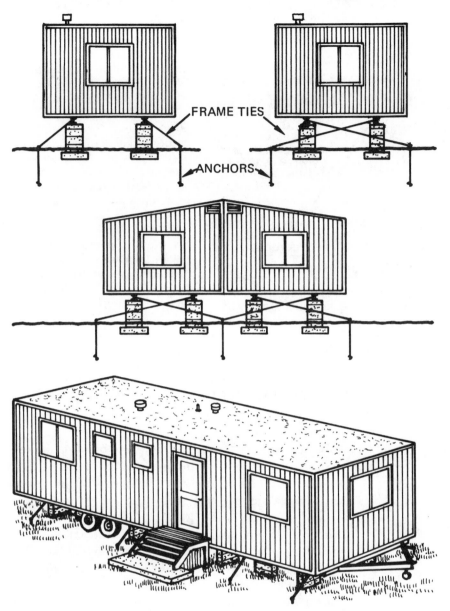

FRAME TIES

ANCHORS

These sketches illustrate the recommended methods for connecting and anchoring frame ties for mobile homes. The x-bracing system is preferred for its greater resistance to lateral earthquake forces.

Construction and Earthquake Resistance   **179**

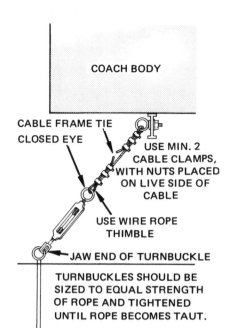

COACH BODY

CABLE FRAME TIE
CLOSED EYE

USE MIN. 2
CABLE CLAMPS,
WITH NUTS PLACED
ON LIVE SIDE OF
CABLE

USE WIRE ROPE
THIMBLE

JAW END OF TURNBUCKLE

TURNBUCKLES SHOULD BE
SIZED TO EQUAL STRENGTH
OF ROPE AND TIGHTENED
UNTIL ROPE BECOMES TAUT.

GROUND ANCHOR

Frame ties allow a coach to slip a little on the piers with the earthquake motions, but prevent it from falling off. Thus, if the piers are solidly reinforced against collapse, a well-tied mobile home can endure a quake with, at worst, some minimal interior damage from the shaking. Use a galvanized steel cable with a minimum diameter of 7/32 inches, or an "aircraft cable" with a minimum diameter of ¼ inches. If you prefer to use straps, use 1¼ x 0.035 inch galvanized steel.

foundation, to connections embedded in the concrete). Diagonal x-bracing, as illustrated here, provides the greatest resistance to the lateral earthquake forces.

- Hook-ended fasteners are subject to bending under stress and should not be used for the ties.
- Several types of ground anchors can be used —screw augers, expansion anchors or concrete deadmen—but they must be able to withstand about 5,000 pounds of tension without pulling out. The supplier of the anchoring devices will be able to recommend the one most suitable for your soil conditions. The anchors should always be installed to a depth of at least four feet, and the ground should be thoroughly tamped.
- For a coach less than 50 feet in length, five sets of frame ties will be adequate. Longer coaches should use at least six and preferably seven tiedowns. In addition, one frame tie should always be placed at each end of the coach parallel to the long direction.

CHAPTER 7

The importance of architectural & structural design & detailing for earthquake resistance

Just as the various prototypes of "safety" cars are extremely austere and not very stylish, the most earthquake-resistant house would be a clumsy, bunker-like structure with a bare minimum of small and narrow doors and windows penetrating the walls. Numerous interior partitions dividing the house into very small rooms would further strengthen the boxy structure in resisting earthquake forces. Obviously, such a house would not be very appealing, nor is it very common in structures built within the past 30 years. The contemporary trend in design favors buildings without any visible means of support, and certainly such light and airy structures are much more attractive and better suited to the climate and life style of California and much of the West. With their large glass areas, slender columns supporting heavy broad-eaved roofs, multi-level floor plans, unusual geometric patterns and dramatic water and hillside sites, these buildings satisfy the tastes and needs of their owners. Usually, they also satisfy the local building codes, which are seldom based on the realities of seismic hazards.

Unfortunately, all too often the architectural and structural design and detailing that make these houses so attractive also incorporate many of the most obvious earthquake hazards. Engineers and contractors sometimes neglect to stress the importance of good detailing, and small contractors do not always have the knowledge to insist on good earthquake-resistant design. Consequently, a large percentage of the building damage from earthquakes is directly attributable to poor design or detailing.

For example, the failure of a slender corner column supporting a heavy roof or the upper floor in a split level can cause damage not only to wall and large glass panels but also to the roof, the floor, the interior walls, the furnishings and the occupants of the building. In contrast, a sturdy older home with conventionally small window areas and numerous and solid supporting walls might sustain some broken windows, falling plaster and chimney damage, or it might even fall off its foundation, but chances are very good that the house would remain intact and the damage would not be costly or dangerous to the occupants.

As this book has continually emphasized, the modern design requirements for houses and other small buildings in earthquake country must be accompanied by especial attention to the strengths of the load-bearing vertical supports and the connections among all the structural elements of the building. This chapter examines these factors in greater detail and suggests ways that poor detailing and design may be avoided in construction or corrected in existing buildings. The chapter also discusses the special earthquake problems of old houses and of certain modern architectural features—split levels, houses on stilts, and glass walls, etc.—which have caused or have sustained disproportionate damage during recent earthquakes.

Foundations

The following brief descriptions of the different types of foundations suitable for earthquake country will give you some notion of the relative advantages and disadvantages of the primary system of support an architect or engineer has chosen or will choose for your building:

A good, reliable type of foundation for most areas of

This is an example of a well-tied and continuous wall foundation. Note the steel sill anchors every four feet. With this type of foundation all of the main load-bearing walls of the townhouses will have solid, continuous support—an essential requirement in earthquake country and especially on sloping sites.

earthquake country is a *continuous, tied, wall foundation*, in which poured reinforced-concrete forms a uniform length of support under every foot of the main load-bearing walls of the building. The concrete is reinforced with vertical steel rods and then securely tied together with horizontal steel rods that extend around corners. Such tied foundations enable a building to move as a single integral unit during an earthquake, so that the different components of the structure remain stable and damage is minimized. If your building is in a high earthquake intensity area (particularly on fill or alluvium) and if it has separate, unconnected concrete mats and foundation columns under the outside load-bearing walls, the risk of earthquake damage is quite high. Insurance coverage is a necessity in these circumstances. An alternative but very expensive measure is to have the foundation columns tied together with reinforced concrete beams, so that a solid, continuous foundation will be formed.

A *mat*, or *floating foundation*—a reinforced-concrete slab resting directly on the soil—is ideal for buildings located on soft soils or other inferior ground, such as landfill. Full mat foundations, when well-reinforced with steel, have the advantages of rigidity and continuity—they provide continuous support to a structure and minimize the hazard from differential soil movements by bridging over the pockets of especially soft or loose soil in the ground. When foundations displace even slightly, the support of the building becomes uneven, causing severe cracking and warping of the floor and partial collapses in the frame. The damage can be similar to that caused by faulting directly under the house. Buildings on mat foundations (and on the pier or piling foundations described below) generally experience less of this type of damage during earthquakes. The mats should always be reinforced with steel well in excess of the usual code requirements.

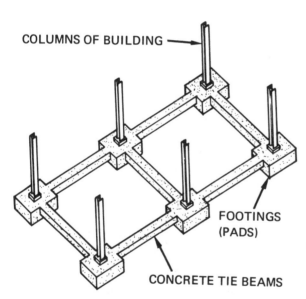

COLUMNS OF BUILDING

FOOTINGS (PADS)

CONCRETE TIE BEAMS

Another common type of foundation uses separate concrete pads or footings to support the major columns of a building. Such a foundation is not reliable during an earthquake unless the column pads are held together with reinforced concrete tie-beams that restrict any differential movement of the pads. Generally, a full concrete slab supporting the entire walls of a structure is a better, more stable foundation for earthquake country and particularly for soft soils (alluvium, landfill, etc.) that will be subject to high amplifications and/or ground settlements.

Drilled pier or *caisson-pile foundations*, which are steel or concrete pilings set deep in the ground, are generally used only with tall or very heavy buildings, especially with alluvial, clay, landfill or other soft soils. These foundations have a very good record for endurance in large earthquakes. For example, much of the damage in the alluvial and filled areas of San Francisco in 1906 was caused by large ground settlements. However, the buildings on deeply submerged pilings did not settle with the alluvial or filled soils, and the damage to these buildings was substantially less.

The quality and the earthquake resistance of these three types of foundations are governed by a few basic principles:

- The foundations should be supported by solid ground, and the major supporting segments of the foundation should rest on *uniform* ground conditions. For example, a portion of a foundation wall should not be partially supported on bedrock and partially on landfill material; for differential movements of the fill away from the rock during a quake can cause heavy damage to the foundation and to the structure it supports.
- Different types of foundations should not be used under one building—a combination of separate unconnected pilings with sections of continuous concrete-block wall, for example, could be risky unless the designing engineer had thoughtfully anticipated the earthquake hazard. Two different types of foundations will behave in different ways during the ground motion of a tremor, and uniform behavior is essential if a building is to withstand the earthquake stresses.
- The type of foundation required for a given site is determined primarily by the ground conditions under the building. A good bedrock base needs only the conventional continuous, tied concrete foundation minimally required by most building codes, whereas very soft soil or loose fill may require special drilled pier or caisson footings. The selection of the proper foundation for the geology of your particular site should always be the decision of an engineer well-versed in earthquake hazard and in the ground conditions of your area. *Never* depend upon the knowledge

Foundation connections

• A wood-frame building has little chance of surviving an earthquake without serious damage if its major support, the foundation, is poorly connected to the superstructure. One large jolt can easily break or disalign a weak sill connection, and this damage can, in turn, either knock the building entirely off its foundation or cause the collapse of studs and columns.

In new construction, the sill should be anchored with bolts which are embedded according to code in the concrete of the foundation. The bolts should be centered in the sill for maximum strength, and a washer should be used with the nut to allow a very tight connection without damage to the sill. Once tightened, the bolt should extend at least ⅛-inch above the nut. There should be such an anchor bolt at least every four feet along the sill and within 12 inches of the end of each sill piece. The joints between sill pieces should also be toenailed, as shown here.

The various steel anchoring devices illustrated in Chapter Six are useful in further strengthening the connections between the sill and the studs or shear-wall bracing. In addition, the device shown here is recommended for the corner connections between the wall and foundation in plywood-sheathed walls with large openings (the front garage wall in a split-level, for example). The bolted connection above the sill dispenses the concentrated earthquake forces directly into the concrete of the foundation.

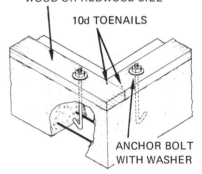

APPROVED PRESSURE TREATED WOOD OR REDWOOD SILL

10d TOENAILS

ANCHOR BOLT WITH WASHER

and judgment of a contractor in this matter.

• Faulty or insufficient connections between the foundation and the sill or between the sill and the studs and columns will drastically decrease the overall earthquake resistance of a building. The building can slip wholly or partially off its foundation, or the poor connections can hinder the effective transference of the inertial weight of the building from the studs and the

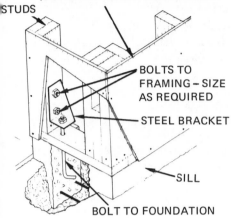

PLYWOOD SHEATHING OR SIDING
(CUT AWAY TO EXPOSE BRACKET)

STUDS

BOLTS TO
FRAMING – SIZE
AS REQUIRED

STEEL BRACKET

SILL

BOLT TO FOUNDATION

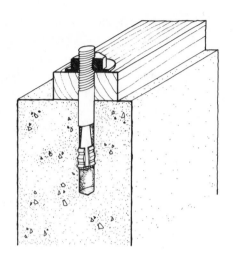

Existing wood-frame buildings lacking sufficient (or any) sill connections can be rather easily repaired with the addition of ½-inch or larger steel expansion bolts wherever you have access to the sill. The ends of the sills are especially important and should be anchored even if you have to temporarily remove the wall covering or bracing in order to add the bolts. The hole that is drill-ed into the sill and foundation does not have to be precise in its length–that is, it can be longer than the bolt–but the diameter of the hole should provide a snug fit for the bolt. After drilling the hole, caulk the inside edge thoroughly, then insert the bolt, add a washer and the nut, and turn the latter until it is as tight as possible against the washer.

columns to the foundation and the ground. The sill connections are especially important and require some further discussion in the section that follows.

Foundation connections for wood-frame buildings

One of the most common failures of wood-frame buildings results from insufficient or poor anchorages between the sill and the foundation. During the intense earthquake vibrations, the sill and the building simply slide off the foundation and crash to the ground. The damage from such failures is obviously very heavy and expensive to repair.

Existing building codes in most areas require firm anchorages between the sill and the foundation. For example, the San Francisco Building Code states that:

> Foundation plates or sills shall be bolted to the foundation or foundation wall with not less than one-half inch bolts embedded at least seven inches into the masonry or concrete and spaced not more than six feet apart. Bolts shall be located within 12 inches of each end of each piece with a minimum of two bolts per piece. Washers are required under all nuts.

These code requirements are very good ones, although maximum spacing of four feet for the anchor bolts would add greater stability for a negligible increase in cost. The placement of a bolt within 12 inches of the end of each sill piece is especially important to ensure the stability of the sill.

When purchasing a building, or when improving and repairing existing buildings, see that the sills are properly bolted in this manner to the foundation. The importance of this detail cannot be overemphasized. If the connection is inadequate, the building represents a very poor risk. The risk can be readily and economically eliminated, however, by any bolting and anchoring procedures which firmly restrict the movement of the house and sill relative to its foundation. For

This detail of sound sill-foundation connections illustrates the importance of anchorages within 12 inches of the end of each sill piece. Note, for example, that the sill is bolted on each side of the cutaway for a pipe and that anchors are placed very near the corner joint of two sill pieces. The bolts are also well-centered and include washers.

Contemporary code requirements provide for some, but not always sufficient, connections between the foundation sill and the walls of a building. However, older buildings–some constructed before the mid-1950s and many built during the 1920s and 1930s–will often have no connections whatever between the foundation and the frame. Obviously, it doesn't take much of a jolt to knock such a structure off its foundation. This older home in San Fernando was badly damaged as a result of simply resting the structure, without connections, on the foundation wall.

example, the sill may be clamped to the foundation with bolted steel angles or other anchoring devices illustrated here.

The typical *cripple-stud* connections between the sill and the floor are another very common cause of earthquake damage in wood-frame buildings. Cripple studs are short, vertical 2 x 4 supports which lift the floor one or more feet from the foundation and provide a crawl and air space under the building. Numerous serious failures among the new homes in San Fernando are attributed to cripple studs which were braced, if at all, by merely a few unreliable diagonals. The solution to this type of foundation connection problem is quite simple—merely add plywood sheathing in lieu of or to

Unless very old buildings have been reconstructed in the past 40 years, it is very likely that they are resting on their foundations without any significant connections between the foundation and the structure. Witness this dramatically ruined Victorian house in San Francisco in 1906. The force of the fall from its foundation literally split the building in half.

supplement the diagonal bracing. The plywood sheathing provides a continuous surface which quickly transfers the earthquake forces to the ground while greatly strengthening the resistance of the cripple studs to the lateral earthquake motions. The plywood shear-wall bracing should be fitted as tightly as possible against the cripple studs and should be thoroughly nailed to the sill, studs and floor joists (beams). The use of steel framing devices is also recommended to further strengthen these connections. (These devices are illustrated in the previous chapter in the section on stucco.)

Existing foundation damage. Existing foundation damage from ground settlement, previous earthquakes or, most often, rotting wood or termites is another common cause of building failures during a tremor. Older buildings especially are likely to have some foundation damage and should be carefully checked, preferably by an engineer or by a city building inspector. When inspecting for foundation damage, give special attention to the condition of the wood connections. The foundation may have been laid or graded improperly so that it traps water and rots the wooden sill or columns. Poor insulation or an improperly placed dirt backfill may also retain or trap moisture and rot the wood connections. Termite damage to the sill or columns is another particularly hazardous factor. The buyer of an older home should always insist on a termite clearance, even when it is not required.

Wide cracks in foundation concrete are an almost certain sign of existing damage from ground settlement or previous quakes. (Do not confuse such cracks with the common "hairline" cracks which are caused by the shrinkage of con-

Cripple studs are a very frequent cause of building failures during earthquakes. They are stable under earthquake stresses only when they are braced with shear-walls of plywood. Diagonal bracing, as in this damaged San Fernando home, is not sufficiently strong to withstand a large quake. Note also the fallen brick veneer.

The photograph at right shows the repairs to another San Fernando house which was severely damaged in the quake. Note that repairs include plywood sheathing to reinforce the cripple studs that raise the floors of the split level home. Unfortunately, other houses in the area built a month or two after the quake, carried on the faulty practice of bracing cripple studs only with diagonals.

Existing foundation damage in older buildings is frequently responsible for severe earthquake damage to the building as a whole. Decayed or termite-infested cripple studs in the dwelling at left led to far more serious damage to the structure during the Long Beach quake. A poorly designed or constructed foundation in the other building collected rain water, which, over the years, rotted the corner foundation sill. The decayed corner connections resulted in a partial collapse of the building.

crete.) These wide cracks may also be indicative of further structural damage in the walls, so it is imperative that an engineer be consulted immediately. Existing foundation damage *must* be repaired, since it is not only an earthquake hazard but it may also lead to more serious damage to the structure simply in the course of time. The repairs will be expensive, and once you have learned from an engineer exactly what must be done, be sure to shop around with foundation contractors or pest control companies to get the most competent and economical work.

Houses on stilts and pilings. The construction of houses on stilts or pilings has made it possible for people to enjoy the advantages and breathtaking views of living on steep hills or over the water along bay shores and riverbanks. Such houses are very appealing, but they also can be very dangerous in earthquake country. As noted, the ideal foundation support

In this Anchorage building, which was under construction when the 1964 earthquake struck, the steel reinforcing rods within the concrete-block wall kept the wall relatively intact despite its collapse. The wall fell, however, because the reinforcing rods did not extend beyond the wall into the concrete foundation. The photograph is an instructive illustration of the futility of strong walls and bracing if the wall-foundation connections are faulty.

for a house in a seismically active region is a continuous and tied wall of reinforced concrete or a reinforced concrete slab. Houses founded on a few slender supports are too seldom designed to carry the large lateral stresses of an earthquake, and even a light to moderate tremor can bring such a building crashing down. The earthquake risks for this type of building are compounded by the propensity of shoreline and steep hillside soils either to amplify earthquake intensities or to slide and slump.

A house in an earthquake region can be safely supported on slender columns only when the soil foundation is exceptionally stable and the columns are specifically designed and braced for earthquake loads. For example, columns and

Steel stilts, with diagonal bracing, welded connections and a deep, well-designed concrete pier foundation, are probably the safest supporting system for houses and small apartment buildings located on very steep hillside sites. Generally, the floor beams should also be of welded steel. The house shown here has all of these features except diagonal bracing–which would be a wise addition.

floor joists of welded steel are one excellent solution for a steep hillside house. The columns must be imbedded in deep concrete pads and the floor joists must be thoroughly bolted and welded to the columns.

For the more conventional and less expensive wood columns, the only safe choice is a shear-wall bracing system of plywood covering the entire length and breadth of the stilt foundation. Steel angles and other anchoring devices should also be used extensively to reinforce the connections between the plywood sheathing and the foundation sill and floor joists.

Diagonally braced wood stilts are always extremely risky in earthquake country. The slender wood supports are simply not strong enough to withstand a large shock. Shear-wall bracing of plywood, applied over conventional studs should be used instead for a steep site, as in the townhouses shown here.

The angles should be used as well to tie the sheathing at the corners of the building.

Diagonal bracing is never adequate for timber stilts, and if you own such a house, you should certainly add plywood sheathing as soon as possible. This is not a do-it-yourself type of job, however. At least initially, the services of an engineer are required to ensure that the design and mounting of the bracing complies with sound engineering principles.

Buildings partially or wholly on raised pilings are also very susceptible to collapse. The slumping, liquefaction and high vibrational intensities experienced during a quake along shorelines and riverbanks can easily topple the pilings or simply shake the structure off these slender and unstable supports. In such cases, the damage to the building is inevitably severe and expensive to repair. If a house is supported entirely by pilings, they must be securely planted in the ground and *rigidly* tied to the understructure of the building. This work is best done by an engineer. When a portion of a building is supported on land and a portion is supported by a wharf structure, adequate ties between the two must be designed by an engineer. The ties will prevent the movement of the wharf and the consequent spreading and collapse of the pilings supporting the building. All buildings on raised pilings should be covered by earthquake insurance.

Columns and walls

In general, the failure of wall supports, and particularly of the main corner columns, of a building is the most serious and potentially destructive and expensive type of damage that might occur during an earthquake. Once a column breaks or becomes disconnected, a chaotic sequence of further failures begins which can demolish the structure. Of all the components of a building's superstructure, the columns must be designed, reinforced and connected most carefully.

Wood-frame buildings. Wood columns fail most often because of the following deficiencies:
- The column is weakened by rotting because of poor

All of the houses supported by raised pilings along Bolinas Lagoon were shaken off their unstable foundations and dumped into the water during the 1906 quake. Despite the proximity of the San Andreas (the sand spit in the background was ruptured along the fault line), the same type of structures (and many of the same buildings) have been erected since 1906 all along the shore from Stinson Beach to Bodega. Pilings may provide adequate support only if they are securely tied, with the aid of an engineer, to the building and to a firm soil along the shore.

drainage along the top of the foundation. Termite damage to the column is another common factor. If any rotted or termite-infested column bases are found in a home, the *whole* column should be replaced immediately, with careful provision for better drainage and thorough treatment of the wood against water or insect damage. Never try to splice in a new section of column; the splice introduces a weak point which the earthquake forces are certain to discover.

- The column is not continuous from roof to foundation. It is always preferable to use single timbers for long columns, even in two-story houses. The small added cost provides significantly increased strength in en-

The connections of columns to beams and to the foundation sill must be exceptionally strong if a building is to survive a large quake without serious structural damage. The "toe-nailed" connections in the photograph at left are extremely poor; the lateral motions of a tremor could easily detach the column and bring the whole structure down. Steel angles, such as that shown in the picture at right, and various other steel anchoring and framing devices, should be used extensively–especially on the main supporting columns. Sturdy bolts will be placed in the framing device shown here; other devices may require only heavy nails.

during the lateral waves of a tremor.

- The joists, sills and other horizontal structural members are inadequately tied to the column. This is by far the most common and troublesome weakness of columns in enduring earthquake forces. It is also the easiest and cheapest to correct.
- A pair of steel pins or small steel angles are generally sufficient to strengthen these vital connections. The liberal use of these anchorages, either when building a new home or when reinforcing an existing structure, will add tremendous strength to the typical wood-frame building.

The special hazards of split-level buildings. Split-level and multi-story houses or apartment buildings with garages located at ground level are a fairly recent development in

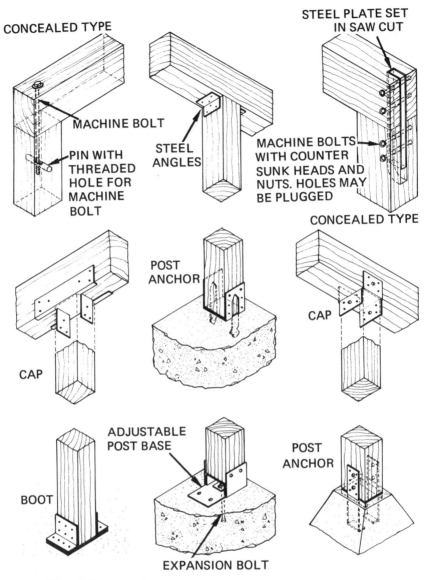

CONCEALED TYPE

MACHINE BOLT

PIN WITH THREADED HOLE FOR MACHINE BOLT

STEEL ANGLES

STEEL PLATE SET IN SAW CUT

MACHINE BOLTS WITH COUNTER SUNK HEADS AND NUTS. HOLES MAY BE PLUGGED

CONCEALED TYPE

POST ANCHOR

CAP

CAP

ADJUSTABLE POST BASE

POST ANCHOR

BOOT

EXPANSION BOLT

Wood-frame column connectors

• There are numerous column anchorages available for wood-frame construction, and the use of these steel devices is highly recommended in building a house in earthquake country or in reinforcing the column connections in an existing structure. For exposed columns and beams, there are several anchoring devices which are designed to be concealed. Other types can be veneered or exposed and painted.

These are two of numerous split-level and two-story homes in San Fernando in which the lower level garage walls were inadequately braced for the heavy load they had to support. Diagonal bracing is never sufficiently strong for this type of architecture. The right ground-level side of the first house also had diagonally braced cripple studs which contributed further to the devastation. In the other photograph, note that the upper level of the house simply ripped away as it crushed the garage walls and the late-model car inside. Neither portion of the house seems to have suffered any other structural damage—a fact that strengthens the idea that plywood sheathing on the garage walls of a split level can mean the difference between minor damage and costly destruction.

building design. Most such buildings have been constructed since the early 1950s, and in the only three earthquakes to strike heavily populated areas of California since 1952—all moderate shocks—these buildings suffered a very disproportionate amount of the total damage.

The reason for the failure of these buildings is obvious. They are inherently weaker than conventional buildings resting wholly on the ground, because the large garage door and any other windows and doors on the lower garage level constitute a large portion of the wall area which must carry and resist the brunt of the earthquake forces. The garage level is, in effect, a foundation with only three walls. During an earthquake, a building tends to twist with the lateral blows of the tremor, and an essentially three-sided structure cannot withstand this twisting motion, particularly under the additional duress of the inertial weight of another floor or two above it. If the walls of the garage do not eventually give way entirely, the top portion of the garage walls and the corners of the garage doors and windows are almost always severely cracked and require costly repairs. In this latter case, the whole building is also most susceptible to further damage or collapse if a strong aftershock should occur.

This type of damage has occurred most often to houses without shear-wall bracing. All of the damaged homes illustrated here had stucco walls with interior wallboard and some diagonal bracing in the garage story; none of the garages were sheathed with plywood. Clearly, to minimize such damage and prevent collapses, the walls of the garage, and especially the front and back walls, should be strengthened with plywood paneling. Wallboard sheathing is totally inadequate for this kind of stress. It is also very important to use steel angles or the other anchoring devices to securely connect the plywood to the foundation sill and the floor joists above. Any columns which support intermediate floor joists should also be thoroughly connected with steel bracing devices.

If the building exceeds two stories in height, you should consult an engineer specializing in earthquake design; for the additional load of multi-stories complicates the problem. The costs of the consultation and the necessary alterations will be reasonable and certainly preferable to the total financial loss of a collapsed building. Finally, even if these precautions are taken, the owner of this type of building, particularly in a high intensity area, would be wise to carry ample earthquake insurance.

Masonry Buildings. Some older brick, stone or concrete buildings are supported in part or entirely by unreinforced brick columns. These columns are extremely dangerous, since they have practically no ability to resist lateral earthquake forces. If you own or wish to purchase such a building, consult a structural engineer experienced in earthquake problems to determine the need and the cost of reinforcement for the columns and for the building as a whole.

Modern, large, wood-frame or steel apartment and

This very commonplace design for modern apartment buildings on the West Coast is both risky to the investor and unsafe for the occupants, unless proper measures are taken to strengthen the supporting walls and the connections between the walls of the different stories. With their essentially three-sided supporting foundation and thin columns, these San Fernando buildings were fortunate, indeed, still to be standing. A stronger shock or a few more years of inevitable deterioration in the structure would probably have meant the collapse of the buildings.

commercial buildings are most often supported by reinforced concrete columns. If you are involved in the architectural and structural planning of such a building, then you should know that although many different types of reinforced concrete columns meet current building codes, one type has consistently demonstrated the greatest endurance during past earthquakes. That type is reinforced with tied *spirals* of steel. The more common rectangularly tied concrete columns are cheaper, but they are also often completely inadequate for large earthquake stresses.

Floor and roof diaphragms

Almost without exception, all earthquake failures associated with the diaphragm members of a structure have occurred at their connections with the walls, rather than in the diaphragms themselves. The destructive forces of an earthquake are easily absorbed by these horizontal members, but their connections to the vertical supports are often con-

Numerous heavy balconies and canopies, such as this in El Centro, California, wholly or partially collapsed during the large Imperial Valley earthquake in 1940. The brick supporting columns were unable to sustain the lateral forces of the tremor.

siderably less durable. This is especially and mainly a problem in masonry buildings with wooden roofs and floors. With the lateral blows of a tremor, the rigid masonry walls pull away from their connection with the diaphragms, and the unsupported roof or floors plummet.

The diaphragm connections in these buildings fail most often because of the use of a wood *ledger*—a framing beam which is bolted to the masonry walls. The floors and roof rest on and are attached to this ledger. Such a connection is insufficient in earthquake country; the roofs and floors require the additional support of steel anchors or metal straps that tie the joists of the diaphragms directly to the wall.

These anchors and straps restrain the diaphragms from pulling out from the ledger or from pulling the ledger out of the masonry. They also add considerable strength to the masonry walls and may help to prevent their collapse. If you wish to reinforce a masonry building in this way, be certain that the diaphragm anchors are not seated in lime mortar. As noted earlier, this type of mortar is particularly weak, and the anchors are likely simply to pull out of the masonry at the first strong jolt of an earthquake.

The reasons for the failure of the Olive View Hospital in San Fernando have been discussed earlier. What is interesting here is the differences in the performances of the two types of columns supporting the structures. The completely fractured corner column in the foreground had vertical steel reinforcements which were tied together with individual steel loops. The individual ties pulled apart, allowing the concrete core to burst.

The intermediate columns, which retained their shape and kept the building up after the quake, were also reinforced with vertical steel rods, but these rods were tied together and supplemented with continuous pre-formed steel spirals. The detail shows that the spirally reinforced columns suffered only damage to the concrete facing and disalignment as a result of the lurching of the building. The core of the column remained intact.

The diaphragm connections for wood-frame buildings have a far better history for earthquake damage. However, it is very important, that these connections be thoroughly nailed and, in high intensity areas, reinforced with the numerous metal anchors and clips illustrated in the previous chapter. The most common problem with diaphragm connections in wood-frame buildings is a too-heavy roof. Mission-style clay-tile roofs, slate roofing and the very broad-eaved shingled roofs popular in the hot desert climates require considerably more support and reinforcement to secure their

This modern light-industrial building in San Fernando was one of many that were badly damaged by the quake. In almost every case, the problem with the concrete structures was the poor design of the roof-wall connections—a very common weakness in larger masonry buildings with wood roofs and floors. Under the lateral ground motions of a quake, the heavy walls pull away from the roof or floor and break the connections. In this photograph, you can see the wood ledger which, with a few nails, was the only support for the roof beams. All buildings of this type should include steel diaphragm supports and connections.

connections during an earthquake. A clay-tile roof on a 1,500-square-foot building, for example, weighs about eight tons more than a roof of wood or asphalt shingles. The heavy-roof problem is especially hazardous with multi-story buildings because the walls of the upper stories are subject to broad deformations which weaken their resistance to the weighty inertial load from the roof. It is essential that the walls of a building topped by an exceptionally heavy roof be optimally strengthened with shear-wall bracing of plywood, so that the structure can support the roof during an earthquake. Even with such bracing, there is some risk of damage to or by the roof, and it is a good idea to carry earthquake

Connections for masonry walls & wood diaphragms

These drawings show some of the detailing recommended for the connection of wood diaphragms and masonry walls in new construction. The first is a steel joist anchor which is embedded in the masonry wall and, preferably, tied as well to the vertical steel reinforcing in the wall. The anchor is then nailed to the underside of the blockings and joists of the roof and floors. The anchor should always be long enough to span at least three joists. Note also the anchor bolt, which is the conventional and code-required connection in all new masonry wall-wood diaphragm construction.

Another type of joist anchoring device is used where the ends of the joists abut the wall. In this case, a steel anchor (strap) is embedded in the wall and tied to the reinforcing steel rod. The strap is then thoroughly nailed along the side of the joist. There should be such an anchor at least every four feet along a diaphragm.

For existing buildings without the above reinforcement, you can add steel angles which are bolted through the masonry wall and then connected to the joists. An engineer should be employed to design such anchoring and bracing details.

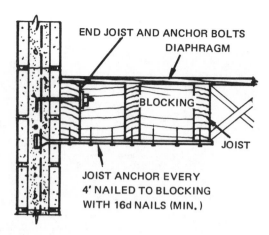

END JOIST AND ANCHOR BOLTS
DIAPHRAGM
BLOCKING
JOIST
JOIST ANCHOR EVERY 4' NAILED TO BLOCKING WITH 16d NAILS (MIN.)

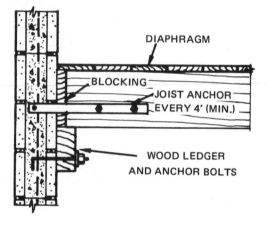

DIAPHRAGM
BLOCKING
JOIST ANCHOR EVERY 4' (MIN.)
WOOD LEDGER AND ANCHOR BOLTS

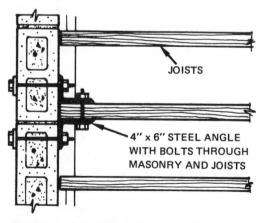

JOISTS
4" x 6" STEEL ANGLE WITH BOLTS THROUGH MASONRY AND JOISTS

Buildings with exceptionally heavy roofs, which includes all clay-tile and slate roofing, require significantly stronger wall bracing. This building, at the Fukui, Japan, College of Engineering, vividly illustrates the whip effect caused by the combination of the heavy tile roof and the 1948 earthquake.

insurance on the building, especially if it is in the vicinity of a fault and/or on a soft soil foundation.

Clay-tile, slate and other masonry or stone roofing materials are also in themselves especially susceptible to earthquake damage. Unless they are thoroughly nailed to the roof, they tend to dislodge and fall during even moderate tremors that will leave the rest of the building completely unaffected. Besides being expensive to replace, these heavy roofing materials can be very dangerous to people running out of the building during the quake.

Large windows and doors

The corners of large doors and windows are always the weak points in the structural frames of buildings. Much of the damage after an earthquake will be concentrated in the vicinity of these large openings. The cause for this damage is easy to understand: Where there are no openings in the walls, the earthquake forces are distributed evenly throughout the entire wall. A large hole in the structural frame interrupts the path of the earthquake forces and increases the stress to the area around the opening. The sharp corners of the opening also cause further stress concentrations which add to the damage.

A careful bracing system around the openings may be sufficient to redirect the earthquake forces back to the foundation and strengthen the framing. Diagonal bracing can be helpful, but the most effective bracing is always plywood sheathing. The shear-wall bracing should be below, above and on both sides of the large windows or doors, and the sheathing on each side of the opening should be at least as wide as the opening itself in order to prevent cracking and other damage to the interior and exterior wall veneers.

Large plate glass panels, such as sliding glass doors and bay and picture windows or glass walls, present the additional hazard and costly damage of breakage during earthquakes. The brittle glass panels break easily as they deform with the surrounding walls. Plywood sheathing around such openings may prevent some of this damage by stiffening the walls and decreasing the wall distortions. However, glass breakage in

This single-story dwelling in Managua, Nicaragua, endured the heavy load of the tile roof and the strong tremor with only light damage. The heavy stucco walls and the low level of the building saved it from further damage. However, another disadvantage of tile roofing is shown here. Without careful anchoring, the tiles are easily thrown off the roof during an earthquake.

large windows and doors is virtually inevitable during strong quakes. Normally, earthquake-insurance policies will not cover broken glass. Therefore, a plate-glass insurance policy is recommended in cases where high-intensity tremors can be expected.

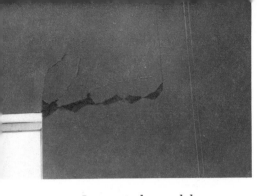

Large window and door openings are especially prone to earthquake damage because the openings interrupt the path of the earthquake forces and cause concentrations of stress around the openings and especially at their corners. Very often, the cracking around these openings also indicates far more serious structural damage within the walls. Diagonal and, preferably, shear-wall bracing should support the walls surrounding large openings. The last photograph (below, right) shows the belated post-earthquake addition of plywood sheathing around a door which sustained heavy damage in the San Fernando quake.

Parapets, ornaments, balconies and other projections

Masonry parapets, balconies and other ornaments are usually the first components of a building to fail during an earthquake. Their positions at the tops of buildings, where the earthquake vibrations are most intense; the poor connections between the projections and the building; the cracking and general weakening caused by weathering and lack of maintenance; and, in the case of wood projections, the rotting supports—all contribute to the frequent failures of the ar-

Masonry parapets, and other overhanging, unsupported architectural features, are highly subject to earthquake failure and are one of the most hazardous elements of earthquake damage. In the United States, many earthquake casualties result from falling masonry parapets, canopies and other exterior decorative features. The parapet damage to this Bakersfield school is typical.

chitectural features.

In themselves, these decorative projections are not such a problem, because if they fall or break, an owner can simply eliminate them from the building and the repair costs will be minor. However, when they fall, these heavy projections are also likely either to pull down a part of the supporting wall or to damage the lower portion of the building or other adjacent buildings. In addition, because these architectural features tend to be located above entrances, they are extremely hazardous to people running out of the building during a tremor.

Mainly for the latter reason, the city of Los Angeles has passed a retroactive building ordinance requiring the elimination or strengthening of hazardous parapets, ornaments and other projections on buildings other than private residential dwellings. The city allows a sufficient amount of time so that the problem can be eliminated in an orderly and thorough fashion and so that the owners can finance the repairs and meet some of the peculiar problems which inevitably arise. Many other cities in California also have such ordinances, but most of them have not been as responsible in seeing that the repairs are carried out. Fortunately, the repair and strengthening of hazardous projections are usually moderately inexpensive procedures. The most common method for strengthening building projections is their reinforcement with steel ties and anchors and/or the additional lateral sup-

During the San Fernando quake, a parapet collapsed and fell through the ceiling of a classroom at Los Angeles High School. After numerous repetitions of this kind of damage to schools decade after decade, the California state and local governments are finally beginning to take urgent steps to replace or reinforce unsafe schools.

ports of metal buttresses. These repairs will not only preserve the decorative projections but may strengthen the walls of the buildings as well.

Chimneys and fireplaces

Exterior masonry chimneys are usually the most damageable and often the most damaging element of the typical wood-frame house. In fact, seismologists determine the intensities of a given earthquake partially by figuring the percentage of destroyed chimneys per unit area. In the San Fernando earthquake, most of the houses in the area were less than 15 years old and their chimneys were reinforced with vertical steel bars in accordance with the local building codes. As a result, 68 percent of the chimneys in the highest intensity areas survived the quake without any damage. Certainly, if the chimneys had not been reinforced with steel, the percentage of non-damage would have been close to zero.

Because a house and its chimney are essentially separate and very different structures, they tend to respond to earthquake motions by pounding and pulling apart. Thus, chimneys must be tied thoroughly to the frame of the building, preferably with long steel straps that are embedded into the masonry and nailed to the joists of the various diaphragms of the building. These ties help to support the chimney and eliminate the possibility of pounding between the two structures.

The straps at the roof line are particularly important; for without this tie, the pounding damage could be severe and the top of the chimney can readily break off and fall on the roof or an adjacent building. Chimneys which project three feet or more above the roof line are especially hazardous for this reason, and they should probably be shortened. In lieu of such reconstruction, inspect the chimney frequently (at least every year) to determine if any cracks have formed in the mortar. Such damage may be due to settlement of the building, to small earthquakes or to poor workmanship or materials; but whatever the cause, the chimney is already weakened by this cracking, and its chances for withstanding the next big quake will be significantly lowered.

Any chimneys pre-dating about 1960 are unlikely to have adequate ties to the building and should be reinforced with metal straps or angles, as illustrated here. Frequent inspection of the mortar is also advisable, and if you find any severe cracking, determine whether the likely collapse of the chimney will endanger people or cause costly damage to the building. If the chimney does seem to present a hazard, consult an engineer. He may be able to devise an economical and attractive system of vertical and horizontal steel ties and braces which will keep the chimney upright.

Anyone building a new masonry chimney anywhere in

Heavy overhanging concrete canopies, such as this around a service building in the Olive View Hospital complex, are very common on commercial buildings and over the entrances to schools, hospitals and other buildings. Because of their weight and slender supports, they require far more reinforcement and much stronger connections than most local building codes specify.

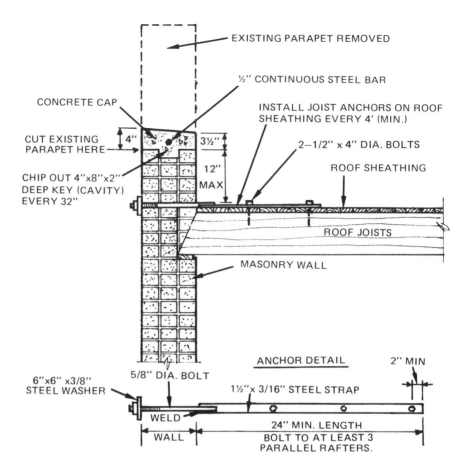

EXISTING PARAPET REMOVED

½" CONTINUOUS STEEL BAR

CONCRETE CAP

INSTALL JOINT ANCHORS ON ROOF SHEATHING EVERY 4' (MIN.)

CUT EXISTING PARAPET HERE

4"

3½"

2–1/2" x 4" DIA. BOLTS

ROOF SHEATHING

CHIP OUT 4"x8"x2" DEEP KEY (CAVITY) EVERY 32"

12" MAX

ROOF JOISTS

MASONRY WALL

ANCHOR DETAIL

2" MIN

6"x6" x3/8" STEEL WASHER

5/8" DIA. BOLT

1½"x 3/16" STEEL STRAP

WELD

WALL

24" MIN. LENGTH
BOLT TO AT LEAST 3 PARALLEL RAFTERS.

The reinforcement or removal of masonry parapets is an essential, life-or-death obligation for property owners and city officers. One relatively simple method of reinforcement is shown here. The parapet is shortened, anchored with steel bolts and straps, and capped with concrete. This procedure had been used extensively in Los Angeles before 1971 and was undoubtedly responsible for preventing much damage and many injuries during the San Fernando quake.

earthquake country should, above all, use the services of an engineer. An ordinary contractor may not have all the information necessary to construct an earthquake-resistant structure. The vertical reinforcing steel bars in the chimney should be considerably in excess of code requirements, and the connecting ties should meet the standards illustrated here. In

Long chimneys are especially susceptible to earthquake damage—even in such a moderate quake as that in Seattle in 1965. The photograph at left shows another chimney failure, in San Fernando, which also caused substantial damage to the house. The costs of repairing this damage could easily mount up to $2,000, and with the standard deductible clause for most earthquake-insurance policies, this cost would probably be out-of-pocket. Additional steel reinforcement during construction or a system of steel ties and anchors for an existing chimney would have prevented this chimney failure at a cost of less than $50.

addition, some horizontal reinforcing bars are recommended, particularly at the points where the chimney is tied to the building. Even better than the traditional brick and concrete structures are the recently developed prefabricated sheet-metal chimneys now available. These chimneys are very light, strong and flexible and will not collapse or cause any pounding damage. For a traditional appearance, the sheet metal can be encased in a masonry veneer, of course. However, this would add to the cost of construction and the risk of earthquake damage. Equally attractive and far more economical and functional would be a well-designed covering of wood or stucco.

Fireplaces are also very prone to earthquake damage. Thus, if you are building a fireplace, be certain that you or your contractor follow the procedure for anchoring exterior masonry veneer—that is, one masonry anchor for every square foot of wall area supporting the brick or stone. If your

Reinforcing and tying exterior masonry chimneys

● Because exterior masonry chimneys are highly susceptible to earthquake damage, and because their failure can be both expensive to repair and hazardous to the roof, walls and occupants of the building, strong steel reinforcements within the chimney and sturdy ties between the chimney and the building are essential. Ample horizontal and vertical reinforcements for masonry chimneys have been required by most local codes for the past 15 years, so that chimneys built after about 1960 are likely to be sufficiently stable. However, the codes have generally been lax in specifying adequate ties between the chimney and the building. Without numerous properly placed ties, the chimney is very likely either to pull away from the house during an earthquake or cause pounding damage to the roof and chimney.

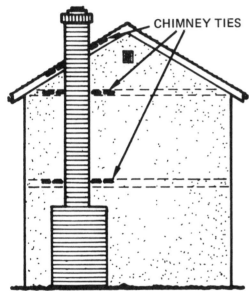

CHIMNEY TIES

The chimney ties should be at every diaphragm level. Most code requirements call only for short steel tie straps to be nailed or bolted directly to the roof joists. This type of connection tends to concentrate all of the earthquake forces in a narrow area around the straps—a concentration which may result in damage to the roof, in broken connections, and in a falling or badly damaged chimney. A better method for using and connecting the chimney ties is shown in the following drawings.

home includes a fireplace, there are no simple measures you can take to ensure its stability in an earthquake. Chances are, if the fireplace is relatively new (built within the past 15 years), it was well-anchored and it will not collapse. Older fireplaces—particularly solid brick or stone structures—are risky, and you would be well-advised to keep any valuable objects or furnishings away from the path of potentially falling masonry.

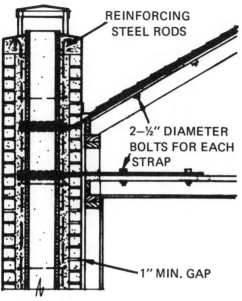

REINFORCING STEEL RODS

2–½" DIAMETER BOLTS FOR EACH STRAP

1" MIN. GAP

In new construction, the connecting steel straps should be anchored in the masonry and around the steel reinforcements in the chimney, as shown here. The straps should then extend into the building at least 2½ feet and should be attached with bolts to a 2 x 4 which is laid diagonally across at least four diaphragm joists. The 2 x 4 is then securely nailed to the joists.

This top view of the chimney-diaphragm ties shows the straps bolted to the diagonally positioned 2 x 4s. Note also that the ends of the straps are bent around the vertical steel reinforcements in the concrete core of the chimney.

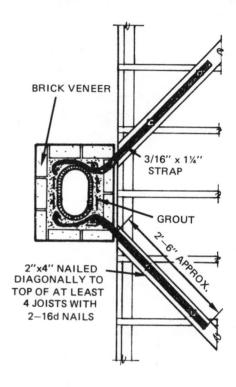

BRICK VENEER

3/16" x 1¼" STRAP

GROUT

2'–6" APPROX.

2"x4" NAILED DIAGONALLY TO TOP OF AT LEAST 4 JOISTS WITH 2–16d NAILS

Special problems with old buildings

The slow but steady evolution of the building codes has led to a very gradual improvement in the earthquake resistant design of commercial and residential structures, particularly in California. This process was especially accelerated following the moderate but terribly destructive Long Beach earthquake in 1933. Up to that time, even some prominent geologists insisted that Los Angeles and the surrounding areas

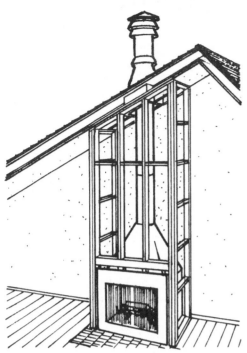

Existing chimneys which are either unreinforced or reinforced but inadequately tied to the building should be strengthened by one or all of the methods shown here. In this drawing, an unreinforced chimney is braced with horizontal steel straps which are bolted to the chimney-diaphragm ties shown in the other two drawings. It is advisable to have the help of an engineer in devising such a bracing system for an unreinforced chimney.

Because the heavy and inflexible masonry chimneys are always subject to earthquake damage, even with the most thorough reinforcement measures, anyone constructing a chimney and fireplace in earthquake country would be wise to take advantage of the new and very safe prefabricated sheet metal units. One such unit is shown here for a single-story house. The strength, light weight and flexibility of the metal eliminates all of the traditional deficiencies of masonry chimneys. The metal units are also less expensive and require less construction time.

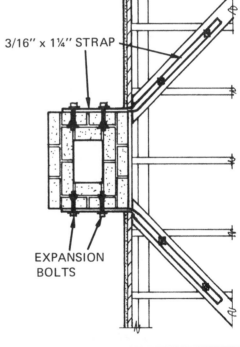

3/16" x 1¼" STRAP

EXPANSION BOLTS

were in no danger from earthquakes and the building codes throughout Southern California reflected that attitude.

San Francisco, which had less excuse, was even more neglected. Soon after the scars of the destructive 1906 earth-

Unreinforced chimneys, such as this stone structure on an older home in San Fernando, are, of course, almost certain to collapse or at least be severely damaged in any moderate earthquake. In this case, the falling chimney took much of the building with it.

quake were removed, the business community of the city and its surrounding areas adopted the attitude that the fire, not the earthquake, destroyed the city. Eastern financial interest and insurance companies were familiar with great urban fires, and if the memories of the earthquake could be erased by San Francisco's leaders, the much needed funds for the city's rebuilding could be more readily attracted. The disaster became known then, as the great San Francisco fire, and the local building codes regarding earthquake hazards were actually weakened in the years following the 1906 shock. Numerous large buildings built during the speculative 1920s were designed to dangerously substandard requirements, and these are the buildings which will probably cause the most spectacular failures during the next large shock. They will also account for a large proportion of the casualties.

Old buildings tend to suffer disproportionate earthquake damage either because the construction procedures or codes were inadequate at the time they were built or because age, poor maintenance and/or previous quake damage have weakened the structures. The large bungalow at left was one of several hundred wood-frame dwellings which were thrown off their foundations by the Long Beach tremor. The house is of the same vintage and design as many homes in the Berkeley Hills near the Hayward fault. The Victorian house in Santa Rosa, center, also had foundation problems. The other old house shown here—a service building at the Olive View Hospital complex in San Fernando—had no foundation, at least by modern standards. It was supported, like many old small town and rural buildings, on small concrete pedestals or blocks. Obviously, such support is totally inadequate in an area subject to earthquakes.

Old buildings, then, can be a very risky investment, and old masonry buildings present the additional problem of considerable danger to their occupants. Bad design or unsound engineering principles, poor construction techniques, heavy construction materials, faulty connections and poor or damaged foundations—all contribute to the costly damage typically sustained by old struccteres. In addition, lack of adequate maintenance over the years reduces the ability of many buildings to endure earthquake shocks. Rotted foundations or underpinnings, cracked mortar and plaster, and slightly settled or distorted foundations, among many other features of neglect, all undermine the earthquake resistance of these buildings. Finally, the cumulative damaging effects of previous tremors and the haphazard repairs of earthquake damage by previous owners weaken an old building and set the stage for even greater damage during a future, often smaller, quake. A check with the office of the city engineer may sometimes be sufficient to establish whether a building had been damaged in a previous earthquake. The office may also have a report on the ensuing major repairs, if any, made by previous owners.

The minor Santa Rosa earthquakes in 1969 provided some interesting data on the relationship between the age of a building and its susceptibility to damage during an earthquake. Of 38 wood-frame dwellings badly damaged in the tremor, 29 had been built before 1920 and nine pre-dated 1940. No wood-frame structures built after 1940 sustained considerable damage. The significance of this data should be obvious enough. The buyer of an old building should also consider that earthquake insurance rates for such buildings may be prohibitively expensive, if insurance can be obtained at all.

If you have your heart set on a home built before about 1935, then you should try and incorporate as many as possible of the earthquake-resistant details and remedies described in this book. Or if you prefer, have a civil/structural engineer examine the buildings first and then faithfully carry out his recommendations. If you do, your new old home can be guaranteed a longer, more useful, and less costly and hazardous life.

CHAPTER **8**

How to minimize interior, utility and other household damage

Some interior damage is inevitable in a strong earthquake. Dishes will fall and break, furniture will topple, pipe lines may be ruptured. Generally, this type of damage can only be anticipated; to try to prevent it entirely would be to turn your household into a museum (or a motel room) in which everything is securely locked away or attached to the walls and floor. However, by anticipating the effects of an earthquake, you can at least minimize such damage and, in some cases, select among the household items that you wish to protect above all others. This chapter covers a miscellany of objects, utility components and interior features which are most typically subject to earthquake damage and which can be protected to some extent by taking the measures recommended here.

Utilities

Obviously, the rupture of plumbing conduits during an earthquake can cause extensive interior water damage. The best and probably only way to remedy this risk is to know where the water control valves are located. Turn them off immediately after the earthquake and leave them off until you have made certain that there are no leaks. The gas mains should also be thoroughly checked immediately following a strong quake. Keep in mind that leaking gas lines can explode

Structural failures in a building, particularly in the foundation area, are very likely to damage utility pipes. This gas main under the deck or porch of a house in Santa Rosa was ruptured by the quake there in 1969, creating a serious fire hazard. Broken water lines are less hazardous but can be very damaging. All utility outlets and lines should be checked carefully immediately after a quake, and the valves should be closed if there is any suspicion of leakage.

into a fire hours after the shaking stops. If you discover a broken gas line or gas leakage, shut off the main feeder valve and do not turn it on again without the assistance of a utility serviceman.

If severe ground settlements or slides occurred in the vicinity of your property, the gas lines are very likely to be damaged. You will know there is such damage, of course, if the gas is not reaching your home. In this situation, the best course of action is (1) if possible, notify the utility company immediately; (2) prepare warning signs in the vicinity of the likely gas line breakage to keep other people away from the danger; (3) move yourself and your valuables a safe distance from the probable break.

Of all utility components, water heaters are most vulnerable to earthquake damage. Because they are quite heavy and usually stand on slender supports unconnected to the

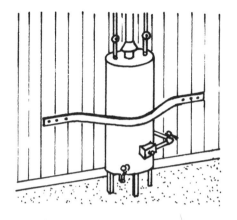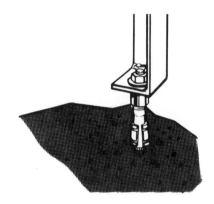

Of all utility components, water heaters are most susceptible to being knocked over by a quake. The heater is almost always ruined by a fall, but the real hazard is the likely rupture of the gas feeder line. All gas heating components, water heaters, furnaces and free-standing room heaters, should be anchored to the floor or to the studs of a solid wall.

floor, the heaters readily topple over. The glass lining of the heater is usually broken in the fall and some of the piping (including the gas line) tends to pull out. In order to avoid such unnecessary and sometimes hazardous damage, you should see that the water heater is bolted to the floor (many models provide bolt holes for this purpose). Water heaters that stand on a flat or solid support should be fastened with one metal strap, located at mid-height, to the wood studs of the nearest wall. The same rules apply to all other types of gas heating units and furnaces. They must always be bolted down or strapped to a solid wall in order to restrict any movement that could rupture the gas lines. Never rely on the piping to provide this support.

Some thought should also be given to the location and installation of air conditioners. For example, it is not advisable to place them in the vicinity of a masonry chimney, which may collapse during a quake. Placing an air conditioning unit on the roof is also undesirable, since they are subjected to higher earthquake motions there and will topple unless strong ties to the roof are added. The best location for an air conditioner is at ground level along the side of a building, where it is solidly connected to a low concrete mat foundation.

Plaster and wallboard

The heavy plaster finishes in old houses, and particularly solid plaster ceilings, can represent a considerable hazard to furnishings and occupants. Plaster ceilings, for example, may weigh as much as eight pounds per square foot, which means that the ceiling of a small 15 by 15 foot room would weigh a ton or more. On the other hand, good quality plaster, like stucco, is surprisingly strong and will crack only under very heavy shaking and large wall deformations. Moreover, plaster will seldom fall before other more serious structural damage has occurred in the walls or diaphragms of the building. Indeed, the combination of lath and thick plaster has a stiffening effect which can significantly increase the overall earthquake resistance of the walls.

The problem of falling or cracking plaster can best be avoided, then, by being certain that the plaster is in good condition (no deep or long cracks and no spots softened by water leakage). Further, if you own or will purchase an older house with plaster on inherently weak walls, such as a non-bearing partition wall, you should anticipate some plaster damage in an earthquake. Partition walls generally do not have sufficient framing and bracing to keep them from deforming badly during a quake, and the deformations of the wall inevitably break the plaster.

Wallboard and gypsum board covered with a ½-inch veneer of plaster has replaced solid plaster in almost all construction since World War II. These facings can also be highly earthquake resistant if the backing walls are well-balanced, particularly with plywood sheathing or with an exterior wood facing. When used without sheathing, however, wallboard is rather easily damaged. Fortunately, such damage is neither difficult nor expensive to repair.

When wallboard is nailed directly to the studs of a main load-bearing stucco-exterior wall, there is considerable risk of damage such as this in a San Fernando home. Without plywood sheathing, these walls are subject to deformations which crack and throw off the wallboard. Plaster is less likely to crack or fall, but risk is still rather high unless the walls are faced or lined with either plywood sheathing or a sturdy clapboard. Stucco-veneer buildings lacking shear-wall bracing or an exceptionally strong, welded wire lathing (as per the 1973 Uniform Building Code) face damage both to the stucco exterior and the wallboard or plaster interior.

In installing wallboard or sheetrock, be certain that each panel is thoroughly nailed to the studs or the plywood sheathing. The spacing for the nails should be no more than six inches. The plaster finish should be of good-quality and carefully mixed according to the specifications of the supplier. Use strips of metal lath diagonally across the corners of large openings and along the junctures of walls and the walls with the ceiling in order to strengthen the bond of the plaster.

Furnishings

A strong earthquake is bound to cause some damage to furnishings, particularly to the breakable items—china, glassware, picture frames, lamps and ceiling light fixtures, displayed art objects. Much of this damage can be prevented if you are willing to take some extra measures. For example, paintings and wall plaques should be attached to the wall with oversized, *closed* threaded hooks which can be screwed deep into the studs. A strong wire should then be strung through the hooks and securely attached to the frame or backing of the picture or plaque. The same procedure should be used in wiring hanging light fixtures.

Falling books and bookcases are another common problem in earthquakes, and such heavy objects can be a serious hazard to occupants. It is advisable to arrange bulky books and any other heavy objects on the lower shelves of a bookcase or cabinet. It is also wise with tall, free-standing bookcases or other such heavy furniture to attach it to the walls with steel angles or straps. A lightweight bar or dowel or a rim across the shelves is another solution for books or other objects displayed in high places. Few earthquakes shake hard enough to throw anything off a shelf, but the continued earthquake motions usually cause sliding or rocking which will eventually bring the materials down.

Just about the only way to guarantee the safety of dishes and glassware is to use the type of shelving found on ships. The next best solution is to have very strong latches on the cabinets containing the dishes; for most of the damage to china occurs when the cabinet doors fly open and the dishes fall to the floor. Valuable glass or plaster objects should always be kept in locked drawers or cabinets, preferably in a low-profile piece of furniture. Lower cabinets are far less likely to overturn during a large tremor. Valuable art objects on open display can be affixed with a strand of piano wire or some other fastening device to the supporting furniture. Stereo systems can be attached in the same way and should be kept on a low, stable piece of furniture. Thick carpeting can be helpful in reducing the movement of furniture across a room and in softening the blow when objects fall. Lamps and overhead light fixtures are common casualties of an earthquake, and in both cases a little discreet wiring or bolting can reduce the damage potential. Heavy chandeliers should be very carefully anchored with both wiring and bolting.

One more note: It would be extremely foolhardy in earthquake country to place your bed or those of your family anywhere near high heavy objects—a heavy chandelier or fixture, for example, or a bookcase or tall piece of heavy furniture, or a large mirror or mirrored ceiling. The first jolt of an

Some interior damage and vast disarray of objects and furnishings are inevitable in a large earthquake. This typical damage in a home in San Fernando can be minimized if you anticipate the effects of the quake and take measures to secure those belongings that are most breakable and valuable. Strong latches on cupboard doors; wire or angle anchors on tall, heavy furniture, stereo components, valuable lamps and art objects, and hanging light fixtures and pictures; dowels or rims on bookshelves—these and other common-sense measures can lessen the most heart-breaking kind of earthquake damage.

earthquake will most certainly awaken you, but it may also plunge that heavy object into your bed seconds before you are able to move to safety. It would also be wise to place the beds away from large glass walls or windows.

Swimming pools

Earthquake damage to swimming pools is usually related to any ground disturbances in the vicinity—slumping,

Hanging light fixtures are very likely to fall during an earthquake unless they have been bolted and, preferably, chained to the ceiling joists. Use only closed hooks in attaching the fixture with chains; open hooks are too likely to bend. A good test of any hanging fixture is simply to tug on it sharply. If it remains firmly attached to the ceiling, it is likely to stay there during an earthquake as well.

settlement, ruptures, etc. There is little you can do about this problem, of course, except to pick a sound geologic foundation for your homesite. However, pools can also *cause* damage to a house, and this is a problem that you can anticipate and avoid. For example, if a pool is situated on a steep hillside and the pool is not sufficiently supported by the ground on one side, it can freely slide to that side if the earthquake vibrations are of long duration. Pools sited on a hillside above the house should be sunk deeply into the ground on all sides.

Another possible hazard from swimming pools, especially on hillside sites, is the damage from escaping water. In the larger Southern California quakes, pools lost as much as 25 percent of their water from the sloshing caused by the earthquake motions. It is always best to locate a pool at an elevation lower than the house and as far away as possible from other homes downhill from your property.

Antennas

The worst location for a large and heavy antenna—a chimney or a fragile cornice of the roof—is the place where most antennas are attached. Instead, they should be well-braced either to the middle of the roof or, preferably, along the wall of the house.

Free-standing and retaining masonry walls

Masonry retaining walls and fences require some reinforcement and full grouting if they are to remain upright dur-

Concrete-block retaining and garden walls call for the same type of careful reinforcement that is required in constructing a concrete-block building. All of the garden walls in this block in San Fernando Valley were toppled by the earthquake. Note that the columns remained intact when they fell, because they had been grouted with concrete. Had they also been reinforced with a steel rod that extended into the base, they and the whole wall might have remained upright as well. The blocks between the columns had neither grouting nor reinforcement.

ing a quake. Because they are heavy, inflexible and segmented, and because they have either no support (freestanding garden walls), or support on only one side (retaining walls), the walls are almost certain to collapse without sufficient reinforcement and anchorage to a solid foundation. Collapse is not generally a hazard to life or property, of course, but the replacement of these walls is expensive, and the damage is easily avoided.

Reinforce all such masonry walls with ½-inch vertical steel bars every two or three feet. The bars should extend the

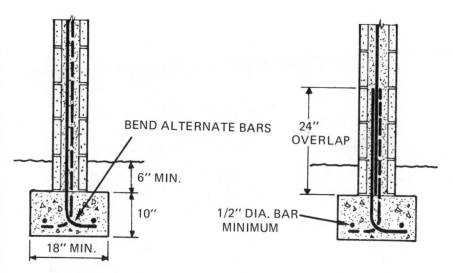

BEND ALTERNATE BARS

24" OVERLAP

6" MIN.

10"

18" MIN.

1/2" DIA. BAR MINIMUM

In reinforcing a concrete-block retaining or garden wall, the steel rods should be bent at the bottom end and these ends should then be embedded perpendicularly in a concrete-block or, preferably, poured-concrete base. The bend in every other rod should be placed in the opposite direction, so that the rods will pull against one another and remain anchored under the stress of the

earthquake's lateral motions. The concrete base should be set at least 16 inches into the ground and a few inches of dirt should cover it. If the wall is fairly tall and the use of the lengthy steel rods would be awkward, you can use a shorter rod (called a "dowel") as the anchor and overlap it by about 24 inches with another rod that will extend to the top of the wall.

full height of the wall and should be fully grouted with poured concrete or good-quality mortar. In addition, *all* of the other cavities of concrete blocks should be grouted. The foundation for these walls should be embedded several inches into the ground. With brick walls, some horizontal steel rein-forcement—about every two feet—is also required.

PART IV
The other remedies— earthquake insurance and common sense preparations

CHAPTER **9**

Earthquake insurance

Contrary to popular belief, earthquake insurance is now generally available at a reasonable cost throughout the West. The annual rate for a single-family wood-frame dwelling in the San Francisco or Los Angeles metropolitan areas presently varies from $1.50 to about $2.50 per $1,000 of coverage. Thus, the annual premium for $30,000 of insurance could be as low as $45—not an excessive amount considering the protection and peace of mind that the insurance will afford the homeowner (see the table). For higher risk buildings, of course, the rates will be considerably more expensive. For example, an unreinforced brick building in the same areas might be rated as high as $7.50 per $1,000 of coverage, or an annual premium of $225 on a $30,000 policy. All insurance companies also require a minimum deductible clause ranging from a standard sum of about $500 to a small percentage (generally 5 to 15 percent) of the building's value at the time of the loss. Most small residential buildings fall into the 5 percent category or require only the moderate standard deductible of $500. The policies including these low standard deductibles tend to include somewhat higher annual rates than the percentage-of-value deductibles.

Buildings located on other than firm, natural ground are sometimes penalized by a 25 percent increase in the rates. Landfill, waterfront properties, landslide-prone areas and other poor ground conditions are included in this category.

Class of risk	Building description	Cost per $1,000 coverage
I	Small wood-frame and frame stucco buildings (less than four stories)	$1.50
II	Steel-frame and reinforced poured-concrete buildings	$2.50
III	Reinforced concrete-frame (col-umned) buildings and other reinforced shear-wall masonry buildings	$3.00
IV	Wood-frame buildings with masonry veneers or other liabilities	$3.50
V	Steel-frame and reinforced concrete-frame buildings with segmented masonry walls (brick, concrete block, etc.)	$3.50
VI	Single-family dwellings (less than three stories) of reinforced masonry; other reinforced masonry buildings with liabilities	$4.00
VII	Unreinforced brick and larger reinforced masonry buildings without steel or concrete framing	$7.50
VIII	Unreinforced masonry, masonry-veneer, or adobe buildings	$25.00

However, insurance underwriters rarely inspect either the building or the geologic foundation of small dwellings (under four units), and any such buildings are generally classified automatically as sound structures on solid soil foundations unless the area has a past history of landslide or seismic damage. This lack of inspection or soil investigation by insurers is a distinct advantage to consumers with faulty buildings or building sites. However, anyone located in a well-known active fault zone will find it difficult to conceal that fact from the insurer.

Earthquake insurance rates are also based on the geographic location of the property. Each state is subdivided into zones for the purposes of the insurance, and areas which experience fewer earthquakes are generally granted rates between 20 and 60 percent lower than the figures quoted in the table. On the other hand, a zone classified as a high risk area may have even costlier rates than those shown in the table. For example, Imperial County in California carries the most unfavorable rate, about 50 percent higher than the figures given in the table. Overall, the different insurance zones are rather broad and arbitrarily chosen, so that pockets of expected high intensities in a low-risk zone are usually not penalized. This is another favorable feature of earthquake insurance policies.

Two types of earthquake insurance are available: (1) *straight earthquake insurance*, and (2) an *earthquake-damage assumption endorsement*. Straight earthquake insurance is usually written as a separate "disaster" policy covering only those extraordinary losses caused directly by earthquake (or flood, *tsunami*, dam breakage, volcano, etc.). Insurance companies are sometimes reluctant to provide this form of coverage in Alaska and California, and the rates for such a policy may be 30 to 40 percent higher than those for the second type of coverage, the assumption endorsement policy. This type of policy is merely an addendum to the standard fire policy on a building, in effect extending the fire policy to cover the peril of earthquakes. (The standard fire policy for a home also covers *fire* damage caused directly or indirectly by earthquake, while straight earthquake policies usually exclude fire loss.)

Naturally, the lower rates generally make the assumption endorsement type of policy advantageous. However, some homeowner fire policies may not accept earthquake addendums. In addition, the deductible clause may be lower on the straight earthquake policy. Thus, you should shop around for insurance coverage and should carefully weigh the various earthquake risks and the economic considerations affecting your property. A house or other building that is very subject to damage and is located in a high earthquake-intensity region might well be more advantageously covered with a straight policy that includes a low deductible clause.

In addition to this direct damage coverage on buildings, both types of policies also provide for miscellaneous coverages. Some of these coverages are personal property, additional living expenses, business-interruption insurance, rental value, lease-hold interest and other types of special insurance coverage generally available with standard fire policies as well. These additional coverages are often offered at reduced rates when purchased in conjunction with the building insurance.

Both types of earthquake policies usually carry the following stipulations:

- An earthquake is defined as any one, or any series of several shocks, which occur in a given 72-hour period. Earthquakes or aftershocks which occur in the following 72 hours are considered to be a separate earthquake for insurance purposes. Thus, the minimum deductibles which the policies carry may be deducted more than once for damaging shocks which occur at intervals greater than 72 hours.

- When the minimum deductible clauses are based on a percentage of the building's value, the deductible is determined from the *total market value* of the property (excluding the land) at the *time of loss*. Thus, a typical frame and stucco house with a present market value of $30,000 must sustain earthquake losses up to $1,500 (5 percent) before the insured can recover for any earthquake damage. It is important, then, that the coverage reflect the current value of the building and current labor costs for repairs or replacement. An undervalued property would result in a lower deductible but it might also be completely unrealistic in terms of the amount of money you would receive for replacing or repairing a badly damaged structure.

- Masonry veneer, such as brick, is not covered by earthquake insurance policies, unless the building is classified in a very high category, such as VIII, with the attendant premium rates. However, the value of the veneer is deducted from the market value of the building when computing the deductible amount.

- Window and door glass is generally not covered against earthquake damage. If such coverage is desired, it must be obtained in a plate-glass addendum to the standard fire policy or in a separate plate-glass policy. Some plate-glass insurance coverage is strongly recommended for houses with large areas of glass.

- Losses caused directly or indirectly by explosions, floods or *tsunamis* resulting from an earthquake are not always covered by the earthquake policies. Be certain that you understand the range of coverage and consider the various earthquake risks to your property. If you live near the ocean shore in a sea-level site in Alaska, for example, *tsunami* coverage is probably essential.

- Separate buildings on the same property must generally be insured separately for specific amounts, so that the deductible clause will apply individually to each building.

- Personal property, such as equipment, furnishings, clothing or the stock in a commercial building is not covered by the typical earthquake policy and must be insured in a separate addendum to which another deductible clause is applied. Again, the deductible ranges from a standard sum to 5 to 15 percent of the value, depending not only on the building but on the damageability of the personal property. For example, china and glass would take a higher deductible than the stock of a book store. For households, the usual deduction is 5 percent of the total value of the building's contents or of the specific contents being insured.

- Optional higher deductibles are allowable in some cases, at reduced insurance rates. Generally, for every percent of deductible in excess of the mandatory percentage, the rates are reduced by 2 percent for building classes I to VI, and 1 percent on classes VII and VIII. The maximum deductible permitted is 40 percent of value at the time of loss.

- Many policies carry an average clause, which is an agreement whereby the insured agrees to carry a certain percentage of the value of the property for his insurance coverage. In return the insurance company grants the most advantageous rate. The earthquake rate tables are based on 70 percent of value figures, and many companies therefore require a minimum coverage of 70 percent of the value of a building. If the required minimum is not purchased, losses are usually paid in proportion to the amount of coverage carried. For example, if a policy were written with an 80 percent average clause and only 40 percent of the value of the building is carried, then the insurance company will pay only half of the damage claims that are submitted.

- A few insurance companies have recently initiated special earthquake insurance plans which are set up on the basis of a *trust*. The trust may have a limit of $20 million, for example, and if this limit is exceeded in a large and destructive earthquake, then there is a *pro rata* distribution of the amount among those who have sustained losses. These policies are offered at considerably lower rates, sometimes at half the cost of the standard earthquake insurance. However, such policies are not generally recommended because earthquake damage is often followed by a multitude of litigations which may take many years. Meanwhile, the insureds under such a plan would have to wait for their share of the trust until all legal questions are settled. If such a plan is offered to you, you would do well to find out the specific regions covered by the trust. If the company has spread its risks throughout a very large area, such as the entire state of California, and if a single high-risk locality, such as the Los Angeles area, does not account for more than about 75 *percent* of the total amount of insurance covered by the trust, then a trust insurance plan may be acceptable. If the trust is concentrated in a high-risk area, however, where the damage and the claims would be extensive after a quake, the trust could be quickly depleted, and your share (after years of wrangling) might be far less than you have claimed and need.

The details of the coverage and of the rates should be discussed with your insurance agent or broker, and you must be very careful to consider all relevant factors and to understand the requirements of your policy. Insurance companies are not noted for their flexibility in interpreting the provisions of their contracts. If an agent is unwilling to discuss the subject, you should ask a knowledgeable person to help you interpret the policy or consider switching agents, brokers or companies. Many others will be interested in supplying and fully explaining the coverage.

The decision on whether to purchase insurance and how much coverage is necessary cannot be based on any blanket generalizations here. You should understand from this book that the geology of your site and the materials, design and structural features of your building are the important considerations. You have to thoughtfully weigh these factors, as well as the history of seismicity in your area and your own financial situation. Certainly, if the soil foundation and/or the condition of your building suggest considerable risk, you should carry a minimal earthquake insurance policy even if there has been little seismic activity in your area. On the other hand, if you are in an area of high earthquake activity and intensities but have a well-built and reinforced house on a solid bedrock foundation, you do not have to assume the worst and purchase a costly policy for the full replacement value of your property.

You must use common sense and wise budget planning, just as you would with any other insurance policy. The insurers are naturally interested in selling you as much insurance as you are willing to purchase. By all means, do not go overboard and pay hundreds of dollars a year for coverage that, if and when you collect, might amount to far less than you have paid over the years. In most situations, coverage of one-half or less of the value of the building should be sufficient, and if the insurers require greater coverage (often 70 percent), purchase only this minimal amount or shop around for a better deal. Keep the land value of your property in mind as well; for even the total destruction of your building will leave you with a building site that is worth some thousands of dollars.

CHAPTER **10**

How to behave before, during and after a quake to protect your family, yourself and your property.

Before an earthquake

The most important measures in preparation for an earthquake are these two: (1) Make your building and its contents as stable and earthquake-resistant and well-insured as possible, using common sense and the text of this book as your guide. (2) Think about and discuss with your family, neighbors and co-workers the likelihood and the effects of the next big earthquake, and consider what you and the others would and should do in your home, at work, in your car or in any other place when the tremor strikes. Conscious and sub-conscious pre-planning will enable you to react calmly and effectively during the emergency. In addition, you should make the following preparations:

- Set aside a flashlight, a battery-powered radio, extra batteries, a first-aid kit and a few days' supply of canned food and plastic-bottled water.
- Have some knowledge of first-aid procedures. Medi-cal facilities are always overloaded during a disaster.
- All responsible family members should know what to do to avoid injury and panic. They should know the location of the main gas and water valves and the

electrical switch, and they should understand the safety measures to be taken in protecting themselves, small children and the building.

- Support all legislation and government-agency planning that will strengthen buildings, eliminate hazards and prepare emergency and public-safety organizations for fast and effective action.

During an earthquake

The most important thing to do during an earthquake is to remain calm. If you can do so, you are less likely to be injured and those around you will also benefit from your coolness. Think about the possible consequences before making any moves or taking any actions. Keep in mind that earthquake motions are not constant. There are usually a few seconds between tremors during which you can move to a safer position.

If you are inside a building, stand in a corner or in a strong, preferably interior doorway, or get under a sturdy desk or table. Watch for falling plaster, bricks, light fixtures and tall, heavy furniture. Stay away from windows, large mirrors and masonry chimneys and fireplaces. In tall office buildings, it is best to get away from windows or glass partitions and watch out for falling ceiling debris. In factories, stay clear of heavy machinery that may topple or slide across the floor. The corners or a strong doorway in such buildings are usually safest.

Do not rush outside if you are in a store, office building, auditorium or factory. Stairways and exits may be broken or littered with debris and are likely to become jammed with panicky people. The power for elevators and escalators often fails. In addition, many deaths and injuries in an earthquake result from falling debris around the exteriors of commercial and public buildings. It is therefore better simply to wait until the jolts of the earthquake have diminished before exiting the buildings. Then, choose your exit with care, and as you leave, move calmly but quickly and watch for falling debris and collapsing walls.

If you are in other than a masonry house, you can safely

leave the building during the quake, but be wary of collapsing chimneys or porch canopies and watch for fallen electrical wiring. Once you are outside, or if you are outside when the quake strikes, stay well away from high buildings and from masonry walls. Watch for falling power poles, lamp posts and power lines. Remain in an open area until the ground motions have ceased, and do not re-enter your house until you are certain that the quake is over and the walls are stable. If there is obvious and serious damage to the house, you should stay out of it or enter it very carefully and only long enough to turn off the utility valves. An aftershock or the damage itself might cause further collapse of the roof or walls.

If you are in an automobile during the earthquake, stop in an open area away from tall buildings and remain in the car until the quake is over.

After an earthquake

After the quake, the first thing to do is to check for injuries among the people around you. Seriously injured persons should not be moved unless they are in immediate danger of further injury. First aid should be administered. Your next concern should be the danger of fire. Check the gas lines, and if there is any likelihood of leakage, turn off the main gas valve, which is usually near the meter. If there is a possibility of damage to the gas lines outside of your building, put up warning signs, notify your neighbors and the emergency authorities and stay well clear of the fire and explosion hazard until it has been checked by a serviceman. Do not use electrical appliances if there is a possibility of gas leakage, because the sparks could ignite the gas.

Check the water and electrical lines next, and turn off the main valve or switch if there has been damage. Be especially careful of any damage to the wiring. Also, since there is likely to be much shattered glass and other debris after a quake, put on heavy shoes or boots before you begin to inspect the damage. There is always a danger of falling debris long after the quake, so be cautious in moving about or near a building. Particular attention should be given to the roof line and chimney.

Do not use the telephone unless you have a genuine emergency. The lines are always overloaded during a disaster, and your unnecessary call could be responsible for blocking an emergency call by someone else. Do not go sightseeing; the streets must be kept open for emergency vehicles. Use the radio to obtain information and damage reports.

Stay away from beaches and other low-lying waterfront areas where *tsunamis* could strike after the quake. Your radio will broadcast any alerts regarding the danger of sea waves. Also stay away from steep, landslide-prone areas, since an aftershock may trigger a slide or avalanche.

Small children often suffer psychological trauma during a quake and should be comforted and attended at all times. An aftershock may panic them if the parents are absent. Pets also suffer trauma during an earthquake, and packs of crazed dogs are a common hazard following a quake. Comfort your dog and keep it on a leash or indoors for several days after the quake.

If the water is off, emergency drinking and cooking water can be obtained from water heaters (be careful of broken glass particles) and from toilet tanks, melted ice cubes and canned vegetables. Do not flush your toilet until you are certain that you will not need the water stored in the tank (you should also be certain that the sewer lines are intact before flushing). If the electricity is off, use the fresh and frozen foods first before they spoil. Save canned and dried food for last. Use outdoor barbecues or fireplaces for cooking. With the latter, however, be certain that the chimney is undamaged. Check especially at the roof level and in the attic, for unnoticed damage could result in a fire if you use the fireplace.

Finally, be prepared for strong aftershocks and do not remain in or near a building that might be further damaged by these milder shocks. Masonry buildings are especially susceptible to aftershock damage, and it is a good general rule simply to stay away from such buildings until they have been declared safe by an expert.

APPENDIX A

The significant faults and earth-quakes of the western states

Major portions of Alaska, California, Montana, Nevada and Utah and smaller sections of Washington and Oregon are interlaced with hundreds of faults, many of them known to be active and highly subject to an earthquake. Some of the most heavily faulted areas contain the largest urban settlements in the West, including Los Angeles, San Francisco, Oakland, Salt Lake City and Portland. Other large cities, such as Seattle and Anchorage, are near major fault zones and have experienced damaging earthquakes in the past.

This appendix contains brief descriptions of the larger and more important faults in the West and includes brief accounts of some of the most damaging earthquakes recorded along these fault zones. The descriptions here are not intended to be used as the sole aid in locating your property with regard to the nearest fault zone. This is no more than a general summary of existing information on the location and activity of major faults. Small but active faults and branches of the major fault zones may not be included. Therefore, the detailed maps and records listed in Appendix B will be needed to accurately pinpoint a specific site.

Alaska

The earthquake history of sparsely settled Alaska is necessarily very spotty, although there are partial records dating back to the late 1700s. One fact, however, is certain. Of all 50 states, including California, Alaska has experienced by far the largest number of *great* earthquakes. In the past 75 years, for example, eight shocks have exceeded magnitudes of 8, the largest (8.6) near Yakutat in 1899, the next largest (8.5 and 8.4) in the Aleutians in 1957 and in Prince William Sound in 1964. By comparison, during the same time span, California has experienced only one earthquake with a magnitude greater than 8—the famous quake of 1906.

Many of Alaska's large earthquakes have been concentrated along the chain of Aleutian Islands, which also includes a number of active volcanoes. In fact, the entire Pacific coast of Alaska and the Aleutian archipelago lie along a particularly active section of the Circum-Pacific Seismic Belt. There are several fault systems in the state, some of them larger and more dramatic and certainly no less active and potentially destructive than California's San Andreas fault system.

It would be futile to describe all of these known faults and all of the important earthquakes which have shaken Alaska, for the state is very lightly populated and, generally, the hazards to life and property are few. Also, very fortunately, no known faults bisect the larger towns and settlements of the state. However, all of these populated areas are

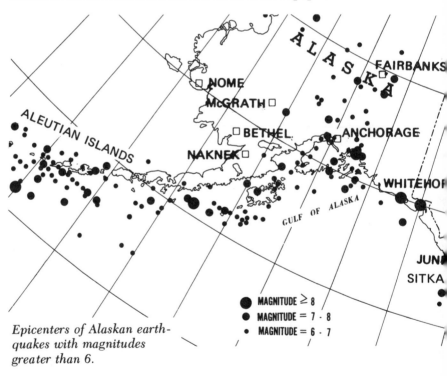

Epicenters of Alaskan earthquakes with magnitudes
greater than 6.

located in the vicinity of major faults, and the huge 1964 tremor vividly demonstrated the destruction that can occur on the periphery of a large fault zone.

It is reasonable to assume that every building constructed in the more populated sections of the state, and particularly along the southern coastal areas, will experience a strong earthquake in its lifetime. The two largest cities of Alaska—Anchorage and Fairbanks—and the capital, Juneau, are located in particularly high seismic areas, and Fairbanks has an especially long earthquake history. In regard to the latter city, three tremors stand out: On July 22, 1937, Fairbanks suffered severe shaking and considerable minor damage from an earthquake of magnitude 7.3 centered about 25 miles away, near Salcha Bluff. Another magnitude 7 earthquake, accompanied by numerous foreshocks and aftershocks, shook the city on October 15, 1947. On June 21, 1967, Fairbanks experienced a series of three earthquakes, all with magnitudes less than 6. These caused only minor property damage in the area.

The great Prince William Sound (Anchorage) earthquake of March 28, 1964, was the cause of immense property damage and a number of deaths in Anchorage and along the southern coast of Alaska. The total amount of damage probably exceeded $800 million. The Good Friday quake is one of the best documented ever. Appendix B contains numerous references which describe the damage to most of the Alaskan settlements and towns in minute, exacting detail. Detailed maps, which accompany most of the references, point out the more severely affected locations, the numerous landslides triggered by the earthquake, and the extent and location of the inundation and property damage caused by the *tsunamis* that struck along the coast. It is strongly recommended that the residents of western Alaska conduct a brief search of this easily available literature before the purchase or development of any property.

California

California has the dubious distinction of having more earthquakes than all other states combined, with the exception of Alaska. The state is covered with faults, many of which are known to be active, and it is interesting to note that the largest cities in the state were founded in the immediate vicinity of the largest and most active of the fault zones. The table here lists the prominent earthquakes which have disturbed the state since the first recorded shock of July 28, 1769, and most of these quakes are also discussed briefly in this text. Voluminous

Prominent earthquakes in California, 1769 through 1973
(Intensity VII and above)

Date	Region	Richter Magnitude	Modified Mercalli Intensity
July 28, 1769	Los Angeles region		
December 8, 1812	Southern California		VIII-IX
December 21, 1812	Off coast of southern California		X
June 10, 1836	San Francisco Bay		IX-X
June 1838	San Francisco region		X
July 10 or 11, 1855	Los Angeles County		VIII
January 9, 1857	Near Fort Tejon	Possibly 8	X-XI
November 26, 1858	San Jose		VIII
November 12, 1860	Humboldt Bay		VIII
July 3, 1861	Near Livermore		VIII
October 1, 1865	Fort Humboldt-Eureka area		VIII-IX
October 8, 1865	Santa Cruz Mountains		VIII-IX
October 21, 1868	Hayward		IX-X
March 26, 1872	Near Lone Pine	Possibly 8	X-XI
April 19, 1892	Vacaville		IX
April 21, 1892	Winters		IX
April 4, 1893	Northwest of Los Angeles		VIII-IX
June 20, 1897	Near Hollister		VIII
April 14, 1898	Mendocino area		VIII-IX
July 22, 1899	San Bernardino County		VIII
December 25, 1899	San Jacinto-Hemet area		IX
July 27 & 31, 1902	Santa Barbara County		VIII
April 18, 1906	San Francisco region	8.25	XI
April 18, 1906	Brawley, Imperial Valley	6 to 6.9	VIII
October 28, 1909	Humboldt County	6+	VIII
January 11, 1915	Los Alamos		VIII
June 22, 1915	El Centro-Calexico-Mexicali area	6.25	VIII
April 21, 1918	San Jacinto-Hemet area	6.8	IX
June 21, 1920	Inglewood		VIII
March 10, 1922	Cholame Valley	6.5	IX
June 29, 1925	Santa Barbara area	6.3	VIII-IX
October 22, 1926	Monterey Bay	6 to 6.9	VIII
August 20, 1927	Humboldt Bay		VIII
November 4, 1927	West of Point Arguello	7.5	IX-X
February 25, 1930	Westmorland	5.0	VIII
March 1, 1930	Brawley	4.5	VIII
June 6, 1932	Humboldt County	6.4	VIII
March 10, 1933	Near Long Beach	6.3	IX
June 7, 1934	Parkfield	6.0	VIII
May 18, 1940	Imperial Valley	7.1	X
June 30, 1941	Santa Barbara-Carpinteria area	5.9	VIII
March 15, 1946	North of Walker Pass	6.25	VIII
July 29, 1950	Imperial Valley	5.5	VIII
July 21, 1952	Kern County	7.7	XI
August 22, 1952	Bakersfield	5.8	VIII
April 25, 1954	East of Watsonville	5.25	VIII
December 21, 1954	Eureka	6.6	VII
April 8, 1968	Northeast San Diego County	6.5	VII
October 1, 1969	Santa Rosa	5.7	VII-VIII
February 9, 1971	San Fernando	6.6	VIII-XI

amounts of information exist on many of these earthquakes and faults. For the best and most authoritative references, see the listings in Appendix B.

San Andreas fault

The San Andreas fault is certainly the best known fault in the United States and very probably in the world. It is also the most intensively studied. Surface faulting in the United States was first discovered along the fault following the 1906 San Francisco earthquake, and, therefore, the San Andreas was the first fault to draw the attention of American geologists. The general fault zone and the most recent traces of the fault have been mapped in great detail by several agencies, including the U.S. Geological Survey and the California Division of Mines and Geology. The geologists had a considerable task, for the San Andreas runs almost the entire 1,000-mile length of California and then continues through Mexico into the Gulf of California. Thus, the fault and its fault zone constitute one of the primary geographic and geologic features of the narrow state.

Due to its length and complexity, the fault is described here mainly in those sections that cross the larger populated areas. If you are interested in other sections of the fault, you should refer to Appendix B and its list of numerous books and technical publications specifically on the San Andreas. In addition, there are superlative up-to-date maps of the fault, and you will also find a listing of them in Appendix B.

Northern San Andreas fault: Eureka and Cape Mendocino to Bodega Head

For the purposes of this book, the northern section of the San Andreas fault zone is limited to the area from Cape Mendocino, just south of Eureka and Humboldt Bay, south to Bodega Head, which is approximately 50 miles up the coast from San Francisco. The entire length of this northern section of the San Andreas fault broke during the 1906 earthquake, including, it is believed, all of the submarine sections. This extensive surface faulting in 1906 would indicate that the entire coastal area of this section of California will be affected by extremely high vibrational intensities during future large earthquakes along this fault. It would be risky, therefore, to build, buy or remain in any but the most well-constructed structures. In particular, the inroads of the fault across coastal lands and the long narrow valleys further inland that parallel the route of the fault are most hazardous. Some of the most severe damage from the 1906 shock was experienced in Fort Bragg, Healdsburg, Petaluma and other towns located in these parallel alluvial valleys.

Because of the merger of the San Andreas fault into the Mendocino fracture zone west of Cape Mendocino, the coastal area between Mendocino and Eureka is especially active. Prior to 1906, the Eureka area experienced at least three destructive earthquakes—in 1860, 1865 and 1898—and the 1865 shock was severe enough to damage every building in the Eureka and Fort Humboldt area. There were two other moderate tremors in 1909 and 1927, and a much larger quake on June 6, 1932. The 1927 shock was located about 30 miles off the coast, a little northwest from Eureka, and caused limited damage in both Eureka and Ferndale. The Eureka earthquake of 1932 left very few brick chimneys standing in Eureka, which was most severely hit, and triggered numerous landslides around Humboldt Bay. The magnitude 6.4 shock was also felt as far south as San Jose and north to Coos Bay, Oregon. The most recent large earthquake to strike the Eureka area (December 21, 1954) had a magnitude of about 7 and caused extensive damage throughout Eureka and around all of Humboldt Bay.

The immediate Eureka area is also affected by a lesser fault, called the Fresh Water fault. The section of this fault nearest to Eureka proceeds in a straight line between Freshwater and Indianola, where it enters Arcata Bay. This fault seems to present only a minor threat of surface ruptures to the area, but all buildings within the vicinity of the fault should be designed to withstand the high vibrational intensities of inevitable future earthquakes.

San Francisco Bay section, San Andreas fault: Bodega Head to San Juan Bautista (see also the Hayward and Calaveras faults)

The San Francisco Bay section of the San Andreas fault extends from Bodega Head, about 50 miles north of San Francisco, to San Juan Bautista and Hollister, some 80 miles south of San Francisco. The fault alternates between the sea and the land until it re-enters land at Mussel Rock, just south of San Francisco, for its long course through California to the Sea of Cortez in Mexico. While at sea, the fault zone is never more than about three miles from the coast.

Beyond San Francisco, the fault slices through heavily urbanized Daly City and San Bruno, borders the airport and the densely settled sections of San Mateo, Belmont, San Carlos and Redwood City, then crosses exurbia—Woodside, Portola Valley and Los Trancos

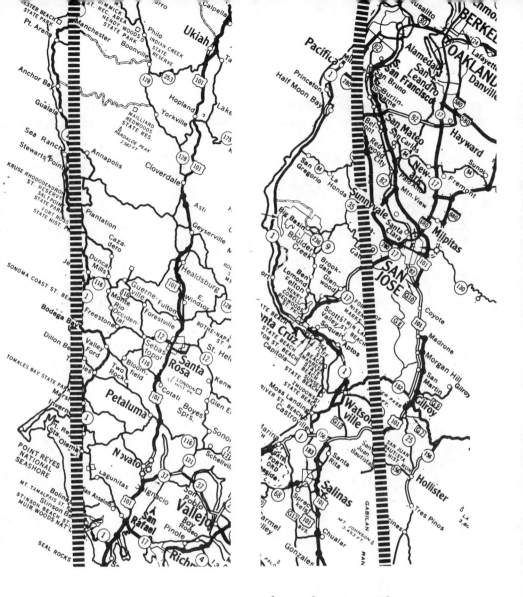

The northern San Andreas fault, from Point Arena to San Juan Bautista and Hollister.

Woods—and continues into the sparsely settled Santa Cruz Mountains. Thus, the San Andreas fault parallels the entire San Francisco Bay Area, including the populous and rapidly growing Santa Clara Valley and San Jose. From Saratoga the fault can be traced as a nearly straight line south to San Juan Bautista, and along the way, it comes to within ten miles of Santa Cruz and three miles of Watsonville. A little

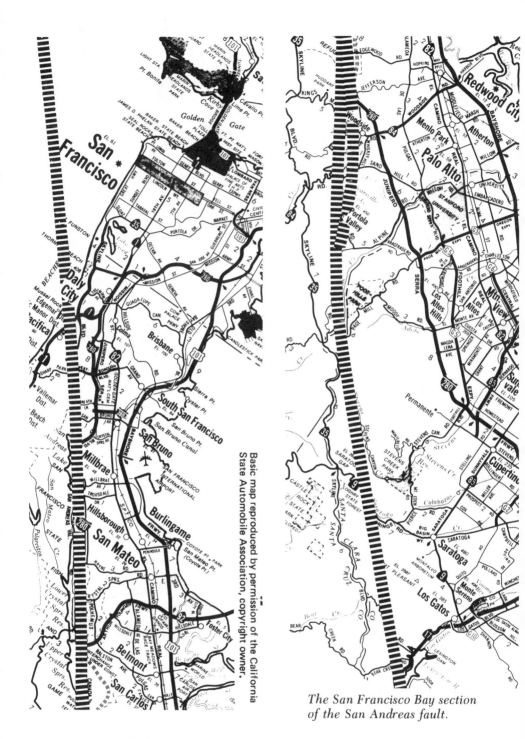

The San Francisco Bay section
of the San Andreas fault.

further south, the Salinas area is exposed to high earthquake risks from the fault because of the alluvial subsoil of the city.

A number of active subsidiary faults—among them the Pilarcitos, Seal Cove and San Gregorio faults—parallel the San Andreas through the San Francisco Bay Area, particularly along the San Francisco Peninsula. For their precise locations, the reader is referred to the maps in Appendix B. These minor faults are probably less risky than the San Andreas itself, but you would be well-advised not to locate a building directly over or within a few hundred feet of any of these faults. In the event of the next major San Andreas quake, these subsidiary faults are likely to bring heavy vibrational damage and may even break out into surface ruptures.

Numerous damaging earthquakes have occurred in the San Francisco Bay Area along the San Andreas fault. The earliest known record is of a series of earthquakes in the vicinity of San Juan Bautista during October of 1800. Friars at the mission reported themselves so terrified by the numerous strong shocks, sometimes as many as six in a day, that they spent the nights out-of-doors in the mission carts. The thick adobe walls of all the buildings at the mission were damaged. Another strong earthquake with an estimated magnitude of 7+, occurred on the Peninsula in June and July of 1838. Contemporary accounts of the quake describe a long fissure reaching from San Francisco to a point near Santa Clara. The ground motion was severe in the harbor of San Francisco and in San Jose and Santa Clara, and damage was reported in Redwood City and as far away as Monterey.

A series of smaller earthquakes between 1850 and 1865 damaged, often extensively, different sections of the Bay Area, including San Jose, Santa Clara, Santa Cruz, Santa Rosa and San Francisco. The shock of October 8, 1965, which apparently was centered in the Santa Cruz mountains, was the most damaging of this period.

The San Francisco earthquake of April 18, 1906, was not only the next big shock along the San Andreas but also one of the world's most famous and significant earthquakes. It was the shock that gave birth to the sciences of seismology and earthquake engineering; it was the first earthquake in the United States to be carefully studied and to have the large amounts of surface faulting recorded; it was also the first truly great earthquake to strike a major American metropolitan area. San Francisco alone suffered damage estimated variously between $350 million and $1 billion (1906 dollars), and several towns along the fault, notably Santa Rosa and San Jose, suffered proportionately greater damage. Total fatalities in San Francisco were between 500 and 1,000, and there were an additional 300 fatalities in other areas.

The earthquake had a magnitude of about 8.25 generating high vibrational intensities that caused great damage all along coastal Northern California and far into Central and Southern California. The shock was felt in all of the surrounding states, over a land area of about 375,000 square miles. The 270 miles of surface and submarine faulting stretched along the coast from Point Delgada and Fort Bragg to Hollister. Horizontal displacements of 20 feet occurred at Olema. The earthquake was followed by thousands of aftershocks.

Two other notable San Andreas earthquakes caused limited damage to several communities south of San Francisco. The July 1, 1911, earthquake was centered near Coyote in Santa Clara County and damaged San Jose, Gilroy and Morgan Hill. The October 2, 1934, earthquake was centered on the fault near Colma and caused considerable damage in that city and in Daly City, South San Francisco and the Portola district of San Francisco. Generally, however, the San Francisco Bay section of the San Andreas fault has been quiet since the disastrous shock of 1906. The most damaging recent earthquake occurred on March 22, 1957, when a minor, magnitude 5.3 shock was centered in Daly City, just off Mussel Rock.

Central San Andreas fault: San Juan Bautista to Tejon Pass (see also the Santa Ynez fault and the White Wolf fault)

The central section of the San Andreas fault is nearly linear as it stretches between San Juan Bautista and Tejon Pass, north of San Fernando Valley. The fault is always clearly visible through this section because of the similarly linear hills which bound it on both sides. The narrow valley fault zone passes near Parkfield, goes through Cholame, parallels Taft, and is intersected by the traces of the Garlock-Big Pine fault at Fraser Park near Tejon Pass. The section of the fault north of Cholame is not known to have experienced any major faulting or earthquakes during recorded history. However, the area has experienced numerous small earthquakes, and certain sections show signs of slow, creeping fault displacements. In addition, several recent shocks have caused minor surface faulting near Parkfield and Cholame.

The San Luis Obispo earthquake of April 11, 1885, is sometimes attributed to the central section of the San Andreas, but the shock may have occurred on the Nacimento fault, which parallels the San Andreas nearer to San Luis Obispo. Property damage was concentrated near San Luis Obispo, although Visalia and Monterey were also shaken

The central San Andreas fault, from San Juan Bautista and Hollister to Tejon Pass.

substantially. Several other minor shocks, all with magnitudes between 5.5 and 6.5, have damaged some buildings and caused limited faulting along this section of the fault. These include the Stone Canyon earthquake of March 2, 1901, centered northwest of Parkfield, the Cholame Valley earthquake of March 10, 1922, the mildly damaging earthquake at Parkfield on June 7, 1934, the Hollister shock of April 8, 1961, and a second Parkfield earthquake on June 27, 1966.

None of these earthquakes, excluding that of 1885, was seriously damaging. However, the lack of significant damage is directly attributable to the low population density of the area and not to a "characteristic" mildness of the shocks. A severe earthquake along this whole central section of the San Andreas fault could easily occur at any time, and the seismic risk is nearly equal to that along any other section of the San Andreas.

Los Angeles section, San Andreas fault: Tejon Pass to San Bernardino (see also the Sierra Madre fault zone)

Between Tejon Pass and the San Bernardino area, the San Andreas fault experienced very large scale displacements during the great Fort Tejon earthquake of 1857. The 1857 quake was the strongest of

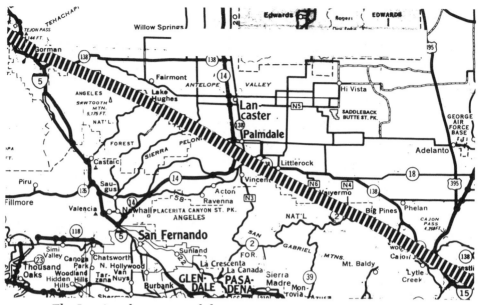

*The Los Angeles section of the
San Andreas fault, from Tejon
Pass to San Bernardino.*

Southern California's history, and with an estimated magnitude of about 8, it is generally ranked third, behind the Owens Valley shock of 1872 and the San Francisco earthquake of 1906, in the history of the state. Another major earthquake along this portion of the fault poses a very great earthquake hazard to the Los Angeles area and much of Southern California.

The epicenter of the 1857 earthquake was in the vicinity of Fort Tejon, on the Tejon Pass through the Tehachapi Mountains. Surface faulting is estimated to have been about 225 miles, from the vicinity of Cholame to San Gorgonio Pass, north of Palm Springs. Some of the displacements along the length of the fault may have been as large as 30 feet. Most of Southern California was violently shaken by the quake, but the damage was slight, of course, because of the sparse population at the time. However, all of the towns along this fault segment reported severe vibrational intensities, and these towns would now include Los Angeles, the San Fernando Valley, San Bernardino, Riverside, Lancaster, Bakersfield and Fresno, as well as the numerous smaller cities of the southern San Joaquin Valley and the Southern California desert. By virtue of their peculiar geologic foundations and their location near the fault, the cities of Lancaster, Quartz Hill and Palmdale must expect especially heavy shaking during a major shock along this section of the San Andreas.

The Los Angeles section of the San Andreas fault has experienced numerous earthquakes in addition to the severe Fort Tejon tremor. Among them, the earthquake of July 22, 1899, which was centered near Cajon Pass, stands out because of its high magnitude. The maximum intensities for that shock ranged from VII (damaging) to IX (destructive) in the area of the fault in the San Bernardino Mountains, an area which today continues to be developed at a rapid pace. During this Cajon Pass tremor, the road in Lytel Creek Canyon was blocked by debris slides in many places, while the Cajon Pass road was filled with debris for a distance of half a mile. San Bernardino, Highland and Patton were damaged extensively, and some damage was also reported in Riverside, Redlands, Pomona, Pasadena and Los Angeles.

The southern end of this section of the San Andreas bypasses Cajon and enters San Bernardino near West Highland, where it splits into two branches, the North Branch and the main South Branch. The North Branch later merges into the Mission Creek fault; the South Branch follows the foothills of the San Bernardino Mountains. A number of shorter, subsidiary faults of unknown activity follow the main trace of the fault through Del Rosa, Highland, Harlem Springs and East Highland.

As a whole, this segment of the San Andreas fault presents very high earthquake and landslide risks, and the purchase or development of property in the fault zone itself would be unwise. Any property adjacent to the fault zone by several miles should be thoroughly investigated for its geologic foundation, and structures should be carefully planned or renewed for a violent shock.

Southern San Andreas fault (the Banning fault): San Bernardino to El Centro (see also the San Jacinto and the Imperial faults)

South of San Bernardino, both branches of the San Andreas fault break up into a multiplicity of parallel, merging and diverging faults which encompass much of the south-central area of California. The Mill Creek fault is the southern extension of the North Branch of the San Andreas fault below San Bernardino. This fault passes through Fallsvale, merges into the Mission Creek fault, crosses San Gorgonio Pass, passes through Desert Hot Springs, and then continues south until it meets the Banning fault in the Myoma area. The South Branch of the San Andreas parallels the North Branch, finally merging with it into what is called the Banning fault. The two branches of the San Andreas continue as the Banning fault, bypass Palm Springs, and then

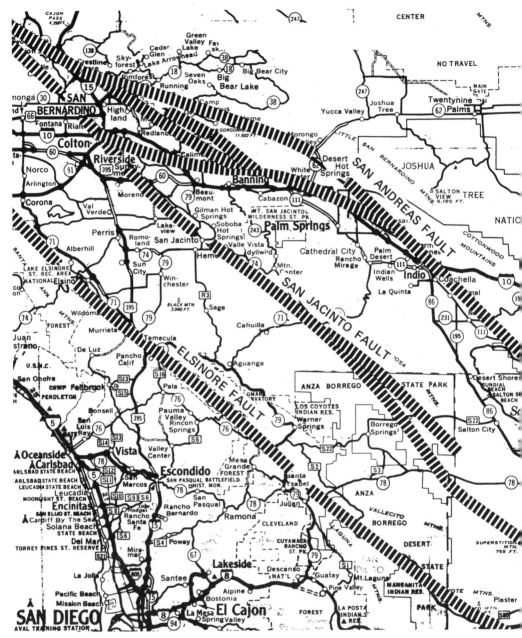

*The southern San Andreas
fault and the San Jacinto and
Elsinore fault zones.*

merge into the Banning Mission Creek fault, which, with several smaller subsidiaries, passes the Salton Sea along its eastern shores and continues along the eastern boundary of the Imperial Valley and into Mexico.

Numerous earthquakes have been recorded along this southern section of the San Andreas fault zone, but the Desert Hot Springs earthquake of December 4, 1948, is the only damaging earthquake to have occurred in the area in the recent past. This quake had a magnitude of about 6.5 (similar to the San Fernando earthquake of 1971) and the maximum intensities were felt in the Desert Hot Springs-Mecca area. The area was very sparcely populated then, and the light damage was mainly concentrated in the towns of Twentynine Palms and Indio. A similar or larger earthquake today would cause significant damage to the populous and largely masonry buildings of the greater Palm Springs area.

Hayward fault (see also the Calaveras fault)

The Hayward fault along the eastern side of San Francisco Bay, is one of the major active branches of the San Andreas fault system. Because the Hayward fault is very active and stretches through one of the most densely populated areas of California, it has been studied and mapped in considerable detail, and much material on the fault is available to the public.

The known southern end of the Hayward fault is between Warm Springs and Milpitas, along the Alameda-Santa Clara County lines. Further south, the fault merges into the Calaveras fault zone, another major branch of the San Andreas system. The Hayward fault passes through virtually every city on the eastern shores of San Francisco Bay before it enters the bay at Point Pinole near San Pablo. It emerges from the bay in Sonoma County and continues toward Petaluma along the Petaluma Valley. The fault then appears to merge into two lesser fractures, the Rodgers Creek and Healdsburg faults, which continue north past Santa Rosa to Healdsburg.

The Hayward fault has been the cause of several destructive earthquakes including the Hayward earthquake of 1836, which was one of the largest ever to occur in Northern California. According to a recent study of that quake, fissures opened along the fault from San Pablo to Mission San Jose, and the tremors caused havoc in the settlements in Monterey and Santa Clara. In another great quake in 1868, the fault ruptured for about 20 miles, from Warm Springs to the vicinity of Mills College in Oakland. Horizontal displacements along the trace were up to three feet, and every building in the village of Hayward was either severely damaged or completely demolished. Numerous structures in San Francisco, particularly in the filled areas of the bay, were also destroyed or damaged, and San Leandro, Oakland, San Jose and other nearby towns suffered varying degrees of damage.

Another earthquake on October 7, 1915, was centered in the vicinity of Piedmont, where most of the damage occurred, but the shock was felt as far as Sebastopol and Santa Clara. A generation later (May 16, 1933), the fault erupted again, reaching intensities of VIII in the vicinity of Niles and Irvington, where all chimneys were thrown down and numerous dwellings were damaged. The most recent damaging earthquake along the Hayward fault occurred on March 8, 1937, in the Berkeley-Albany-El Cerrito area.

The Hayward fault presents one of the greatest earthquake hazards in California. It stretches through a densely populated area which has been built up in the past 25 years with a minimum of regard for the dangers from the fault. It is imperative that any property owner or prospective owner in this area carefully examine his or her property according to the standards outlined in this book.

Calaveras fault zone and the Concord, Pleasanton, Green Valley and Antioch fault branches

The Calaveras fault is another major and active branch of the San Andreas fault system. It splits off from the San Andreas a few miles south of Hollister and runs in an almost straight line through Morgan Hill and the Calaveras Reservoir, south of Fremont, where it intersects the Hayward fault and continues north-northwest past Sunol and along Interstate 680 through Dublin, San Ramon, Danville, Alamo and the Lafayette-Walnut Creek area. From here, one branch of the fault passes through Vallejo and into Solano County, the other branch passes Pleasant Hill, crosses Martinez and the Carquinez Straits, and disappears in the eastern outskirts of Vallejo. Particularly in the northern section, in the vicinity of Martinez and Vallejo, the Calaveras is most appropriately called a fault zone; for it consists of a series of several smaller faults. The Calaveras fault is at its most active in the city of Hollister, where regular

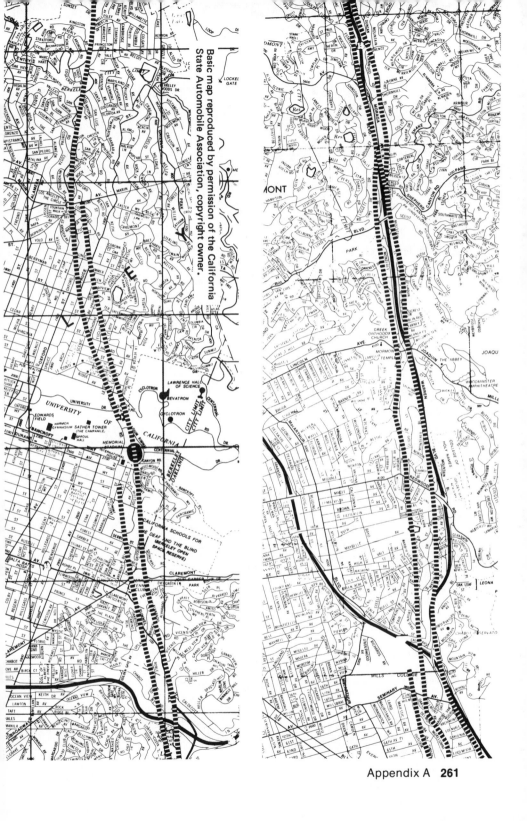

Basic map reproduced by permission of the California State Automobile Association, copyright owner.

creep has been measured for the past two decades.

A number of earthquakes have occurred along the Calaveras, but none has approximated the magnitudes and intensities of earthquakes along the nearby parallel Hayward fault. The strongest recorded tremor on the fault occurred on July 3, 1861, and is known as the Amador Valley earthquake. The epicenter of the shock is believed to have been in the Livermore Valley near Dublin, where about five miles of surface faulting was reported. Damage from this quake was reported throughout the Amador, Livermore and San Ramon Valleys.

Two other damaging earthquakes have been recorded in the northern section of the fault: The Mare Island earthquake of March 30, 1898, had a magnitude of about 6 and was very damaging to the Vallejo area. The Walnut Creek earthquake of October 23, 1955, with a magnitude of 5.4, was centered between Walnut Creek and Concord, probably on the Concord fault branch. It caused considerable damage to chimneys and other brick structures at Martinez, and extensive minor damage, estimated at $1 million, was recorded throughout the area.

The Pleasanton fault is a minor break which parallels the Calaveras fault through Pleasanton. The fault is apparently active. A recent study by the U.S. Geological Survey has also determined that the Concord branch of the Calaveras is showing significant creep in the Concord area and presents some risk to recent housing developments in Ignacio Valley across the probable zone of activity of the fault. Because grading operations of the developments have virtually eliminated any natural features of the landscape that once marked the location of the fault, there is some uncertainty about its exact position there. There is no uncertainty, however, that the fault is active and may be the cause for extensive property damage in a future earthquake.

Recent studies by geologists from the California Division of Mines and Geology and the U.S. Geological Survey have also discovered active fault slippage along the Green Valley fault, which is a possible extension of the Concord fault west of Fairfield. It is possible that the powerful and very destructive Vacaville-Winters earthquakes of April 21, 1892, were centered on this fault. Future development north of Concord and Suisun Bay must consider the risks introduced by this recently noted active branch of the Calaveras fault zone.

Very recent (1973) research by the Geological Survey has also uncovered apparent creep along a related and previously unmapped fault which passes through the central area of the town of Antioch. The creeping fault appears to be the cause for curb and sidewalk offsets

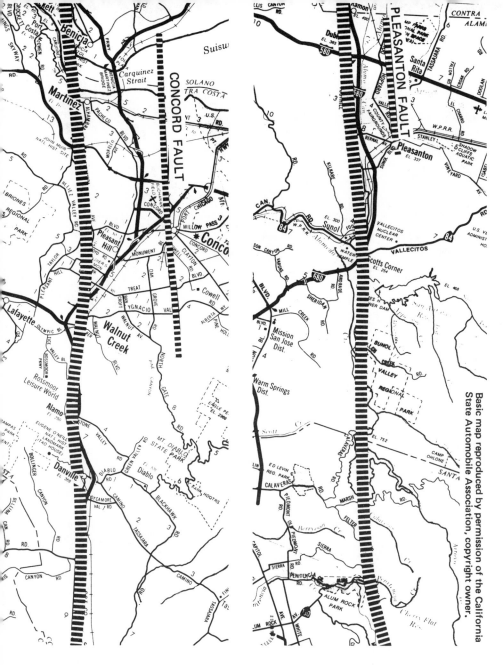

Approximate location of the main trace of the Calaveras fault, and the Concord and Pleasanton faults through Alameda and Contra Costa counties.

Appendix A **263**

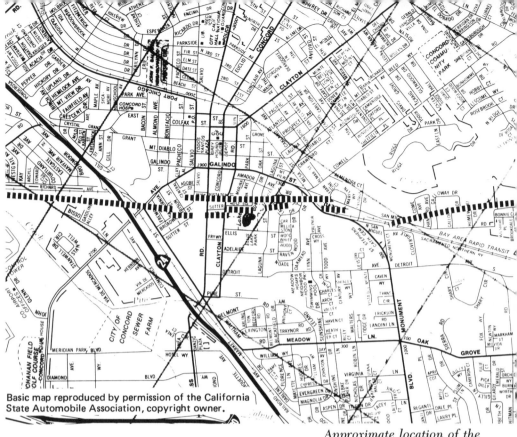

Approximate location of the Concord fault through the Concord area.

throughout the town, and some structural damage to several straddling buildings. The earthquake record of the area also strongly supports the likelihood of fault movements in and near the city. Among the numerous earthquakes, mostly small, which have occurred in the area, that of May 1889 caused the greatest damage in Antioch and the town of Collinsville. The Geological Survey concludes that other quakes along the fault are likely.

San Jacinto fault

The city of San Bernardino, like San Francisco and Oakland, has the dubious distinction of being surrounded on both the east and west by the San Andreas fault and its parallel subsidiary branches. One of these subsidiary fault zones, which bounds the southwest side of San Bernardino, is the San Jacinto fault, which many geologists consider the most active in California. Numerous sizeable tremors have been centered on the fault and have caused extensive surface faulting. The first significant earthquake recorded on the San Jacinto fault was on Christmas Day in 1899, with an estimated magnitude of between 6.2 and 7. It was centered near Hemet and San Jacinto, where the vibrational intensities were highly destructive. The Riverside area was also hit hard by the earthquake, and it was strongly felt as far south as San Diego. The most recent shock to cause ruptures along the fault was the Borrego Mountain earthquake of 1968.

The San Jacinto fault starts somewhere between Cajon Pass and San Bernardino, crosses Colton, Loma Linda, San Bernardino and Bryn Mawr, and continues into the San Jacinto Valley, the Borrego Valley and into the Colorado River Delta in Mexico. There is also some possibility that the San Jacinto merges with the very active and dangerous Imperial fault. The fault zone never follows a single linear pattern but instead proceeds as a series of overlapping and parallel fissures which include such fault segments as the Glen Helen fault, the Claremont fault, the Casa Loma fault, the Clark and Buck Ridge faults, the Coyote Creek fault, the San Felipe Hills fault, the Superstition Hills fault, the Superstition Mountain fault, and several others. The Coyote Creek fault is particularly active and presents a serious threat to the Borrego and Clark Valleys.

The magnitude 6 Southern California earthquake of September 19, 1907, is believed to have been centered on the San Jacinto fault, since it was felt most strongly at San Bernardino and at San Jacinto. San Bernardino experienced three large shocks at that time, and numerous landslides were reported in the hills and mountains along the fault. Another large shock with an estimated magnitude of 6.8 and an epicenter along the San Jacinto was the San Jacinto earthquake of April 21, 1918. The greatest damage occurred in the business district of San Jacinto, where only two buildings remained standing. However, most of the wrecked buildings had been of poor construction or of inadequate materials.

The recent Borrego Mountain earthquake (April 8, 1968) had a magnitude of 6.5. Since the epicenter was located in the sparsely settled area west of the Salton Sea, the quake was responsible for very little damage. However, the Coyote Creek fault, a subsidiary branch of the San Jacinto, experienced surface breaks for about 30 miles, and for the first time following any earthquake, investigators found evidence that several nearby faults, including the San Andreas and the Imperial, had experienced some faulting as a result of the San Jacinto tremor. This phenomenon indicates that anyone living in or very near a fault zone also risks property damage from an earthquake on a different, adjacent fault.

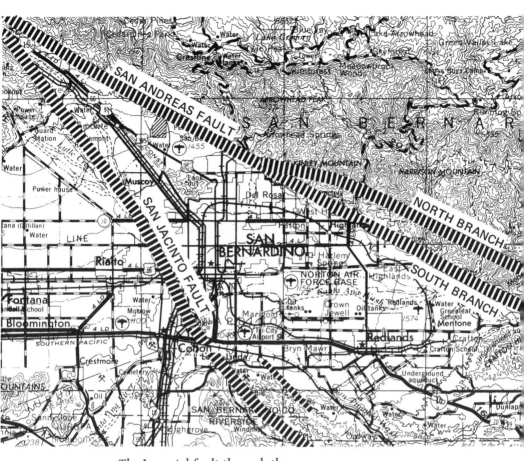

*The Imperial fault through the
Imperial Valley.*

Basic map reproduced by permission of the California
State Automobile Association, copyright owner.

San Andreas and San
into fault zones through the
Bernardino and Redlands
as.

Several other notable earthquakes have occurred along the San Jacinto fault zone—San Bernardino, 1923, magnitude 6.25; San Jacinto, 1937, magnitude 6; Brawley, 1942, magnitude 6.5; and Coachella, 1954, magnitude 6.2—but because of low population densities in the affected areas, they caused little damage.

Imperial fault

The Imperial fault is one of the numerous traces of the San Andreas fault zone in Southern California. The fault became known for the first time following the major El Centro (Imperial Valley) earthquake in May 18, 1940, when the fault ruptured in a linear pattern for approximately 40 miles from Brawley to Volcano Lake in Baja California. The trace of the Imperial fault rupture was about five miles east of the towns of Imperial, El Centro and Calexico, and the epicenter of the earthquake was in the vicinity of El Centro. All of the towns in the area were heavily damaged, and the intricate irrigation system of the Imperial Valley was nearly destroyed by displacements of up to 19 feet.

Several other earthquakes have disturbed the serenity of the Imperial Valley in the vicinity of the Imperial fault. The Imperial Valley earthquake of June 22, 1915, was centered in the Calexico-El Centro area and hit Calexico very hard. The quake had a magnitude of approximately 6.3 and intensities up to IX. It is uncertain whether the shock was focused on the Imperial fault or on the nearby San Jacinto fault zone. The most recent earthquake in the area occurred on March 4, 1966. The magnitude was less than 4, and the shock caused no damage, but displacements along the Imperial fault measured between one and three feet. Much of the permanent displacement was the result of slow creep during numerous small aftershocks.

Sierra Madre fault zone and the lesser faults of the San Fernando Valley

The Sierra Madre fault zone is one of the major geologic formations of the Los Angeles Basin, outlining the base of the San Gabriel Mountains and the northern edge of the San Fernando Valley. California's first recorded earthquake in 1769 was apparently on this fault. The Sierra Madre fault zone starts a little northwest of Altadena

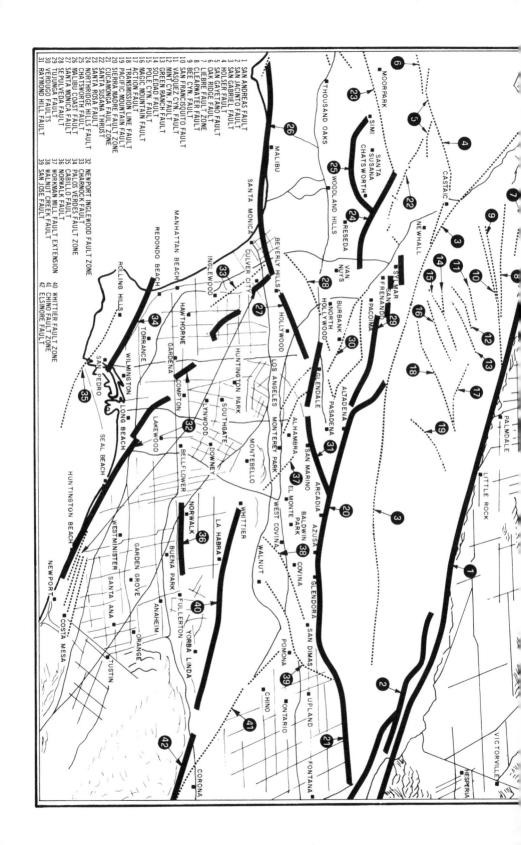

1 SAN ANDREAS FAULT
2 SAN JACINTO FAULT
3 SAN GABRIEL FAULT
4 HOLSER FAULT
5 SAN GAYETANO FAULT
6 OAK RIDGE FAULT
7 LIEBRE FAULT ZONE
8 CLEARWATER FAULT
9 BEE CYN. FAULT
10 SAN FRANCISQUITO FAULT
11 VASQUEZ CYN. FAULT
12 MINT CYN. FAULT
13 GREEN RANCH FAULT
14 SOLEDAD FAULT
15 POLE CYN. FAULT
16 MAGIC MOUNTAIN FAULT
17 ACTION FAULT
18 TRANSMISSION LINE FAULT
19 PACIFIC MOUNTAIN FAULT
20 SIERRA MADRE FAULT ZONE
21 CUCAMONGA FAULT ZONE
22 SANTA SUSANA THRUST
23 SANTA ROSA FAULT
24 NORTHRIDGE HILLS FAULT
25 CHATSWORTH FAULT
26 MALIBU COAST FAULT
27 SANTA MONICA FAULT
28 SEPULVEDA FAULT
29 TUJUNGA FAULT
30 VERDUGO FAULTS
31 RAYMOND HILL FAULT
32 NEWPORT INGLEWOOD FAULT ZONE
33 CHARNOCK FAULT
34 PALOS VERDES FAULT ZONE
35 CABILLO FAULT
36 NORWALK FAULT
37 WORKMAN MILL FAULT
38 WORKMAN MILL FAULT EXTENSION
39 SAN JOSE FAULT
40 WHITTIER FAULT ZONE
41 CHINO FAULT ZONE
42 ELSINORE FAULT

ults in the Los Angeles area.
e darker lines outline the
ter known and the most ac-
e of the faults.

and follows the San Gabriel foothills through Sierra Madre, Monrovia, Duarte, Azusa and Glendora. There it turns east, where it becomes the Cucamonga fault, and continues along the foothills.

Branching off and running parallel to this fault are many other lesser "local" traces, which include the San Fernando fault responsible for the 1971 earthquake. The San Fernando is surrounded by a number of even smaller faults, such as the Santa Susana fault, the Granada Hills fault, the Mission Hills fault, the Northridge Hills fault, the Verdugo fault, the La Tuna Canyon fault, the Park fault, the Chatsworth fault and the Olive View fault. It is important to keep in mind that the small San Fernando fault and the many other minor faults in the valley must be viewed as faults of major significance, because they are active and entirely within a heavily populated area. Each of them raises the specter of a future disaster.

The San Fernando fault was really defined for the first time as a result of the 10 miles of surface ruptures accompanying the 1971 earthquake. It can be subdivided into two general areas: the Sylmar seg-

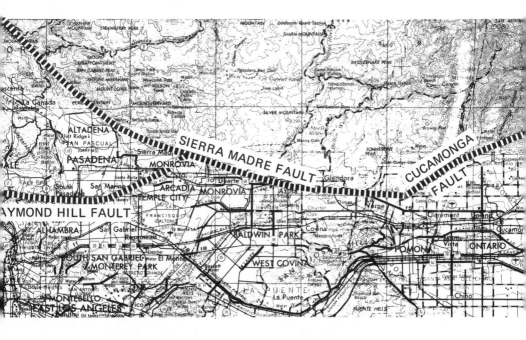

The most destructive segment of the San Fernando fault during the 1971 earthquake.

ment and the Tujunga segment. The Sylmar segment lies almost entirely within the heavily populated Sylmar-San Fernando area. It is characterized by numerous ground breaks forming a zone up to one mile wide. The Tujunga segment generally follows the foothills of the San Gabriel Mountains to the east of San Fernando, along the Tujunga Valley, and consists of only one or two parallel breaks. Since 1971, this area has become one of the most studied and mapped fault zones in the metropolitan regions of California. A detailed map, together with some of the best references on the 1971 earthquake, are listed in Appendix B.

The Raymond Hill fault is another short fault which transects the area between South Pasadena and Monrovia and finally joins the Sierra Madre fault. The fault trace is in the general vicinity of San Marino, Temple City, Sierra Madre and Arcadia. The fault is believed to be active, but it has not moved (faulted) in the past 200 years. Nevertheless, it is probabyy capable of generating an earthquake similar to the 1971 San Fernando; and like all of the small faults in the area, it presents a serious hazard which must be considered in the design, construction and purchase of buildings in the area.

The Northridge Hills fault—potentially active and hazardous, but little known—transects the densely populated San Fernando Valley from west-northwest of the town of Chatsworth to Northridge and on in an easterly direction to at least the east central valley, where it disappears beneath deep alluvium. From available geologic data, this fault appears capable of producing another San Fernando earthquake on the scale of 1971. Earthquake experts familiar with the area suggest that a zone along the fault some 2,000 feet wide could be subject to future ground ruptures.

Newport-Inglewood fault zone

The Newport-Inglewood fault zone is one of the major faults of the Los Angeles area. It has been the source of numerous earthquakes, including the second most destructive earthquake in Southern California—the Long Beach tremor on March 10, 1933. The Newport-Inglewood fault is parallel to the San Andreas, with the major trace beginning just north of Culver City. It crosses the Baldwin Hills, Inglewood, the Dominguez Hills and Signal Hill, then parallels the coast along Seal Beach, Sunset Beach and Huntington Beach and enters the Pacific near Newport Beach. The southern end of the fault is not known, but some geologists have suggested that it may continue as far south as San Diego. It is difficult to follow the trace of the fault through much of this area, since most surface expressions and details

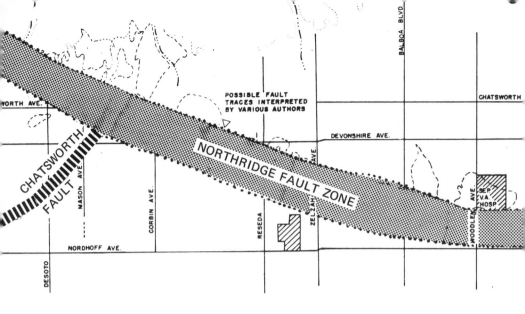

The Northridge Hills fault zone through the San Fernando Valley.

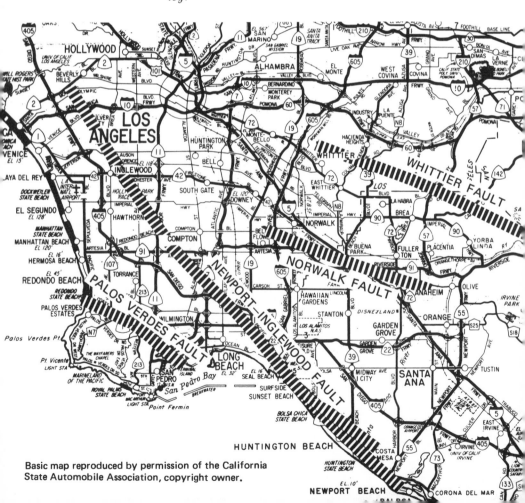

Basic map reproduced by permission of the California State Automobile Association, copyright owner.

along the zone are covered by commercial and residential developments and thick alluvium.

The 1933 Long Beach shock was relatively small, with a magnitude of 6.3 and maximum intensities of VIII to IX. There was no known surface faulting. Nevertheless, this quake caused about 120 fatalities and more than $50 million in property damage. The epicenter was near Newport Beach, and the most heavily damaged cities were the coastal cities, primarily Long Beach. The town of Compton was nearly leveled by the earthquake. It is estimated that, overall, about 20,000 dwellings and 2,000 apartment houses, stores, office buildings, factories, warehouses, theaters and churches were damaged in degrees varying from cracked plaster to complete destruction. The reason for the disproportionate damage was that the quake was centered in a heavily populated area, built up without any regard for the dangers from earthquakes.

Several small earthquakes have caused lesser degrees of damage to the area since 1933. Typical examples are the tremors of October 21 and November 14, 1941. The latter caused about $1 million in damage to the towns of Torrance and Gardena. In addition to earthquakes, the failure of the Baldwin Hills Dam on December 14, 1963, is attributed to the slow creeping movements along the section of the Newport-Inglewood fault below the reservoir. The Newport-Inglewood fault zone is regarded as one of the more active regions in California, and its long history of earthquakes should be enough warning that every building in the area must be properly braced and strengthened to ride through the inevitable "next" tremor.

Norwalk fault

The known segment of the Norwalk fault extends for only about five miles from the Norwalk, Cerritos and Artesia areas, through La Mirada and Buena Park into Fullerton. However, because this small fault is believed to be active and is situated in a densely populated urban area, it must be taken seriously as a hazard to life and property. The last damaging earthquake attributed to the Norwalk fault occurred on July 8, 1929. It was a mild tremor with a magnitude of about 4.7. Because much of the damage was concentrated in the Whittier area, and because the Norwalk fault was unknown at the time, the shock was

*e Newport-Inglewood fault
ne, and the smaller Palos
rdes, Norwalk and Whittier
ults.*

blamed on and named for the Whittier fault, which extends along the base of the Puente Hills.

Numerous other smaller earthquakes have occurred along the Norwalk fault since 1929, but none have been very damaging. However, according to Professor Richter, "There is good reason to suppose that the Norwalk fault is capable of producing an earthquake of the magnitude of the Long Beach earthquake." Because the fault is located in a generally flat area with an alluvial soil foundation, the effects of such an earthquake in the area will probably be similar to those produced by the costly and destructive San Fernando earthquake of 1971.

Elsinore and Whittier faults

The Elsinore fault is one of the longest in Southern California. It parallels the San Jacinto fault, some 20 to 25 miles to the west, and follows a nearly straight course for 150 miles through Lake Elsinore, Murietta, Temecula, Palomar Mountain and toward the Mexican border. A secondary branch of the fault zone passes through Aguanga, Oak Grove and Warner's Hot Springs. The fault appears to be active, although only one moderate earthquake with a magnitude greater than 6 is known to have occurred over its length. That earthquake, and a series of related smaller aftershocks, occurred in May of 1910. The quake was strongest in the vicinity of Lake Elsinore, but it was also felt over most of Southern California.

The Whittier fault is the northern extension of the Elsinore fault, joining the Elsinore south of Corona. It runs along the base of the Puente Hills, crossing numerous towns including Whittier, La Habra, Brea, Fullerton and Yorba Linda. The activity and history of the fault is at best sketchy, since the same general area is affected by the active Norwalk fault. Clearly, with this encompassing web of fault activity, all of the towns in this area are threatened by a strong earthquake at any time.

Santa Ynez fault zone and related faults of the Santa Barbara region

The southwestern corner of Santa Barbara County, which includes the cities of Santa Barbara, Montecito, Carpinteria, Goleta and Gaviota, is an intensely active earthquake area affected by a group of intricately connected and interrelated faults. The dominant fault is the Santa Ynez, which can be traced from eastern Ventura County west to the town of Gaviota, where the fault enters the Santa Barbara Channel.

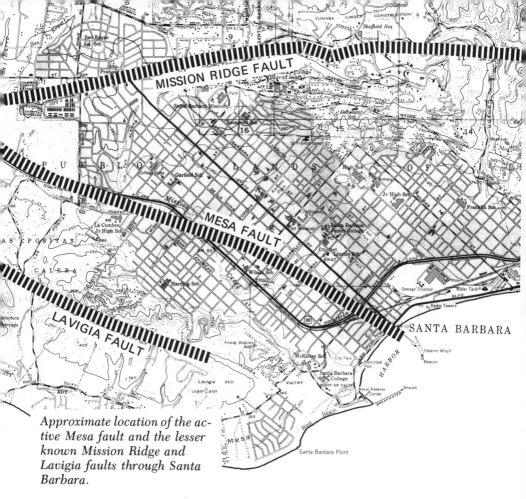

Approximate location of the active Mesa fault and the lesser known Mission Ridge and Lavigia faults through Santa Barbara.

The fault zone is apparently the cause for the uplift of the Santa Ynez Mountains, which rise to more than 4,000 feet to form the picturesque backdrop for Santa Barbara. The fault zone is presently quite active and seems to be undergoing considerable movements.

The Santa Ynez fault zone is paralleled by a number of other faults, several located along the coast, others entirely submerged in the Santa Barbara Channel and a few crossing the Channel Islands off the coast of Santa Barbara. At least three faults are known to underlie the city of Santa Barbara—the Lavigia fault, the Mesa fault and the Mission Ridge fault—and at least one of these, the Mesa fault, is believed to be active. The Mesa fault crosses the main business district of the city and is probably responsible for the destructive Santa Barbara earthquake in 1925. Detailed street-by-street investigations have been carried out for approximately half a mile on each side of the fault, and the results indicate that the fault must be considered a very serious threat to any future development and construction in its vicinity.

The Lavigia fault is located within the hills in the southwestern part of the city and is traceable for approximately four miles. It is not known whether the fault is active today. The Mission Ridge fault, located along the Mission Ridge east of the business district, is also an unknown. The concensus is that both are dormant and relatively secure.

At least six earthquakes have caused significant damage to Santa Barbara, and four of these had epicenters close to the city, presumably on the nearby faults. The earliest, in 1812, destroyed the Santa Barbara Mission, as well as the Mission Purisima Concepçion, some 10 miles northeast of Point Arguello. It also caused a *tsunami* along the north coast of the Santa Barbara Channel. It is estimated that the earthquake had a magnitude of 7. Nearly a century later, on July 27, 1902, a smaller shock was centered near Los Alamos, where tremors were felt for more than a week. Every house and chimney in the area was damaged, and the town of Lompoc suffered extensive property loss.

The best known Santa Barbara earthquake, that of June 29, 1925, had a magnitude of 6.3 and severely damaged much of the town, particularly the business district along the Mesa fault. Another forceful earthquake, magnitude 7.5, occurred two years later on November 4, 1927. The tremor was centered near Point Arguello, and its effects were most pronounced in the Lompoc, Surf and Honda areas. However, damage was widespread for many miles, and the shock also caused a six-foot *tsunami* in the channel. The most recent important and damaging Santa Barbara earthquake occurred on June 30, 1941. This magnitude 6 earthquake was centered in the Santa Barbara Channel, about five miles south of the coast, between Santa Barbara and Carpinteria.

White Wolf fault

The existence of the White Wolf fault had been known by geologists since its general trace was plotted as early as 1906, but the fault was not considered to be active in the sense of constituting an earthquake threat. Then on July 21, 1952, the fault suddenly and unexpectedly erupted, causing the major, magnitude 7.7, Kern County earthquake and miles of surface breaks. This tremor remains the largest earthquake in California since the 1906 San Francisco earthquake and the largest earthquake in Southern California since the great Fort Tejon earthquake of 1857. The effects of the shock on structures in Kern County are described and pictured throughout this book. It caused ground movements of up to two feet in a horizontal direction

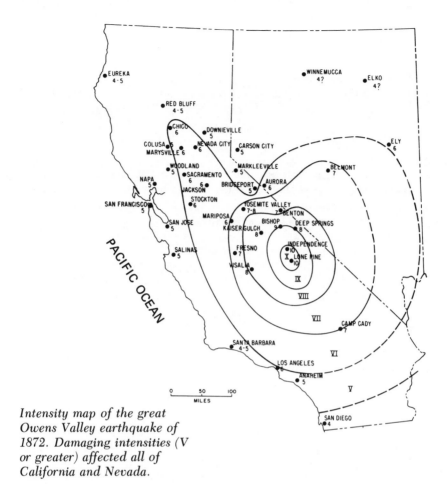

Intensity map of the great Owens Valley earthquake of 1872. Damaging intensities (V or greater) affected all of California and Nevada.

and up to about four feet in a vertical direction. The entire Bakersfield area and much of Southern California suffered extensive property losses.

The White Wolf is traceable for only about 34 miles, extending between Highway 58 and Interstate 5, just south of Arvin. Much of the fault line is invisible, particularly in the vicinity of Wheeler Ridge and up to Sycamore Canyon. From there, until Bealville, the fault outlines the edge of the Tehachapi Mountains.

Owens Valley fault

On March 26, 1872, Owens Valley, east of the Central Sierra, was shaken by what is believed to be the greatest earthquake in California history. In effect, the earthquake struck the western United States; for it was felt throughout California and as far east as Salt Lake City. The earthquake is estimated to have been magnitude 8.3, a little larger than the 1906 quake. Extensive faulting occurred in a number of short parallel fractures all across the long narrow valley, from Haiwee Reservoir north 100 miles to Big Pine. The ground surface displacements were immense. In some locations, particularly between Lone Pine and Independence, there were up to 23 feet of vertical and 20 feet of lateral shifts.

Despite the low population density of the area, the loss of life was considerable—about 60 deaths, mostly from the collapse of adobe buildings. In a summary of his observations of the earthquake, the editor of the *Inyo Independent* wrote on April 6, 1872:

> Severe and appalling as this great convulsion of the earth unquestionably was, it is a settled conviction with all here, that not a person would have been killed or hurt had their houses all been made of wood.

Further on, he recommended to his readers that they ". . . forever eschew adobe, brick, and stone in buildings."

The Owens Valley fault remains the most active formation in the system of faulting that is responsible for the formation of the Sierra Nevada ranges and the hills and low valleys to the east. Indeed, some of the fissures which opened in the 1872 earthquake were reactivated by new tremors in the 1960s.

Montana

The state of Montana has a long earthquake history—particularly the southwestern part of the state, which falls within the active seismic belt along the western edge of the Rocky Mountains. Much of the past seismic activity in Montana is not well-known, because until recently, this area had a scattered and very small population density. Nevertheless, numerous quakes have been recorded since 1869, and in the past 50 years, five tremors were magnitude 6 or higher. Most of them took place within a zone between Yellowstone National Park and Helena in a great belt of seismic activity that forms an arc through western Montana, northwestern Wyoming, southeastern Idaho and Utah. This area is thought to be the eastern limit of the effects of the collision between the Pacific tectonic plate and North American plate along the San Andreas and other western faults. Unfortunately, until very recently, this area was not generally recognized as an active seismic zone, and the building construction and codes have reflected this attitude.

Besides the Hebgen Lake quake in 1959, the largest eruption in this century was on June 27, 1925. The magnitude 6.75 quake was

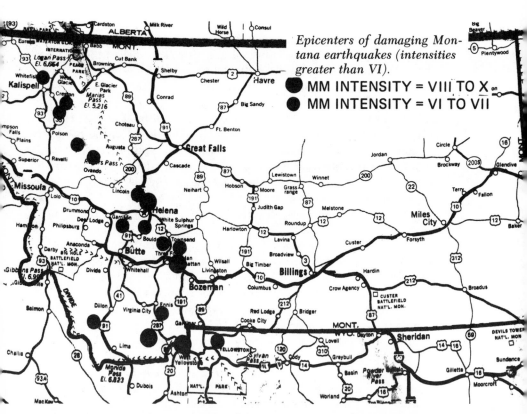

Epicenters of damaging Montana earthquakes (intensities greater than VI).

● MM INTENSITY = VIII TO X
● MM INTENSITY = VI TO VII

centered a short distance from Manhattan, in the Clarkston Valley. The most heavily damaged areas included Three Forks, Logan, Manhattan and Deer Park. Brick buildings in Willow Creek, Bozeman, Radersburg, White Sulphur Springs and Trident also suffered extensive damage, and there were various minor damage reports in many other localities within a 75-mile radius from the epicenter. Numerous landslides blocked several roads and railroads in the damaged areas, but no fault movements were observed on the ground surface. It is believed that substantial sub-surface displacements occurred, however, the area is covered with a thick deposit of soft sediments which would have absorbed the movement of the bedrock below.

A destructive series of earthquakes struck the same area 10 years later, starting with a moderate shock on October 12, 1935, and culminating in two powerful earthquakes on October 18 (magnitude 6.25) and October 31 (magnitude 6). Both were centered in the vicinity of Helena. This series of earthquakes rates as one of the most destructive in U.S. history. The tremors struck almost directly beneath the ill-prepared city, and each successive strong shock further damaged the previously weakened buildings. A survey conducted by the city engineer's office in Helena indicated that more than half of the buildings in Helena were damaged, many of them totally.

Another large quake (6.25) shook southwestern Montana on November 23, 1947, bringing considerable damage to brick, masonry and concrete structures throughout central Madison County. Then again, on August 17, 1959, the largest of all of the recent shocks hit the Hebgen Lake area. The quake, which reached a magnitude of 7.1, was centered on the Madison Range on the western edge of Yellowstone National Park and was felt over an area of about 600,000 square miles. Some 156 aftershocks were recorded at Old Faithful Ranger Station, Yellowstone National Park, during the first 21 hours after the main shock.

The most spectacular effect of the earthquake was a great avalanche of rock, dirt and trees which cascaded into the Madison River Canyon, forming a new lake just below Hebgen Dam. Most of the 28 casualties attributed to the earthquake were caused by this slide. An extensive and spectacular fault scarp was also formed near Hebgen Lake, with vertical displacements of 21 feet near Red Canyon Creek. Minor to moderate damage occurred throughout southern Montana, northeastern Idaho and northwestern Wyoming as well.

In the opinion of many seismologists and engineers, the western section of the state of Montana is an area of very high earthquake hazard. Thus, the contents of this book are as applicable to buildings and property in Montana as they are to Alaska and California. The resident of southwestern Montana must do all that he can to protect himself and his family and property against this hazard.

Nevada

The bulk of the earthquake activity in the state of Nevada is concentrated along a series of faults extending in a northerly direction from California's Owens Valley to Winnemucca. The area of greatest activity, the Reno-Winnemucca-Tonopah triangle, also contains a major portion of Nevada's population. A number of large earthquakes have struck this area in the past 60 years, all of them accompanied by significant fault displacements and strong vibrations that affected hundreds of thousands of square miles. However, because of the very low population density of most of the area, damage has generally been low.

The largest of the quakes in this century, the 1915 Pleasant Valley earthquake, was centered along a fault on the eastern side of the

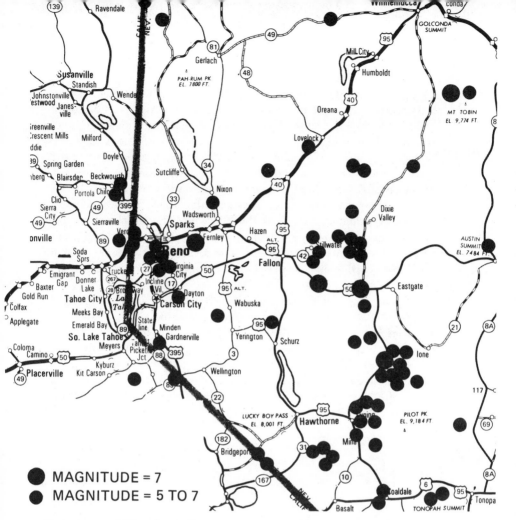

*Epicenters of Nevada earth-
quakes with magnitudes
greater than 5.*

valley, which lies south of Winnemucca. The magnitude 7.6 shock was
felt at Reno, but damage was concentrated in the Kennedy, Winnemucca and Lovelock areas. Surface faulting of about 22 miles accompanied the tremor. Another tremor exceeding magnitude 7.3 struck
Cedar Valley, a practically uninhabited area, in 1932. The shock caused
spectacular faulting, extending over a length of about 38 miles with a
width of 4 to 9 miles. Some heavy structural damage was sustained at
Hawthorne, Luning and Mina. The Excelsior Mountains earthquake
(magnitude 6.3) in 1934 brought damage to much of the same area, including Mina and Marietta.

The year 1954 stands out in the earthquake history of Nevada.

During that year, four earthquakes with magnitudes between 6.8 and 7.3 occurred throughout the western part of the state. Three separate tremors occurred east of Fallon, causing extensive damage in the Fallon-Stillwater area, and the last of these, that of August 23, 1954, was accompanied by 11 miles of surface faulting. Another major earthquake, of magnitude 6.8, struck the Frenchman's Station-Dixie Valley area east of Fallon later that year. Spectacular faulting broke the surface for about 55 miles, with vertical fault movements exceeding 20 feet and horizontal slippage of about 12 feet. The fault scarp crossed U.S. Highway 50 east of Frenchman and may still be seen today, some three miles south of the highway. The most significant damage from the latter earthquake occurred in California, where a Sacramento water reservoir partially collapsed.

The more densely populated Reno-Sparks area has felt a number of earthquakes. None have been particularly destructive, but a few were uncomfortably close. The largest shock in the vicinity of Reno was that of April 24, 1914, with an intensity of about VII. The quake lasted for 10 seconds and caused some light structural damage. Two other earthquakes, in 1942 and 1953, caused limited damage. Presently, the Nevada Bureau of Mines is conducting intensive research regarding the potentially active faults and the earthquake risks in this area.

Oregon

Oregon holds the distinction of having the least number of earthquakes of the four states bordering the Pacific Ocean. During the period between 1841 and 1963, a total of only 17 earthquakes in Oregon had intensities greater than V, which is barely damaging. A few California earthquakes have caused some damage along the southern portions of the state, of course, and *tsunamis* inundated some coastal areas as a result of the 1964 Alaska quake.

The most active earthquake areas of the state include Klamath Falls, Grants Pass, Salem, Portland, The Dalles, Milton-Freewater and Baker. The largest earthquakes (intensities of VIII) in Oregon occurred in Port Orford in 1873, in Portland in 1877 and 1880, and in Milton-Freewater in 1936. Earthquakes with intensities of VII were also recorded in Umatilla in 1923 and in Portland in 1962. The latter occurred on November 5, 1962. The epicenter was located about two miles southeast of Hayden Island, near the Columbia River. The maximum intensity was VII and damage was minor in the city, consisting

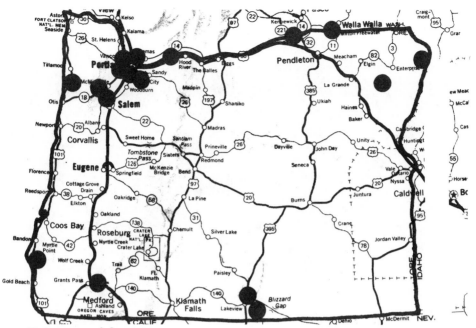

Epicenters of damaging Oregon earthquakes (intensities greater than V).

mainly of shattered chimneys, broken windows, cracked plaster and damaged furnishings. A number of aftershocks, none of them damaging in Portland, followed the main shock.

Despite this encouraging record, the Portland area in particular is geologically ripe for a larger earthquake, and its citizens would be unwise to become smug and careless about their building habits. According to Dr. George O. Gates of the U.S. Geological Survey, "Portland . . . is within the Circum-Pacific Seismic Belt, and there is no reason to believe it could not be subjected to strong seismic shock at some time in the future."

Dr. Gates believes that much of the hazard to the Oregon coastal settlements and to Portland is presented by off-shore faults. In fact, the Pacific floor off the coast of Oregon is a very active seismic area, much like the Eureka area of California, a few miles to the south. According to two other experts, J. H. Balsillie and G. T. Benson of Portland State University:

> Of the 240 earthquakes felt in Oregon between 1841 and 1958, 51 were reported in the Portland area. Although this proportion may reflect population distribution in part, Portland is certainly among the more active seismic areas in the state. In the last few years, about one shock has been felt in the Portland area per year.

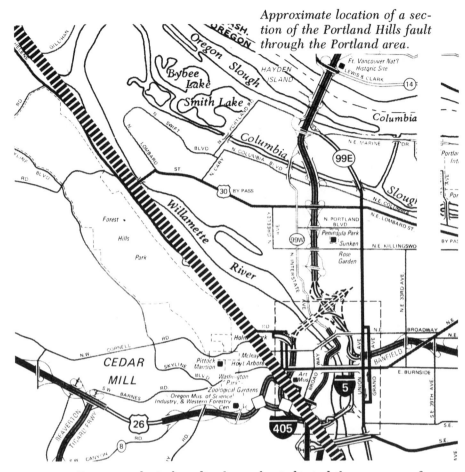

Approximate location of a section of the Portland Hills fault through the Portland area.

Recent geological studies have also indicated the presence of a major fault along the east face of the Portland Hills through the city of Portland. This fault is apparently part of a major fault system which extends across the state from the Portland Hills, along the Clackamas River and as far as Steens Mountain. The trace of the fault in Portland is most clearly outlined from the west bank of the Willamette River at the south end of Suavie Island to about Vaughn Street. Further southeast the trace is covered by thick alluvia. Many Oregon geologists and scientists believe that the Portland Hills fault is active and presents potential dangers which must be considered in urban planning and construction.

In short, a strong earthquake could and probably will strike the coast of Oregon, and such a shock would likely affect the Portland area as well. A major earthquake in this area would cause extremely damaging intensities in the numerous landfill and poor-soil areas of Portland and other nearby cities, especially in the flood-plain and landfill areas along the Willamette and Columbia Rivers. Numerous other smaller filled areas along the Portland waterfront are also highly subject to severe damage.

Utah

Few laymen realize that Utah is in a highly active seismic belt. Moreover, the main faults in Utah are aligned through the central part of the state, where about 85 percent of the population lives. In the period from 1850 through 1963, nearly 300 earthquakes were felt in the state, although only about 38 caused any property damage.

The six most active fault zones in Utah are the following (the approximate number of earthquakes documented for each fault zone from 1850 through 1965 are noted in parentheses):

- Hansel Valley fault zone (9), north of the Great Salt Lake.
- East Cache fault zone (18), along the eastern margin of Cache Valley in northern Utah.
- Wasatch fault zone (105), extending for about 160 miles along the western foot of the Wasatch Mountains between Collinston and Levan.
- Thousand Lakes fault zone (15), southeast of Nephi in central Utah.
- Sevier-Tushar (or Elsinore) fault zone (51), which includes Sanpete Valley in central Utah.
- Hurricane fault zone (40), extending southward from the Cedar City area to the Grand Canyon.

Clearly, the Wasatch fault zone is one of the nation's most active seismic belts. It is astounding and very fortunate that no major destructive earthquakes have occurred along its length during the course of Utah's history. The fault crosses the most heavily populated parts of Utah, starting north of Brigham City, bypassing Logan, and continuing through the Brigham City, Ogden and Salt Lake City areas. Further south, the fault passes near Provo and continues south of Nephi. The entire Salt Lake City area in particular presents one of the highest earthquake hazards in the United States. However, unlike many of the large cities in California, which are similarly crossed by an active fault system, Salt Lake City continues to be built without much regard for

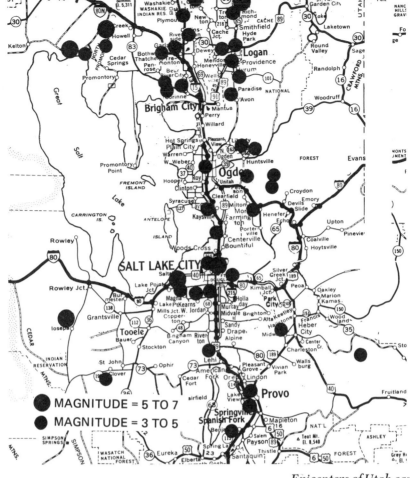

Epicenters of Utah earthquakes with magnitudes greater than 4.

the earthquake hazard, both in the code requirements for construction and in the zoning plans for fault traces and other inferior geologic foundations. Numerous residential and office buildings are located directly across the Wasatch fault. In addition, because the city is situated on a deep alluvial valley at the foot of the Wasatch Range, it is especially subject to very high vibrational intensities that could literally level the many masonry buildings in the city.

Another hazard associated with the Salt Lake area, as well as Ogden and other cities affected by the Wasatch fault zone, involves the numerous landslide-prone hillsides along the scarps of the fault. The Utah Geological Survey is presently conducting research to delineate these dangerous landslide areas.

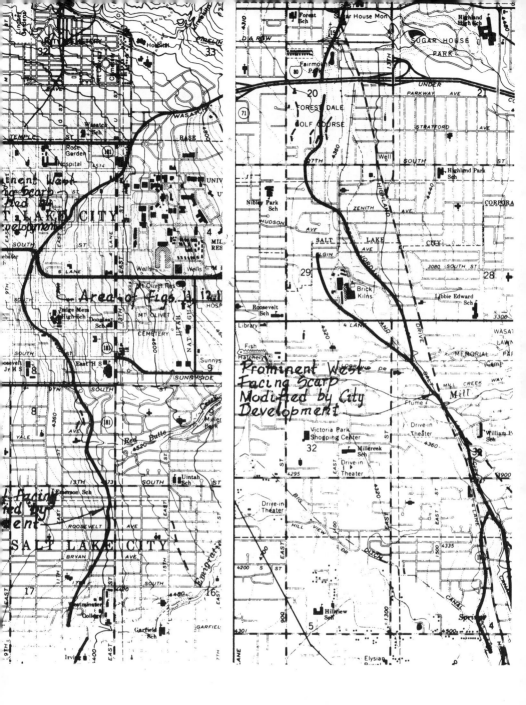

Approximate location of the East Bench fault through Salt Lake City.

It is important to point out that like most other faults of comparable length, the Wasatch is actually made of a series of separate smaller faults in an interlocking or branching pattern. For example, the very active East Bench fault is a branch of the Wasatch system. It forms the boundary between the East Bench and the East Lake Plain districts of Salt Lake City. The north end of the fault is in the vicinity of 13th East and 1st South streets, where the University Apartments building stands astride it. There, the East Bench fault merges into the Wasatch and can be traced northeasterly through Federal Heights, an expensive residential district. In the opposite direction, the East Bench fault proceeds in a southerly course across the most highly developed and populous sections of Salt Lake City.

Another branch of the Wasatch system, the Warm Springs fault, is located at the northern end of the city, at the boundary of Davis and Lake Counties. It splits into two branches near the county lines—the Lime Kiln fault, which turns east and fades away one mile south of Bountiful, and a second branch which continues north for about eight miles.

The largest earthquakes in the recent history of Utah are those of 1921 and 1934. The earthquakes of September 29 and October 1, 1921, struck the Elsinore area in the Sevier Valley, some 150 miles south of Salt Lake City, and caused considerable damage to the towns of Elsinore, Richfield and Monroe. The shock on March 12, 1934, known as the Utah or Hansel Valley earthquake, was centered near Kosmo, at the north end of the Great Salt Lake, and therefore caused little damage despite its magnitude (6.4 to 6.8) and high intensities.

Numerous other smaller earthquakes have caused varying degrees of damage. The August 30, 1962, Northern Utah earthquake, which was centered in Cache County, caused significant damage on the east side of Cache Valley from Logan to Lewiston. The greatest damage occurred at Richmond. Another series of small earthquakes caused slight damage to the Salt Lake City area during the winter and spring of 1955.

Washington

About 850 earthquakes had been felt and recorded in the state of Washington as of 1965. The greatest number of them occurred in western Washington, in the Puget Sound area, which contains the major proportion of the population of the state. The Olympia, Seattle, Port Angeles and Sultan areas are the most active districts in this part

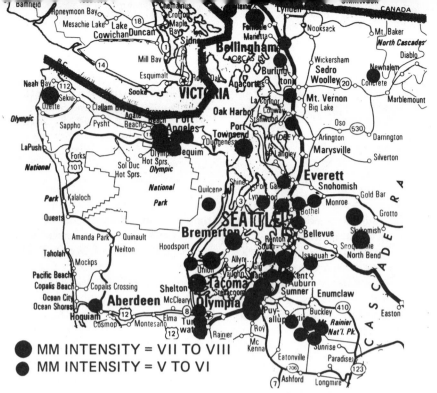

● MM INTENSITY = VII TO VIII
● MM INTENSITY = V TO VI

Epicenters of damaging Puget Sound earthquakes (intensities greater than V).

of the state. On the eastern side of the Cascades, the Chelan-Wenatchee area is the most active district, but the Spokane and Walla Walla areas have also felt several earthquakes of moderate intensity.

Geologists and seismologists generally believe that the probability of a great earthquake, such as the 1906 San Francisco disaster, occurring around Puget Sound is small. However, the nature of some geologic features of the area suggest that the possibility cannot be dismissed completely. The area is part of a moderately active earthquake zone which extends from the vicinity of Portland north through Puget Sound to the Canadian border and Vancouver Island. Recent geophysical data also suggest that a branch of the active Circum-Pacific Seismic Belt traverses this coastal area, putting Puget Sound in the same seismic zone as California and western Alaska.

The first recorded Washington earthquake occurred on June 29, 1833, in Thurston County, near the southern end of Puget Sound. The four largest earthquakes since then were in 1939, 1946, 1949 and 1965. The Olympia earthquake of November 12, 1939, had a magnitude of about 5.8 and brought minor damage to Centralia, Elma and Olympia. No structural collapse of buildings was reported. Other small areas of

High intensity zones of Seattle. The darkened areas have suffered, or are expected to suffer, greater earthquake damage because of the geologic foundations—loose soils, filled lands, old river beds, etc.

intensity were noted in Tacoma, Auburn, Kent and Port Orchard. The Puget Sound earthquake of February 14, 1946, registered a magnitude of about 5.8 and was centered about 20 miles north of Olympia. The tremor caused several deaths and moderate property losses, mostly in Seattle. The most severe damage in Seattle occurred in industrial buildings on filled ground in the Duwamish River valley, along the former tidal areas at the south end of Elliott Bay, and along the waterfronts of the city.

The Olympia earthquake of April 13, 1949, was the largest earthquake on record for the state, with a magnitude of 7.1. It caused extensive damage to the area, variously estimated at between $15 and $70 million. Eight people were killed and many more were injured. The earthquake was centered between Olympia and Tacoma along the southern edge of Puget Sound. Numerous areas were damaged extensively, including Seattle, Tacoma, Auburn, Castle Rock, Centralia, Chehalis, Olympia, Puyallup and many smaller settlements.

The Puget Sound earthquake of April 29, 1965, is the most recent damaging tremor in the area. The magnitude of the earthquake was approximately 6.5, the center about 13 miles southwest of downtown Seattle. Property losses were estimated to exceed $13 million, with much of the damage in Seattle and in King County. The damage pattern of the earthquake closely resembled that of the 1949 shock but was less severe. Again, much of the damage was concentrated in the "poor land" areas of Seattle, including the filled and low alluvial lands along the rivers and the sound. Buildings which had been damaged in 1949 often sustained additional damage in 1965.

None of the known earthquakes in the state of Washington have been accompanied by surface faulting. However, the most earthquake-active areas of the state, particularly those located in the Puget Sound lowlands, are covered in most places with hundreds of feet of soft glacial deposits, and this glacial cover has effectively prevented surface investigations of possible faulting during the past earthquakes. Several faults are known to exist in the state. For example, the Tolt River earthquake of 1932 is believed to have been caused by a

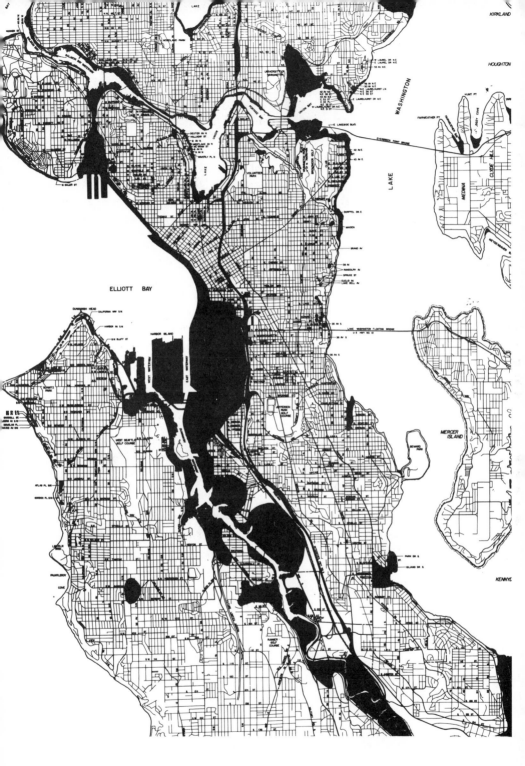

major fault which borders on the western edge of the northern Cascades. But again, the fault is covered by thick layers of sedimentary deposits, so there was no evidence of surface faulting. The 1949 earthquake is believed to have been on the Bordeaux fault, near the junction of Lewis, Thurston and Grays Harbor Counties. This presumed fault, also covered by thick soil deposits, runs from Independence Creek, near the junction of the counties, northeastward toward Olympia. Generally, then, there seems to be no danger of surface faulting in the state. The earthquake hazard, which is considerable, arises only from ground motions and from amplification of the earthquake intensities in soft alluvial soils.

Note:

The following base maps are copyrighted by AAA and are reproduced by permission: pp. 251, 255, 256, 258, 279, 281, 283, 284, 286, 289.

The lines and shaded areas used to show faults and fault zones on photographs and maps in this book are based on published geological material. Damage descriptions are based on engineering publications. The illustrations are intended to show only general trends of faults and causes of damage and should not be interpreted literally.

APPENDIX B:

Earthquake, fault, geologic and landslide information sources and references

Earthquake, fault, geologic, landslide and related information is available from a large number of agencies and institutions in the form of reports on past earthquakes, maps of known or suspected active faults, known and suspected landslides, geologic and soil conditions, etc. This information is available for sale and in numerous reference libraries, which often have staffs familiar with the material. *Many* public libraries carry these references.

In your search for information, you may begin with this appendix. Many references are listed here. However, others exist in the files of the agencies which are concerned with seismic and land-use oriented problems. If you do not find the necessary references here, check with:

1. Local libraries, and university, college, corporate and private libraries.

2. City and county offices: the information is usually in the files of the engineer (or geologist or planner). These files often contain invaluable information on past landslide damage in the area, fault maps, etc. This information is *public* and *is* available for your use. Current legislation is making it mandatory, at least in California, for city and county offices to compile information on active fault hazards in their areas.

3. State geologic agencies: all states discussed in this book have organizations—geologic surveys, mining bureaus, etc.—which compile and publish information (their addresses are included). They offer a surprising number of services and constitute an outstanding but often disregarded source of information.

4. The U.S. Geological Survey: the major source and distributor of earthquake information. The Survey publishes the results of hundreds of geologic studies every year (many are concerned with the earthquake risk) in the form of reports, maps, atlases and *open-file maps* and *reports* (maps and reports not in final form, subject to revision before final publication). The Survey maintains several *Public Inquiries Offices* for distribution of its work. Each office maintains a reference library where the publications may be consulted and provides sales services. Each office is a depository for *open-file reports*.

Alaska

Selected sources: U.S. Geological Survey, 502 Second Ave., Anchorage; Alaska Div. of Geological and Geophysical Surveys, 3001 Porcupine Dr., Anchorage; Fairbanks Chamber of Commerce.

Selected references:

Anchorage Maps I-787A and I-787B (USGS, 1972): geology, landslides from the 1964 earthquake, etc. Bulletin 1258-D (USGS, 1969): landslides of Government Hill.

Fairbanks *The Fairbanks, Alaska, Earthquakes of June 21, 1967* (U.S. Coast and Geodetic Survey, 1968). Map I-455 (USGS, 1966); Map GQ-110 (USGS, 1958): geology.

1964 earthquake Prof. Papers 541 to 546 (USGS, 1965-1970): effects on most towns, detailed damage maps, etc. *The Tsunami of the Alaskan Earthquake, 1964, Technical Memorandum No. 25,* 1968, U.S. Army Corps of Engineers, Coastal Engineering Research Center: detailed damage maps. *The Prince William Sound, Alaska, Earthquake of 1964 and Aftershocks,* ESSA, U.S. Department of Commerce, 1976: three volumes. *The Great Alaska Earthquake of 1964,* National Academy of Sciences, 1968-1973: seven volumes, extensive information.

California

Selected sources: U.S. Geological Survey (USGS): 300 North Los Angeles St., Los Angeles, 555 Battery St., San Francisco; California Division of Mines and Geology (CDMG): 107 South Broadway, Los Angeles; 2022 Ferry Bldg., San Francisco; 1416 - 9th St., Sacramento; numerous libraries, incl. most university and college libraries.

Selected references:

Statewide Special Reports 102, 52B, 52A and 52, Index to Geologic Maps of California (CDMG): contains reference to all maps of interest through 1968. Geologic Atlas of California (CDMG, 27 maps of the state): useful reference. *Earthquake Country: How, Why and Where Earthquakes Strike in California* (Lane Books, 1964): general, San Andreas fault.

Northern California

Eureka area Water-Supply Paper 1470 (USGS, 1959): geology, soils, Rio Dell north past Arcata. "An Engineering Study of the Eureka Earthquake of Dec. 21, 1954," *Bull. Seismological Soc. Amer.*, V47, 2, Apr. 1967: damage, effects.

Tahoe area Circular 537 (USGS, 1967): Effects of the Truckee earthquake of Sep. 12, 1966. *Geologic studies in the Lake Tahoe Area,* Geological Society of Sacramento, 1968: earthquakes, faults, etc.

San Andreas fault Map I-692, (USGS, 1972): Bolinas Bay north to Point Delgada. Prelim. Report 16 (CDMG, 1972): fault, geology, landslides, risk zones of Sonoma Co. coast between Russian and Gualala Rivers.

Santa Rosa area *The Santa Rosa Earthquakes of Oct. 1, 1969* (U.S. Geodetic Survey, 1970): effects, damage maps. Also see 1906 earthquake, San Francisco Bay Area (Marin Co.).

Monterey Bay Map MF-518 (USGS, 1973): faults, earthquakes, history, Santa Cruz to Big Sur.

1906 earthquake. All towns—Eureka to Monterey *The California Earthquake of April 18, 1906,* Carnegie Institution of Washington, 1908 (reprinted 1969): extremely detailed damage observations, fault maps, etc., all towns in Northern and Central California, maps can be used to pin-point the effects of the shock at different blocks of San Francisco, shows damage prone areas, Santa Rosa, Sebastopol, Berkeley, Oakland, San Mateo, San Jose, Santa Cruz, Salinas, etc. Bulletin 324 (USGS, 1907): similar to above, emphasis on San Francisco.

San Francisco Bay Area

General faults, quakes Map MF-307 (USGS, 1971): faults and epicenters, Golden Gate to Hollister, east to Tracy. Map MF-331 (USGS, 1970): faults, includes northern Bay Area. Open-file map (Nichols, USGS, 1970): filled marshlands, poor lands. *A Study of Earthquake Losses in the Bay Area,* NOAA, 1972: detailed earthquake damage predictions. Spec. Report 97 (CDMG, 1969): problems with bay fill in earthquakes.

Marin Co. and North Bay Area Map I-692 (USGS, 1972): San Andreas fault. Map MF-483 (USGS, 1973): geology, faults, landslides, Eastern Sonoma and Western Napa Cos., Santa Rosa, Napa, Sonoma. Map MF-494 (USGS, 1973): geology, faults, landslides, North Bay Area to Lake Berryessa, incl. Antioch to Marin, Vallejo, Solano County, etc. Open-file map (Blake, USGS, 1971): geologic map of western Sonoma Co. and northern Marin Co., San Andreas, Healdsburg faults, geology, landslides. Open-file map (O'Rourke, CDMG, 1969): Geology of San Anselmo area, also parts of Fairfax, Ross, San Rafael, available at San Anselmo City Hall.

East Bay faults Map I-522 (USGS, 1967): Hayward fault from San Pablo south to Warm Springs (Fremont); the best reference on the fault across the populous East Bay. Open-file map (Radbruch, USGS, 1968): Hayward and Calaveras faults, from Fremont south to Hollister. *Planning Commission Earthquake Study* (City of Hayward, 1972, available at City Hall): Hayward fault through Hayward. *Map of Earthquake Faults in the City of Fremont* (Fremont, 1973, available at City Hall). Map MF-505 (USGS, 1973): Concord fault in Ygnacio Valley, Concord and Suisun Bay. Map MF-553 (USGS, 1973): Antioch fault in Antioch.

East Bay geology, etc. Open-file map (Radbruch, USGS, 1967): geology and faults of Oakland and vicinity, from San Pablo south to San Leandro (see Map I-522). *The Seismic Safety Study, San Pablo, Richmond, El Cerrito* (Armstrong, 1973, available at City Hall): summary of seismic hazards, many maps. Map MF-493 (USGS, 1973): geology, landslides, western Contra Costa and northern Alameda Cos., from Concord-Walnut Creek and San Ramon Village west to San Francisco Bay. Map GQ-769 (USGS, 1969): geology, faults of eastern Oakland area, including Hayward fault. Map I-239 (USGS, 1957): geology of western Oakland area. Map I-298 (USGS, 1959): fill areas from Berkeley south to San Lorenzo, incl. Oakland, Alameda. Map MF-429 (USGS, 1972): geology, poor soils of Alameda Co. *Hayward Hill Area Study* (Burnett, CDMG, 1971): landslides, available at Hayward City Hall. Map MF-519 (USGS, 1973): geology, landslides, poor soils, eastern and central Alameda Co., including Livermore to Hayward, Oakland to Fremont. Map Sheet 16 (CDMG, 1973): geology, landslides, Walnut Creek, Lafayette, Pleasant Hill areas. Open-file map (Radbruch, USGS, 1963): landslides in the Moraga, Orinda and Lafayette areas.

South Bay to Hollister *Santa Clara Co. Report* (CDMG, 1954): contains map of geology, incl. Hayward, Calaveras, San Andreas faults. Map MF-339 (USGS, 1972): geology, landslides, Fremont to San Juan Bautista, San Jose area. Map MF-361 (USGS, 1972): geology, landslides, northeastern San Jose-Alum Rock. Map MF-361 (Rogers, CDMG, 1968): Calaveras fault through Hollister. Open-file map (Brabb, USGS, 1970): geology, parts of San Mateo, Santa Clara and Santa Cruz Cos., south of Redwood City to Santa Cruz and east to Sunnyvale, San Andreas, Pilarcitos, San Gregorio faults. Map MF-355 (USGS, 1971): alluvial, poor soils of Santa Clara Co.

San Francisco & San Mateo Counties Map MF-355 (USGS, 1972): active faults, San Mateo Co. including San Andreas, Serra fault zones. Map MF-360 (USGS, 1972): landslide hazard, San Mateo Co. Map MF-344 (USGS, 1972): larger landslides, San Mateo Co. Map MF-328 (USGS, 1972): geology, faults, landfills, poor soils, San Mateo Co. Open-file map (Pampeyan, USGS, 1971): geology, San Andreas fault, San Carlos south to Portola Valley and East Palo Alto south to Los Altos Hills. Map Sheet 8 (CDMG, 1966): geology, San Andreas fault, from Portola Valley east to Sunnyvale, and from Redwood City south to Saratoga. Spec. Report 57, *San Francisco Earthquakes of March, 1957* (CDMG, 1959): details effects of the quake, especially in the southern San Francisco, Daly City and Westlake areas. Map MF-334 (USGS, 1964): geology of the San Francisco Peninsula, International Airport north to Sausalito. Map MF-311 (USGS, 1971): geology, landslides, San Andreas fault, fill, from Pacifica and San Bruno north to the Sunset District and Hunters Point of San Francisco. Map I-272 (USGS, 1958): geology, fills, Ortega and 24th Streets of San Francisco to Sausalito, Belvedere and Tiburon (continues map MF-311). Map I-264 (USGS, 1958): landfill of the Potrero Hill–Islais Creek areas of San Francisco. See 1906 earthquake, *Commission Report* for detailed damage maps of San Francisco.

Southern California

Monterey to Tejon Pass Map I-575 (USGS, 1970): San Andreas fault, Hollister to Cholame.

Santa Barbara area Bulletin 186 (CDMG, 1966): geology, faults of Santa Barbara area from Naples to Carpinteria. Water-Supply Paper 1859-A (USGS, 1968): geology of the Santa Barbara-Montecito area, incl. Mesa and other faults. "The Santa Barbara Earthquake of June 29, 1925," *Bull. Seismological Soc. Amer.*, V15, 4, Dec. 1925: detailed damage, maps, etc., from Pt. Conception to Ventura.

1952 earthquake—Kern Co., Bakersfield "An Engineering Study of the Southern California Earthquake of July 21, 1952, and Its Aftershocks," *Bull. Seismological Soc. Amer.*, V44, 2B, April 1952: effects, damage, White Wolf maps. Bulletin 171 (CDMG, 1955): White Wolf fault map, damage, effects.

Vicinity of Los Angeles Map I-553 (USGS, 1969): San Andreas fault from Tejon Pass to Cajon Pass, nearest Los Angeles. "The 1857 Earthquake in California," *Bull. Seismological Soc. Amer.*, V45, 1, Jan. 1955: summary reports on this great quake throughout Southern California. Map MF-76 (USGS, 1960): San Andreas fault, geology, Palmdale-Lancaster area. Bulletin 170 (CDMG, 1956): Plate 1 of Ch. VI, geology of Ventura Co.

San Bernardino area Water-Supply Paper 1419 (USGS, 1964): faults and geology, San Bernardino, Riverside, Fontana, Redlands, shows San Andreas, San Jacinto, Loma Linda faults. See below.

South of San Bernardino Open-file map (Home, USGS, 1969): San Andreas, other faults between Cajon Pass and Salton Sea, incl. Highland, Desert Hot Springs, North Palm Springs. Map I-675 (USGS, 1972): San Jacinto fault, San Bernardino to Borrego Valley. "San Jacinto Fault Zone in Southern California," Sharp, *Bull. Geological Soc. Amer.*, V78, pp. 705-730, map, 1967. Spec. Report 94 (CDMG, 1968): geology, San Andreas and Mission Creek faults through the Desert Hot Springs-Coachella Valley areas. Bulletin 170 (CDMG, 1956): map sheet 20 (San Andreas fault in the Banning area), map sheet 21 (geology of the Corona-Elsinore-Murietta area showing Elsinore fault). Spec. Report 98 (CDMG, 1968): landslides, geology, San Clemente area.

San Diego area Open-file maps (Kennedy, CDMG & City of San Diego): a series of maps showing geology, landslides, including Sunset Cliffs. Open-file map (Ziony, USGS, 1972): report on faulting in the San Diego area, good reference list.

Los Angeles area

Other sources *County of Los Angeles:* Mapping Division, 108 West 2nd St., Los Angeles —carries many USGS reports; subdivision tracts, parcel and single lot maps and geologic reports submitted to the County can be inspected at Geological Section, 108 West 2nd St., Los Angeles. *City of Los Angeles:* geologic maps and reports, tentative tract maps by the City can be inspected at Geology and Soil Engineering Section, 2426 Altman St., Los Angeles. Many other geologic maps are also available; grading ordinances, geology and soil reports, etc., can be inspected at Grading Division, Rm. 421, 200 North Spring St., Los Angeles.

General reference on area *Preliminary Geologic Environmental Map of the Greater Los Angeles Area*, by Wentworth et al., U.S. Atomic Energy Commission, TID-25363, 1970: contains an excellent compilation of the best earthquake and geologic hazard reference maps for the area; a few are listed below, together with maps published since this report; refer to it if following list is insufficient.

Bulletin 170 (CDMG, 1956): Plate 1, Ch. II—geology of the LA Basin, showing Newport-Inglewood, Raymond Hill, Whittier and other faults. "A Study of Earthquake Losses in the Los Angeles Area," NOAA (U.S. Department of Commerce), 1973: detailed earthquake damage predictions, intensity maps, etc.

Santa Monica Mountains Open-file map (Yerkes, USGS, 1973): geology and landslides of the Topanga area from Glenview to the coast. Open-file map (Yerkes, USGS, 1971): geology and landslides of the Malibu Beach area, from Corral Beach to Las Costa Beach, Santa Monica Mountains, Malibu Coast fault. Open-file map (Campbell, USGS, 1970): geology, landslides, Point Dume, Malibu to Cornell. Map MF-471 (USGS, 1973): landslides of Pacific Palisades area of Los Angeles and Santa Monica.

San Fernando Valley Bulletin 172 (CDMG, 1958): geology, landslides of the San Fernando areas, from San Fernando to Tujunga, excludes the 1971 fault. Prelim. Report 11 (CDMG, 1971): faulting in the San Fernando earthquake of 1971—the San Fernando fault. Prof. Paper 733 (USGS, 1971): San Fernando earthquake of 1971, comprehensive report on effects, many photographs, fault & landslide maps, damage reports, etc. *San Fernando Earthquake, February 9, 1971*, Steinbrugge, Pacific Fire Rating Bureau, San Francisco, 1971: damage to residential, small industrial and other buildings, fault and damage maps, etc. *Engineering Features of the San Fernando Earthquake, February 9, 1971*, Calif. Institute of Tech., Report No. EERL 71-02, 1971: numerous illustrations, damage descriptions, etc.

San Gabriel Mountains Map Sheet 15 (CDMG, 1969): landslides of the San Gabriel Mountains, from San Fernando to San Bernardino, north of the line between Hollywood and Fontana (Route 66). Spec. Report 105 (CDMG, 1973): geology, landslides, fills, Sierra Madre, Raymond Hill and Clamshell-Sawpit faults, in the Sierra Madre to Monrovia to Azusa areas. Prof. Paper 750C (USGS, 1971): landslides in the Glendora area.

Central Los Angeles Basin to Long Beach *Geologic Map of City of Glendale*, Byer, Public Works Div., Eng. Section, Glendale, 1968. Spec. Report 101 (CDMG, 1970): geology, faults, landfills, landslides, area between Los Angeles, Glendale, South Pasadena and Monterey Park, Elysian Park-Repetto Hills area of Los Angeles Co. Open-file map (Castle, USGS, 1960): geology of the Baldwin Hills area, Newport-Inglewood fault. Open-file map (Castle & Yerkes, USGS, 1969): the Newport-Inglewood fault in the Baldwin Hills. Open-file map (Castle, USGS, 1960): geology of the area between Hollywood-Beverly Hills south to Manhattan Beach and east to Santa Monica, incl. Culver City, El Segundo, etc. Water-Supply Paper 1461 (USGS, 1959): geology, soils of the area between Santa Monica and Long Beach along the Newport-Inglewood fault, incl. Torrance area. *Earthquake Safety in the City of Long Beach Based on the Concept of "Balanced Risk"*, Wiggins & Moran, 1971: incl. maps of the poor soil areas of Long Beach, expected earthquake intensities, fills, etc., available at City Hall. *Earthquake Investigations in the Western United States, 1931-1934*, Publication 41-2, U.S. Coast and Geodetic Survey: incl. a map and descriptions of the damage in Long Beach and vicinity from the 1933 quake. *Report on the Southern California Earthquake of March 10, 1933*, Nat. Board of Fire Underwriters, New York: effects. Open-file map (Cleveland, CDMG, 1962): geology of the Palos Verdes Hills area.

Southeastern LA and Orange Counties Prof. Paper 420C (USGS, 1973): geology, landslides, poor soils, Whittier fault in the western Puente Hills area, surrounded by Montebello, Bellflower, Fullerton and Rowland Height, incl. Whittier, Pico Rivera, La Mirada, La Habra, Brea, etc. Map OM-195 (USGS, 1964): geology of the Olinda, Placentia and Yorba Linda areas and the Puente Hills, showing the Whittier fault. Water-Supply Paper 1109 (USGS, 1956): geology of the coastal area between Long Beach and Santa Ana. Prelim. Report 15 (CDMG, 1973): maps of Orange Co. showing geology, faults, and landslides, incl. the Whittier, Norwalk and Newport-Inglewood faults, very detailed for the entire county.

Montana

Selected sources: Montana Bureau of Mines and Geology, Montana College of Mineral Science and Technology, Butte; Montana State University Library, Bozeman; Public Library and Historical Society of Montana Library; Helena, University of Montana Library, Missoula.

Selected references:

Historical quakes Prof. Paper 147 (USGS, 1927): the Montana earthquake of June 27, 1925, damage in the Clarkston Valley incl. Three Forks, Logan, Manhattan, Willow Creek, Bozeman, Radersburg. "The Montana Earthquakes of October, 1935," *Bull. Seismological Soc. Amer.*, V26, 2, *April 1936*: damage observations. "Helena Earthquakes," *Bull. Seis. Soc. Amer.*, V26, 4, *Oct. 1936*: detailed maps of damage in Helena. Memoir 16 (Montana Bureau of Mines & Geology, 1936): 1935 Helena quake.

1959 earthquake Prof. Paper 435 (USGS, 1964): extensive report, maps. *Bull. Seis. Soc. Amer.*, V52, 2, *April 1962*: maps, damage reports, etc.

Nevada

Selected sources: Nevada Bureau of Mines, University of Nevada, Reno; State Library, Carson City; Library, Mackay School of Mines, Library, University of Nevada, Reno; Library, Nevada Southern University, Las Vegas.

Selected references:

Historical quakes "The Fallon-Stillwater Earthquakes of July 6, 1954, and August 23, 1954," *Bull. Seismological Soc. Amer.*, V46, 1, *Jan. 1956*. "The Dixie Valley-Fairview Peak Earthquakes of December 16, 1954," *Bull. Seis. Soc. Amer.*, V47, 4, *1957*. "Catalog of Nevada Earthquakes, 1852-1960," *Bull. Seis. Soc. Amer.*, V55, 2, *April 1965*: summaries of effects.

Epicenter map Map 29 (Nevada Bureau of Mines, 1965): historical epicenters.

Geological index Map 42 (Nevada Bureau of Mines, 1971): index and summary of geological information on Nevada.

Oregon

Selected sources: Oregon State Department of Geology and Mineral Industries, 1400 S.W. Fifth Ave., Portland.

Selected references:

Historical quakes "Oregon Earthquakes, 1841 through 1958," *Bull. Seismological Soc. Amer.*, V53, 1, *Jan. 1963*: summaries of effects.

Portland geology Bulletin 1119 and Map GQ-104 (USGS, 1963): geology, poor soils, but no faults.

Portland quakes Articles in the following issues of *The Ore Bin*, Dept. of Geology and Mineral Industries, State of Oregon: V24, 11 (Nov. 1962), V25, 4 (April 1963), V26, 12 (Dec. 1964), V30, 2 (Feb. 1968), V30, 10 (Oct. 1968), V33, 6 (June 1971), V34, 6 (June 1972).

Utah

Selected sources: U.S. Geological Survey, 125 South State St., Salt Lake City; Utah Geological and Mineral Survey, Salt Lake City; Library, Brigham Young University, Provo; Library Utah State University, Logan; Library, Weber State College, Ogden.

Selected references:

Salt Lake City Maps I-766-A to G (USGS, 1972): faults, fills, landslides, geology, etc., incl. the Wasatch and East Bench faults.

Wasatch fault *Wasatch Fault, Northern Portion*, L. S. Cluff et al., for Utah Geological Survey, 1970: covers Jordan Narrows, Granite, Butlerville, Salt Lake City, Bountiful, Centerville, Farmington, Kaysville, Uintah, Ogden, North Ogden, Willard and Brigham City in block by block detail. *Environmental Geology of the Wasatch Front*, Publication 1, Utah Geological Association, 1972. *Guidebook of Northern Utah*, Bulletin 82, 1969, Utah Geological and Mineral Survey. *Wasatch Fault, Southern Portion*, L. S. Cluff et al. for Utah Geological Survey, 1973.

Utah earthquakes "Seismicity in Utah, 1850 through June 1965," *Bull. Seismological Soc. Amer.*, V57, 4, August 1967: history, map of epicenters.

Morgan County Bulletin 93 (Utah Geol. & Min. Survey, 1972): geologic hazards.

Washington

Selected sources: U.S. Geological Survey, West 920 Riverside Ave., Spokane; Washington Div. of Mines and Geology, 335 General Administration Bldg., P.O. Box 168, Olympia; U.S. Geological Survey, Tacoma; Eastern Washington State College Library, Cheney; Public Library, Port Angeles; Library, University of Washington, Seattle.

Selected references:

Geologic maps Water-Supply Paper 1135 (USGS, 1952): Snohomish Co. Water-Supply Paper 1413 (USGS, 1957): Kitsap Co. Map I-354 (USGS, 1962): Seattle and vicinity, shows landfill, alluvium, landslides. Map GQ-706 (USGS, 1967): West Seattle-Arroyo Heights to Duwamish Head. Map GQ-406 (USGS, 1965): Auburn and vicinity. Map GQ-405 (USGS, 1965): Renton, Kent and vicinity.

Earthquake maps Seattle and Vicinity, Tacoma, Bellingham and Vicinity, Washington Surveying and Rating Brueau, Seattle, 1966: filled or unstable grounds which have suffered in past earthquakes.

Historical quakes *The Puget Sound Earthquake of April 29, 1965,* U.S. Coast and Geodetic Survey, 1965 "The Puget Sound Earthquake of Feb. 14, 1946," *Bull. Seismological Soc. Amer.,* V36, 4, Oct. 1946. "Reporting the Northwest Earthquake," Ulrich, *Building Standards Monthly, June, 1949.* "Washington State Earthquakes, 1840 through 1965," *Bull. Seis. Soc. Amer.,* V57, 3, June 1967. "A Summary of Washington Earthquakes," *Bull. Seis. Soc. Amer.,* V43, 1, Jan. 1953.

Geologic index *Compilation of Geologic Mapping in Washington Through 1968,* Washington Div. of Mines and Geology, Open-file report, 1969.

Acknowledgements

I am indebted to my colleagues—engineers, geologists, architects, other scientists and public officials who are engaged in a continuing effort to reduce and eliminate the great risks associated with earthquakes, and who have published their knowledge in the hope of education everyone about these risks. Many of them gave freely of their time and knowledge in order to enhance the quality and accuracy of the text and the illustrations. Most of the ideas in this book were compiled from several hundred books and scientific papers, while the photographs were selected from many thousands.

I am particularly indebted to the following contributors:

Dr. Frank Baron of the University of California, Berkeley; Dennis E. Kuzak of Stanford University; Dr. William M. Morrow, John McCall, Roland O. Marsh, and the staff and management of the Bechtel Power Corporation; Dr. Charles F. Richter of the California Institute of Technology; Frank E. McClure of McClure and Messinger; Karl V. Steinbrugge of the University of California and the Insurance Services Office; Henry J. Degenkolb of H. J. Degenkolb & Associates; William W. Moore of Dames & Moore; Lloyd S. Cluff of Woodward-Lundgren & Associates; Drew P. Lawrence of Industrial Indemnity Company; Robert A. Philbrick of Cornell University; Charles Jennings and the staff of the California Division of Mines and Geology; the staff of the U.S. Geological Survey at Menlo Park and San Francisco; the American Plywood Association; Dr. James A. Wilson of Castro Valley; Henry A. Leonard of San Francisco; Ben K. Kacyra of Earthquake Engineering Systems.

James Arntz of San Francisco edited the text and made a significant contribution to its clarity and quality.

Robert Higginbotham of Berkeley, architect specializing in residential construction and design, collaborated with me in the illustration and review of the text.

Index

Photographic, map and other credits

AA Wire Products Co., Chicago, Illinois: p. 169 (top & center).

American Plywood Association: pp. 127 (top), 148 (top), 153, 199 (top).

After J. E. Amrhein, Masonry Institute of America: p. 205 (top & center).

Architectural Institute of Japan: p. 192 (bottom).

R. Augenstein (Courtesy R. T. Beck): p. 203 (left).

W. N. Ball Collection (Courtesy K. V. Steinbrugge): p. 156.

After Balsillie & Benson, Portland State University: p. 284.

Bancroft Library: p. 76.

After Barnhart & Slosson, Los Angeles Valley College: p. 272 (top).

Bear Photo Collection (Courtesy K. V. Steinbrugge): p. 78.

R. T. Beck: pp. 211, 227.

R. W. Binder Collection (Courtesy K. V. Steinbrugge): p. 192 (top).

California Department of Water Resources: p. 111 (top).

California Division of Highways: pp. 155, 189.

California Division of Mines & Geology: pp. 41, 95, 100-102, 277.

California Institute of Technology, Earthquake Engineering Research Laboratory: pp. 83 (top), 119 (bottom), 171 (bottom), 191 (top), 201, 203 (right), 218 (bottom).

Carnegie Institution: pp. 54 (top), 71, 77, 86, 103, 196.

Concrete Masonry Association of California: p. 171 (top).

R. G. Dean: p. 122.

H. J. Degenkolb: pp. 174, 190 (courtesy).

Courtesy Earthquake Engineering Research Institute: p. 158.

H. M. Engle: pp. 37, 218 (top).

W. Enkeboll: p. 88.

P. E. Estes: p. 226.

After J. M. Fratt: pp. 159, 212.

After J. R. Freeman: p. 73.

D. E. Kuzak: pp. 35 (bottom), 63, 116, 197 (left).

D. P. Lawrence: p. 177.

Los Angeles City Department of Building & Safety: pp. 127 (bottom), 151, 199 (bottom), 213 (left), 217, 228.

Los Angeles Department of Water & Power: p. 110.

R. E. Marsell (Courtesy L. S. Cluff): p. 61.

R. B. Matthiesen: p. 160 (top).

F. E. McClure: pp. 142, 148 (top & right), 163 (bottom), 191 (bottom), 208-209, 218 (center), 221, 224.

J. F. Meehan: pp. 160, 169 (bottom).

W. M. Morrow: pp. 35 (top), 62.

National Bureau of Standards: pp. 157, 170 (top), 210, 268.

N.O.A.A.: pp. 24-25, 32, 75, 96 (bottom), 163 (top).

Pacific Gas & Electric Co. (Courtesy S. Peters): pp. 119 (top), 147.

J. Penzien (Courtesy H. B. Seed): p. 91.

After C. F. Richter: p. 73.

San Francisco Chronicle: p. 115.

San Francisco Examiner (Courtesy K. V. Steinbrugge): p. 121.

H. B. Seed: p. 113.

G. P. Simonds: p. 164.

K. V. Steinbrugge: pp. 34, 53 (bottom-courtesy), 80-81, 117, 152, 213 (right).

W. M. Sutherland: p. 193.

U.S. Army: pp. 93, 96 (top), 111 (bottom), 118, 173, 206.

U.S. Coast & Geodetic Survey: p. 202.

U.S. Geological Survey: pp. 33, 53 (top), 54 (bottom), 55-56, 58, 65, 90, 108, 261 (After Map I-522), 264 (After Map MF-505), 270, 275 (After Water Supply Paper 1859-A).

Utah Geological & Mineral Survey (Courtesy L. S. Cluff): p. 287.

Washington Surveying and Rating Bureau: p. 291.

I.G.B. Wilson: p. 162.

E. G. Zacher: p. 204.